◆ALTERNATIVES *is a series under the general editorship of Eric S. Rabkin, Martin H. Greenberg, and Joseph D. Olander which has been established to serve the growing critical audience of science fiction, fantastic fiction, and speculative fiction.*

# COORDINATES
## PLACING
## SCIENCE FICTION
## AND
## FANTASY

**Edited by**
**George E. Slusser,**
**Eric S. Rabkin,**
**and**
**Robert Scholes**

Southern Illinois University Press
Carbondale and Edwardsville

"America as Science Fiction: 1939," by H. Bruce Franklin, appeared in slightly different form in *Science-Fiction Studies* (March 1982).

86 85 84 83    4 3 2 1

**Library of Congress Cataloging in Publication Data**
Main entry under title:

Coordinates: placing science fiction and fantasy.

(Alternatives)
Essays presented at the 3rd J. Lloyd Eaton
Conference on Science Fiction and Fantasy held Feb. 21–
22, 1981, at the University of California, Riverside.
Includes bibliographical references and index.
1. Science fiction—Congresses.  2. Fantastic
fiction—Congresses.  I. Slusser, George Edgar.
II. Rabkin, Eric S.  III. Scholes, Robert E.
IV. Eaton Conference on Science Fiction and Fantasy
Literature (3rd : 1981 : University of California,
Riverside)  V. Series.
PN3433.2.C66   1983    808.83'876    82-19469
ISBN 0–8093–1105–4

# Contents

# Introduction

As studies of science fiction and fantasy proliferate, the boundaries of this field of investigation have expanded, perhaps overexpanded to formlessness. This volume hopes to establish basic coordinates for these two genres. By placing a number of important individual works in well-defined analytical contexts, it takes up some of the critical slack. What is more, because the essays in this collection address both science fiction and fantasy, they suggest in their interactive resonances new points of intersection between these forms of writing. We hope the establishment of clear coordinates will permit the reader to assess the critical act itself, and to judge the adequacy of any given attempt to bracket and fix the basic problems of science fiction and fantasy.

The lead essay, Leslie Fiedler's "The Criticism of Science Fiction," sets the tone of the volume by offering a basic set of coordinates—that of "elitist" and "popular" standards. Using the examples of A. E. Van Vogt, Olaf Stapledon, and Boris Vian, he asserts that, when science fiction is measured by the norms of the traditional literary establishment, it does not fail the test but rather the norms themselves do. Fiedler's remarks apply equally well to fantasy when it too is considered a "lowbrow" form. In his eyes therefore, both science fiction and fantasy attract the reader not by their "architectonic skill or linguistic subtlety," nor even by their ethical or metaphysical insights, but by their "mythopoeic power"—their ability to provide easy access to the writer's unconscious "at the point where it meets the collective unconscious of us all." In a sense then, each subsequent essay in this volume is a reply to Fiedler's challenge that we revise or reject these traditional standards. Using a diversity of critical methods, all these studies strive not to refute the mythopoeic power of the two genres but, in cases where access to it may not be as easy as Fiedler suggests, to articulate it, to locate it on clearly defined coordinates and by doing so in turn challenge Fiedler's assertion that the

simple presence of these two forms renders us "critic-pedagogues . . .
a little redundant."

Eric S. Rabkin's "semiobiological" study, "The Descent of Fantasy," traces the mythopoeic appeal of this form—here broadly conceived to include works ranging from fairy tale to science fiction—from
origins in the survival of the species, and by establishing this lineage
directly equates the power of fantasy to the structural skill and linguistic subtlety with which a story is told. Defining fantasy as a special class
of narrative "made of unfalsifiable events in part so that the report of
these events can be exchanged long after particular reality changes,"
Rabkin suggests that "the telling of proper tales, well made and
rhetorically interesting tales, in a social world so dominated by language exchange as is ours, signals social success and the likelihood of
social position."

Rabkin's remark, that it is by well-made fantasy that *homo sapiens* shapes his world, suggests another complementary aspect of this
literature's mythopoeic power—science fiction's much-vaunted capacity for "newness." In his essay "How New Is New?", Gerald Prince
places science fiction on three specific narratological and semiotic
coordinates and concludes that *as fiction* it does not necessarily have
greater potential for "newness" than its mainstream counterpart.
Science fiction, Prince argues, first of all is fiction, and the materials of
fiction (despite the designation "novel") are always old. Second of all,
science fiction shares with mainstream fiction a reliance on narrative as
its mode of organizing fictional experience, and narrative, as a predilection for meaningful order, can be reduced to a finite and predictable
number of elements. Third of all, science fiction is constrained by what
Prince calls its scientific "motivation," the need to account for any
given distortion of reality or "newness" by an explanation that signals
the logical, orderly premises of "science."

The remaining ten essays all focus, to one degree or another, on
individual texts or authors. All seek to place the works or writers in
question according to one of the critical axes suggested by Fiedler:
structural, rhetorical, ethical, sociocritical, and ultimately metaphysical and, in the broadest sense, existential. The wide variety of works
discussed—some of which seem at first glance to lie beyond the popular parameters of science fiction and fantasy—suggests a heterogeneity
of canon for the two forms that is matched only by the persistence of
mythopoeic intention each of these various works displays. These
studies then, converging from diverse critical angles through a common center, form coordinates on which the broadest spectrum of texts
can be examined.

Mark Rose's essay, "Jules Verne: Journey to the Center of Science Fiction," moves in exploratory fashion through intense close reading of *Journey to the Center of the Earth* to general statement about the nature of science fiction as a genre. Discovering structural ambiguities in this seminal work that seem to reflect the increasing divergence, in the late nineteenth century, between romanticism and positivism as approaches to nature, Rose suggests not only that science fiction in our modern culture characteristically operates in the space of this basic contradiction, but that one of its functions seems to be to mediate between spiritualistic and materialistic world views.

If Rose places Jules Verne's classic on structural and semantic coordinates which are those of genre, Joseph M. Lenz, in his study "Manifest Destiny: Science Fiction and Classical Form," considers two science fictional "epics"—Asimov's *Foundation* and Herbert's *Dune*—at the crossroads where a set of inherited "classic" forms—in this case a literary model drawn from the past that celebrates the social ideal of stability of empire in the present—intersects with these authors' intentions in re-creating such forms in the context of "popular" modern science fiction. Lenz asks what vision of the "classic" these authors have, and why they might desire to project that vision, in a form associated with prediction and the future, into the world of their readers.

Where Lenz sees a specific and persistent literary model—*The Aeneid*—as informing the science fiction epic, Michelle Massé in her essay " 'All you have to do is know what you want': Individual Expectations in *Triton*," considers Samuel R. Delany's novel, despite its space-epic exteriors, as primarily psychodrama—the study of interrelations between individual expectations and environmental possibilities and restraints in a future social landscape that is to the highest degree urban. Massé examines here another traditional form of science fiction—the utopia—at its point of intersection with what Delany calls "heterotopia." Her analysis of this encounter—in which she shows that it is no longer society that frees the individual but rather the individual who feels it necessary to retreat from this society's "creative anarchy" in order to restore the old restrictive barriers but this time within his own mind—suggests the deep conservatism of the cultural myths underlying this work of professed avant garde science fiction.

Gary K. Wolfe's vision on the other hand, in his essay "Autoplastic and Alloplastic Adaptations in Science Fiction: 'Waldo' and 'Desertion,' " is more optimistic. Using as texts a pair of classic stories, Wolfe discusses two manners in which science fiction seeks to resolve this same tension between individual and environment: what he calls autoplastic and alloplastic fantasies—the manipulation of the body to fit the environment that is the way of primitive cultures; or technological man's solution, the manipulation of environment to fit the body. Wolfe argues that both "Waldo" and "Desertion" offer, rather than fantasies of subjugation, "positive and highly affective models" for individual maturation through integration with the environment. As examples then of a supremely adult mode of fantasy rather that the exercises in adolescent wish-fulfillment they are usually taken to be, such autoplastic scenarios hold out the promise (a promise repeated in films like *Star Wars* and *Altered States*) that one can find in one's own body a means of achieving this integration, "that the most awkward, unpromising body can achieve grace and agility in the proper environment."

If Wolfe would show how science fiction offers models for adaptation, Robert Hunt, in his "Science Fiction for the Age of Inflation: Reading *Atlas Shrugged* in the 1980s," proposes that science fiction also gives us powerful fantasies of the opposite sort—in the case of Rand's novel one that alloplastically transforms all of American history and cultural landscape to ends of ideological persuasion. Hunt not only demonstrates how Rand uses the conventions of science fiction— here the power to dismantle and remake an entire universe—for ideological purposes, but shows how an understanding of the rhetorical devices of *Atlas Shrugged*, as a work perennially in tune with the thought patterns of middle-class America, may be essential to comprehending the general effect of all literature, fiction and nonfiction alike, on American life in today's inflationary age.

The two preceding essays have dealt less with literary or cultural coordinates than with psychological and rhetorical ones. The two that follow consider the ethical and social contexts of science fiction—the pressures and restraints placed on the creative act by the society that produces and consumes the work. George R. Guffey, in his essay "*Fahrenheit 451* and the 'Cubby-Hole Editors' of Ballantine Books," examines the numerous editions of Bradbury's classic protest against book censorship in order to demonstrate how a particular version of this text, one bowdlerized for a special high-school paperback line, the Ballantine Bal-Hi Series, was later substituted, surreptitiously and in a totally unauthorized manner, for the purportedly uncensored version in the regular Ballantine line, and there perpetuated for generations as the "canonical" text. Raising the spectre of such subtle censorship, Guffey asks to what extent this practice is widespread not only in the case of popular literature like science fiction and fantasy, but in the mass paperback market as a whole.

In complementary fashion H. Bruce Franklin, in his study "America as Science Fiction: 1939," compares the themes and preoccupations of the 1939 issues of *Astounding* magazine with those of the New York World's Fair of the same year in order to demonstrate the degree to which science fiction had by that time already moved to the center of American culture. He reveals this year to be a crucial turning point in popular attitudes toward science and technology—the moment in which the figure of the lone genius, so dominant in early science fiction, yields to a vision of collective and corporate scientific efforts. By analyzing the "predictive" thrust of the GM Futurama exhibit—where speculation on future technological marvels is clearly allied with an aggressive economic policy designed to place the automobile at the center of American life—Franklin seeks to show "the ability of the corporate powers, aided by their own form of science fiction, to shape the future in their own image."

Both Guffey and Franklin expose attempts by social forces, in this case purely materialistic and utilitarian ones, to manipulate the mythopoeic potential of a literature devoted to speculation about the future or about other worlds. The next two essays—written as complementary studies from a single feminist perspective—expand the field of investigation to fantasy in general and to the much less obvious and conscious manipulations by our male-dominated culture of the image of woman. Sandra M. Gilbert's "Rider Haggard's Heart of Darkness" considers the paradoxical heroine of *She*—"an angelically chaste woman with monstrous powers"—as the definitive *fin de siècle* embodiment of those fantasies that preoccupied countless male writers and readers of the age. Haggard's figure so obsessed her male audience, Gilbert contends, because she incarnated the myth of a "New Woman" who was the menacing ruler of a fundamentally matriarchal world. Tracing the "progress" of this mythical figure through the nineteenth century and in the works of such "disparate figures" as Haggard, Freud, and Conrad, Gilbert suggests that this fascination—and the need to exorcise it in prose—is symptomatic of a "complex of late Victorian sociocultural and sexual anxieties."

In her companion piece "*She* in *Herland*: Feminism as Fantasy," Susan Gubar discusses the relationship between Haggard's "heart of female darkness" and Charlotte Perkins Gilman's utopian feminist revision of the Haggard romance as a dialectic between patriarchal and matriarchal visions, between what she terms the father's curse and the mother's blessing. Extrapolating from the Gilman work, Gubar considers the general drift of feminist fantasies away from patriarchal culture and its industrialized tyranny, war, pollution, and the aliena-

tion of labor toward the African garden. This peaceful maternal paradise represented, Gubar contends, a dream of female supremacy that
was not only set forth in numerous prose romances, but actually
proposed and in some cases enacted by social reformers of the time.
Such actions may in turn have aggravated male fantasies, Gubar
speculates, to the point of spawning avenging counterfantasies in the
flesh like Jack the Ripper.

Increasingly in these essays we have seen the myths of science
fiction and fantasy spill over into life. The concluding study, George E.
Slusser's "Death and the Mirror: Existential Fantasy," examines the
relationship between fantasy as a seen and fantasy as a lived experience. By displacing the relational axis from fantasy-reality to fantasy-
mirror, Slusser shifts the study of fantasy from ontological to existential grounds, and the question becomes not whether the other world
exists but whether I exist in the act of seeing it, whether I can verify my
existence in what may be only reflections of myself. At this point,
where the entire perceived world becomes a mirror fantasy, only death
as the absence of all reflection can restore the duality of self and other.
Analyzing works of many cultures from Hoffmann and Kierkegaard
to Mishima, Slusser shows how this encounter of death and the mirror
may provide modern man with his ultimate mode of fantasy. Prob-
ing beneath such surface tensions of the fantastic text as Todorov's
"hesitation," Slusser seeks to redefine fantasy as a struggle on the
deepest level of human existence to suspend the perceiving self in an
unending present, and links its mythopoeic power finally to universal
reflexes of the psyche faced with death.

All the essays in this volume were originally written for the third
J. Lloyd Eaton Conference on Science Fiction and Fantasy, held
February 21–22, 1981, at the University of California, Riverside. The
editors of this volume wish to extend their thanks to the following
people for their warm support of the Eaton Conference: David War-
ren, Dean of Humanities and Social Sciences; Joan Chambers, University Librarian; and John Tanno, Assistant University Librarian, all
of UCR. A special thanks goes to the founding spirits behind the
conference: Vice-Chancellor Eleanor Montague, and Jean-Pierre
Barricelli, Chairman of the Department of Literature and Languages,
again both of UCR. The encouragement of all these people, and of the
University of California, Riverside, generally, was essential in bringing to light the essays in this volume.

Riverside, California                          George E. Slusser
October *1982*                                 Eric S. Rabkin
                                               Robert Scholes

# COORDINATES

*LESLIE FIEDLER*

# The Criticism of Science Fiction

I have been pondering for some years now the growing alienation of serious criticism of science fiction from the genre it purports to examine and illuminate; and I have become more and more convinced that a study of how what began as an activity congruous with its subject has become academicized and estranged would cast light on the general dilemma of criticism at the moment, ever more remote from the texts with which it deals and ever less available to the common reader who seeks in those texts rapture and release. There has been critical writing about science fiction ever since it became conscious of being a special genre with a name of its own and an elusive definition on which, in fact, no consensus has ever been reached. For a long time, however, such writing remained by and large pop criticism, as seemed appropriate enough for what was still a popular genre, ghettoized in pulp magazines and read almost exclusively by a minority audience, chiefly white adolescent males, convinced that they hated everything which their teachers considered literature. The stories to which they turned as an escape from the classics of Eng. Lit., were written by hacks, unpretentious professionals who laid no claim to being artists, and possessed neither authorial pride nor the propietary sense characteristic of aspirants to high art in the age of modernism. Such authors not uncommonly published under three or four or five different names, and flagrantly ripped off from each other (or certain dead predecessors) plots, gimmicks, devices, even basic assumptions about what constituted a story. It was as if they were engaged in a communal enterprise, like movie making or the production of comic books, and the myths they shared were more essential than individual vision, voice, or style.

Small wonder, then, that they had no objection to the editors of the journals in which they appeared (in the beginning as omnipotent as pashas or cinema moguls) not only remaking their work *after* the fact—cutting, revising, suggesting or imposing new endings, but even controlling what they produced *before* the fact. On the one hand, such editors assigned certain plots and backgrounds, or requested stories to go with preexistent illustrations; on the other, they effectively defined the parameters of the literary kind to which prospective stories must belong, if they were to be published at all. But this means that they were also critics of a proscriptive or prescriptive sort, much like the literary dictators who presided over high art in the seventeenth or eighteenth centuries. Everyone who knows anything about sf at all, is aware (but the point is worth insisting upon) that Hugo Gernsback, for instance, not merely gave a name to the genre he sponsored, first calling it "scientifiction," then science fiction, but also proposed—and sought to *enforce*—his own definition of what it ought to be, *must* be: "a charming romance intermingled with scientific fact and prophetic vision." Moreover, before there were enough living writers to keep the pages of his magazines filled with such stories, he reprinted as substitutes and prototypes tales by Poe, Verne, and H. G. Wells which fit his formula. And his eminent successors followed his example for as long as the pulps dominated the scene and editorial absolute monarchy remained unchallenged.

Such editors, however, were not the only critics of the genre, even in those golden days. From the start, the back pages of the pulp specialty magazines were filled with pieces on current trends and tendencies, and especially reviews of published stories and books. Such pieces were written more often than not by already established sf authors, approving and disapproving of each other's work in a kind of continuing, *ad hoc*, in-house attempt to define standards independent of and different from those of mainstream criticism. Indeed, implicit in everything they wrote was an acceptance (in part defensive, in part joyously irreverent) of the elite critics' assumption that the genre they were discussing was so utterly alien to real literature that it could not, should not be judged in the same terms.

Some of these review essays, though they continue to appear to this day, have proved as ephemeral as the other contents of the magazines in which they first appeared. But others survive in collections cited still in the bibliographies attached to more recent scholarly books on the subject—most notably, perhaps, James Blish's two volumes, *The Issue at Hand* (1964) and *More Issues at Hand* (1970), and Damon Knight's *In Search of Wonder*, first published in 1956 and expanded in 1967. In the opinion of some surviving members of the old guard, these constitute, indeed, the major contribution to criticism of the genre; so that Jack Williamson, for instance, was able to write not so many years ago, "Equals in wit and insight and contempt for chuckleheads, Knight and Blish have produced what is still perhaps the best science fiction criticism at hand." Clearly what Williamson prizes these craftsman-critics for is their unwillingness to suffer fools (however they and he may define foolishness) gladly. But the pulps in which Knight and Blish appeared were traditionally immensely hospitable, printing along with their contributions, unsolicited comments from fans, some of whom would have to be rated chuckleheads on any conceivable scale.

From the beginning, that is to say, there was printed in the letter columns of the specialty magazines another kind of criticism, amateur rather than professional, since those who produced it had no qualifications other than their enthusiasm for the genre and a need to put into print their judgments of individual stories and authors. In a fairly short time, moreover, some such self-nominated critics, feeling the need for more space, founded journals of their own, fanzines as they came to be called; to which, to be sure, they occasionally invited contributions from more established figures in the field, professionals they especially admired. The pages of these publications were mostly filled, however, with the work of novices, trying their hand—for an audience made up mainly of people quite like themselves—at cartoons, illustrations, fiction not yet up to the level of the pulps, and, of course, naïve criticism as well. Much of it, interestingly but not surprisingly, was dedicated to attempts at defining the genre the fans celebrated in their mimeographed pages, and speculating on its relationship to the canonical literature of what they liked to call the mainstream. Some of those genre definitions were ostensibly quite serious, some clearly flippant (as is appropriate to an identity crisis so prolonged that it becomes finally a parody of itself). They range from statements like "the genre of literature that shows the limits and possibilities of man and goes beyond them" and "the genre . . . [which] explores the mental bush country beyond the tilled lands down by the old mainstream" to remarks like "Science fiction deals with everything that does not exist" and "Science fiction is what we mean when we point to it."

It is curious and illuminating, I think, to realize that fanzines, that unique model of pop criticism in our time, have by and large dealt *only* with science fiction, along with the neighboring genres of fantasy and comic books, often written by the same authors and even more often prized by the same audiences. There are no comparable amateur publications devoted to other popular speciality fiction like the detective story, the spy novel, the western, the girls' romance. This is true in part, I suppose, because those other subgenres did not attract so impassioned, cohesive, and exclucivist a community of readers; their taste defined by both a preference for a particular kind and a rejection of everything else, from the mimetic best sellers their parents read to the classics their teachers assigned. But in part, too, it is due to the fact that no other pop genre has been so self-aware—so obsessed with the notion that it is in essense *problematical* for its own practitioners and fans as well as for traditional literary criticism. Since, however, traditional critics for a long time dealt with that problem chiefly by ignoring it (hoping perhaps that like other passing fads, it would go away), it was up to those practitioners and fans to deal with it; which is to say, to become critics in their own right.

But reinventing criticism in 1930 was a little like reinventing the wheel at the same late date, possible only to the most naïve, and likely to produce therefore eminently unsatisfactory results. In fact, no authoritative critical voice (and by the same token no new critical point of view) emerged from the parochial babble of the fanzines. Indeed, their contents remain unknown to both more recent academic critics and the mass audience which in the seventies and eighties has made sf not merely pop in essence, but popular in fact, that is, best-selling. Furthermore, there is, as far as I know, no anthology of critical pieces from the millions of words that appeared over more than half a century in the earliest of all alternative or underground journals. But there is a history of such publications called *The World of Fanzines*, published in 1973 by, of course, a university press, Southern Illinois to be precise; and rather improbably written by Dr. Frederic Wertham, better known for his ill-tempered diatribe of the 1950s against the comic books.

Called *The Seduction of the Innocent*, the earlier volume, which itself approached best sellerdom, played a major role in the suppression of the E.C. Comics and the imposition of a restrictive code on the entire comic book industry; but it hardly prepares us for Wertham's latter-day defense of journals sympathetic to some of the manifestations of popular culture which he most hated and feared. Wertham, in fact, manages to say a good word for the fanzines only by falsifying them, that is, by picking out solely the most pious and moralizing pieces they printed in an ongoing debate about violence in the popular arts and the role of drugs in the youth culture. Yet he does provide at least a skeletal history of these otherwise largely ignored amateur publications, and reproduces from them occasional memorable phrases which do not offend his own pieties. He also refers in passing twice to Sam Moskowitz, reminding readers that in the latter's account of science fiction fandom, *Immortal Storm*, there was some reference to fanzines. But he does not make clear that Moskowitz, alone among the contributors to such publications, is still taken seriously enough at least to be reproved or condescended to in print by recent serious critics of sf.

Nonetheless, Moskowitz remains to this day an aging but unreconstructed fan. Many decades ago, he began publishing in fanzines and still does, having become in the interim neither an academic (despite the proliferation of courses in science fiction) nor even an author of sf. Yet he has attained high visibility if not actual eminence among critics in the field through sheer longevity and dogged persistence. His collected essays appeared during the 1960s in volumes called *Explorers of the Infinite* and *Seekers of Tomorrow*; and since that time he has established himself as the expert on Olaf Stapledon, whom he actually listened to as a young fan and with whose widow he has kept in touch in more recent years. Since I myself have learned much from Moskowitz about Stapledon, I can scarcely afford to scorn him. But I feel obliged to insist that he represents the *weaknesses* as well as the strengths of the fanzine tradition.

If on the one hand, he has remained an amateur in the best sense of the word—writing out of love, rather than a need to make a buck in the marketplace or to achieve tenure and promotion in the university, and in a language comprehensible to the dewiest admirer of the writers he discusses; on the other hand, he has stayed smugly parochial and naïve: a superannuated groupie, not merely contemptuous but unaware of most contemporary books outside the closed circle of sf, as well as the critical methodologies invented in the last several decades to analyse and evaluate them. He seems, moreover, strangely untouched by two cultural events—one largely a product of the fifties, the other a creation of the turbulent later sixties—which have changed the nature of science fiction by changing the social context in which it is written, marketed, and read.

These two developments not only enlarged the once minuscule homogeneous audience for science fiction, making hard-core fans an even smaller minority; they also introduced new kinds of writers into what had for long been an even more homogeneous group of writers, an organic community, bound together almost incestuously by ties personal as well as professional. Many of the new writers (who eventually proselytized and made converts among the old) were children not of the whiskey culture, to which those older writers originally belonged, quite like their distinguished mainstream contemporaries, but of the hallucinogenic drug culture. The politics of the former, moreover, were no longer responding, like the politics of the laureates of science fiction's Golden Age, to the threat and fact of World War II and the Cold War which followed, but to the civil rights movement and the resistance to the undeclared war in Vietnam. The newer wave of writers though they sometimes disavowed the label of science fiction and occasionally made rude remarks about their predecessors in the genre, were, of course, wittingly or unwittingly radically influenced by them. Yet they also emulated modernist or even postmodernist fictionists like Borges, Nabokov, John Barth, and Donald Barthelme, trying (it was a desperate and equivocal game) to meet the standards of established criticism, as, say, Heinlein, Asimov, and Van Vogt had not, without losing the audience first attracted to science fiction by such forerunners, or cutting themselves off from the markets which specialized in that genre.

Self-conscious in the extreme, such writers not only revised the implicit definition of the genre and tried vainly to rebaptize it speculative fiction they began to write a new kind of in-house criticism, chiefly in the form of manifestos, occasionally essays and introductions to New Wave anthologies. Harlan Ellison and Samuel Delany, among others, produced interesting work of this kind. But no large authoritative volume representing this point of view has ever appeared, though Alexei and Cory Panshin, fellow-travelers of the new movement, tried not quite successfully to do so. Much more influential than their book, however, are two ambitious studies written by longer- and better-established writers of the genre, aware that it is not longer possible to write, as Moskowitz has never ceased to do, for naïve enthusiasts whom one already knew from having met them at a score of conventions. By the early 1970s a large proportion of the buyers of science fiction were moved not by private enthusiasm, but by the course requirements of classes in the genre, which were proliferating up and down the land; and which by their very existence challenged (even as certain latter-day writers continued to challenge) a distinction between sf and mainstream literature that both the writers of the Golden Age and the critics who ignored them accepted, as it were, on faith.

These two major studies of the seventies, Brian Aldiss's *Billion Year Spree*, which was published in 1973, and James Gunn's *Alternate Worlds*, which appeared in 1975, by no means subscribe unqualifiedly to the aesthetics of the New Wave. James Gunn, as a matter of fact, though he is himself a longtime teacher, one of the pioneers of the entry of sf into the academy, and is aware therefore both that his study and the works it treats will be read in the classroom and that recent developments in the genre are irreversible, deplores those developments from within the enemy camp. He was, after all, a writer of science fiction even before he became a teacher, and he believes still that pessimism and experimentalism are essentially hostile to the nature of the genre. Consequently, he ends by excommunicating certain contenders from the canon on the grounds that they are hopelessly mainstream. He finds Aldous Huxley's "dismal view of man" in *Brave New World*, for instance, "alien to the spirit of the genre"—excluding him in a gesture which, instead of rejecting the elitism of established criticism, merely stands it on its head.

Aldiss, on the other hand, though he still leads the old style life of a free-lance extra-academic, is not only willing to accept Huxley, or for that matter, the New Wavers, but cheerfully grants that "Academia and the middle class are moving in on sf," and is prepared to consider as legitimate studies with titles like "Science Fiction as Objective Correlative," since he argues, "For all its fun, sf has long been a cerebal field and rewards such analysis." But he proves finally more ambivalent on this score than such comments indicate—taking time out from a discussion of Olaf Stapledon, to excoriate "the funeral masons and morticians who work their preserving processes on Eng.Lit." Both Gunn and Aldiss bring to the genre knowledge of the mainstream canon, along with a nodding acquaintance with the critical methodologies first developed to deal with high literature. Neither, however, though they may in sense have opened a door to them, are at home with the critical approaches listed in the "Call for Papers" advertising the conference at which I first delivered these remarks: "structuralist, Marxist, psychocritical, feminist . . . semiotical, rhetorical, and hermeneutic."

Candor compels me to confess, that though I myself remain to this day what I have been for more than forty years, an academic, I find most of these approaches unsympathetic for dealing with any living literature in a mass society like our own, and all of them radically inappropriate to a popular genre, whose practitioners are on record as considering "The Cold Equations" their all-time favorite story. It is not merely, I think, the fact that I have recently become a writer of science fiction, proud that my most recent effort is to be included in Harlan Ellison's *Last Dangerous Visions*, that cues my dis-ease with the work of such highbrow revisionist Marxists as Darko Suvin or structuralists and poststructuralists like Eric S. Rabkin and Robert Scholes, indeed with most of the critical pieces produced under the auspices of the Science Fiction Section of the Modern Language Association or published in journals like *Extrapolation* and *Science-Fiction Studies*. It is also, and chiefly, my convictions as a literary populist, impatient with the alienation of current critical writing from the large audience and all the fiction they especially relish, that I find the attempt to transfer to sf approaches which fail to do justice even to Mark Twain, Dickens, or, for that matter, Shakespeare, especially devious, duplicitous, unwittingly hypocritical, or worse, unconsciously self-parodic.

Typically written by a younger generation of university "scholars," who grew up loving hard-core science fiction, but concealed that fact until it no longer seemed an impediment to academic promotion, such articles try to justify a passion rooted in the naïve responses of childhood and early adolescence in a language appropriate only to the most sterile hermetic discourse about equally hermetic books. Sometimes I am tempted to believe that what we need in order to close the breech between the criticism we write and the stories which are its subject is a return to the kind of pop criticism practised in the fanzines: a way of responding without reflection, admiring without apology, and praising without restraint stories which we once subversively preferred to those assigned to us in class as classics or great books—precisely because the former had not yet been travestied like *Moby Dick* or *Hamlet* by scholarly exegesis.

But we are out of that Garden forever; and, indeed, it has come to seem to us in retrospect more ghetto than Garden, at best the kindly prison of the nursery. It would, therefore, be self-deceiving nostalgia to pretend that we can return to it at will, and hypocrisy twice compounded to deny that we have collaborated in, wished for our expulsion. The moment of that expulsion can be dated exactly—occurring with the publication in 1961 of Kingsley Amis's *New Maps of Hell*, in which for the first time a dialogue was opened up between a far-from-naïve fan of sf in don's clothing and the world of proper academic intellectuals, to whom that genre had hitherto seemed the inexplicable addiction of people with whom they did not ordinarily converse at all. Originally delivered in the late fifties as the Christian Gauss Lectures at Princeton University, Amis's study represented a pioneering attempt to preach not to the converted but to the skeptical, whom he tried valiantly to convince that sf was at least *discussable* in an academic context. Despite his limitation (he had an exclusive taste for the satiric, dystopic mode, especially when its politics were right wing) Amis managed to deal with science fiction as literature, without denying the fact that it had first been produced by journeymen trying to please an audience which considered itself hostile to art. Yet his book failed to make a major impact either in the university circles, where he seemed finally himself just a pop writer pretending to be a professor, nor in the still closed world of science fiction fandom, to which he seemed a hopeless outsider (his novels however popular, were *not* sf ) trying to disturb its self-congratulatory parochialism. His final failure is, however, not solely explicable in terms of his credentials not being right for either side, since the time was simply not yet ripe for any such attempt.

Not until the seventies, when, on the one hand, more and more English departments, under pressure from students and radical young faculty, were offering courses in "popular literature," and, on the other, more and more writers of science fiction were becoming discontent with the traditional limits of the genre, could a book with similar ambitions find its audience. That book was, of course, Aldiss's *Billion Year Spree*, to which I return again and again both for its insights (especially into earlier works in the field) and its relaxed colloquial style, appropriate to "a genre which" he reminds us, "has its strong fun side." But Aldiss's book, is marred by a weakness shared with almost all subsequent sf criticism: a failure to deal adequately with the problem of *canonization*, which has indeed plagued science fiction from the very start. Aldiss begins properly enough by rejecting the total exclusion of sf as a genre from high literature, claiming for certain of its writers at least full citizenship in the republic of letters. But he tried to do so (misguidedly, counterproductively, it seems to me) by adopting the standards of elite criticism; which is to say, by establishing a canon of ok literature *within* the genre, cleaning house, as it were.

Clearly Aldiss, who is broadly knowledgeable in the field, has read and loved the American pulp-masters of the thirties, forties, and fifties, whose formulaic stories are rendered in a language without distinction or grace. Yet despite their vulgarity and naïveté (maybe, in some sense, precisely because of them), they manage to evoke a sense of wonder, rapture, magic, release of a kind notably *not* produced by much of the polite literature of the same period. Nonetheless, in his effort to maintain, in-house, a distinction between real literature and trash, Aldiss tends to treat such pop classics a little condescendingly. And his condescension turns into distaste, when he deals with their crude populist politics (sometimes verging on fascism), their old-fashioned realist aesthetic, and especially their strident and (to him) hollow optimism. Quite the opposite of James Gunn in this regard, what he calls for in the place of heartiness and required euphoria, is something he describes as the "natural and decent despair which has always characterized everyday literature." What he means by "everyday literature" is, of course, mainstream writing, especially of the early modernist school; best exemplified for him, it would appear, by the poetry of W. H. Auden, with its stoical confrontation of evil and its orthodox belief in the fallen nature of man.

At any rate, because of this bias, Aldiss fails to do justice to the three great father figures of the American Golden Age, Heinlein, Asimov, and especially A.E. Van Vogt, whose "creative insanity" he is willing to acknowledge, but whose most influential and central book he completely ignores. Given his prejudices, one does not expect Aldiss to speak of *Slan* as hyperbolically as does Moskowitz, who calls it Van Vogt's "most famous and perhaps best work"; but one expects at least a mention of it in so compendious and inclusive a history of the genre as *Billion Year Spree*.

Van Vogt is a test case, and not just for Aldiss; since any apology for or analysis of science fiction which fails to come to terms with his appeal and major importance, defends or defines the genre by falsifying it. If a writer as widely sympathetic to sf in all its varieties as Aldiss flunks that test, what can we expect of later, more academic, elitist, and rigorous critics like Rabkin and Scholes but total disaster. Indeed, they tell us in their ambitious and otherwise useful study, *Science Fiction: History, Science, Vision* (1977), that Van Vogt has not worn well, and that *Slan*, whose centrality to his work they do not deny, proves him "precisely the sort of writer that has given science fiction a bad name among serious readers." My heart sinks at the phrase "serious readers," and when Rabkin and Scholes go on to say of the same novel that "this is not fiction for adults," I lose all hope. It is, after all, the availability to children and the childlike in us all, along with the challenge to the defunct notion of the serious reader which characterizes not just Van Vogt but all sf at its most authentic.

Any bright high school sophomore can identify all the things that are *wrong* about Van Vogt, whose clumsiness is equaled only by his stupidity. But the challenge to criticism which pretends to do justice to science fiction is to say what is *right* about him: to identify his mythopoeic power, his ability to evoke primordial images, his gift for redeeming the marvelous in a world in which technology has preempted the province of magic and God is dead. To do this, structuralism and its spin-offs, those strange French (or naturalized Slavic) gods after whom recent scholars of fantasy and popular literature have gone a-whoring, are of little help—as, indeed, they are of little help with any good-bad literature, whose virtues are independent of the text and therefore immune to semiotic analysis.

Yet there is a countertradition in France itself, which begins with the post–World War II writer, Boris Vian, who himself relished and proselytized on behalf of many aspects of American mass culture, ranging from rock music to science fiction. Not only did he himself write an sf novel called *Et on tuera tous les affreux* [And we'll kill all the uglies], pretending to translate it from the English of Vernon Sullivan, a totally fictional black American passing as white, he also introduced Van Vogt to Parisian intellectuals with a translation of *The World of Null-A*—thus encouraging a marriage of the avant-garde and hard-core sf, most recently exemplified in an ironic *nouveau roman*, entitled *Philip José Farmer conquiert l'univers*.

But despite such flirtations with sf on the avant-garde edges of high literature (matched in Italy by Italo Calvino and in the United States by Thomas Pynchon), most established critics in the Western world have remained unconvinced by the Aldiss strategy; which is to say, the device of rejecting some long-honored sf writers of especial ineptness has not persuaded them to accept others considered classics even by Rabkin and Scholes. The critical establishment continues to exclude from *its* canon not just the Van Vogts and Doc Smiths, but even so revered a figure (in the field) as Olaf Stapledon, who represents in this sense a complementary test case. That unreconstructed mainstream critics have flunked this test as egregiously as revisionist sf critics have the other, should astound no one. But it does baffle Brian Aldiss, who ends up crying out in rage and frustration that their rejection of the author of *Star Maker* and *Last and First Men* "is a matter from which speculation falls fainting away."

Stapledon himself, however, lived long enough to come to terms with that rejection; and indeed he half-expected it from the start, realizing (or at least asserting defensively) that he was not an "intellectual" or a "highbrow," like, say, James Joyce, whom he confessed not understanding, or the aesthetes of Bloomsbury, whom he never tired of satirizing. Quite simply, Stapledon was rejected in his own time and continues in ours to be scorned or ignored by the guardians of Eng. Lit. because, stubbornly provincial and old-fashioned, he was immune to the breakthrough of modernism, the "Revolution of the

Word." He preferred always the high rhetorical style of the late
Victorians, and the conventional structure of the H. G. Wellsian
"Romance" (no more than Wells did he ever call his own work
"science fiction"), though that style and that structure had been re-
manded long before the thirties, when he emerged as a writer, to the
realm of unpretentious pop.

If, therefore, Stapledon moves readers, including us, it is not (we
must learn to admit) as Joyce, Proust, Mann, Kafka or D. H. Lawrence—much less, such post-modernists as Nabokov, Barthelme or
Pynchon—move us. No, despite his superiority in executive skills,
linguistic precision, and subtlety of thought, his books affect us like the
novels of A. E. Van Vogt, which is to say, like sub- or para-literature.
Indeed, there is a clue to this in the metaphor Aldiss uses in praising
*Star Maker*, which he describes as "really the one great grey holy book
of science fiction."

"Holy" is the operative word, suggesting that we do not read *Star
Maker*—if we are responding to it properly—as we read, or, God
forbid, analyze or interpret James Joyce's *Ulysses*. We experience it
"scripturally," as perhaps unintended but quite valid "Scripture," that
is, as the mythological statement, accepted on faith, of a grid of
perception through which we see or aspire to see the world and
ourselves. Much popular literature, in our time, especially science
fiction and fantasy, is read thus; and therefore eventuates not in ethical
enlightenment or a heightened appreciation of virtuosic form, but in
transport, ecstacy, a radical transformation of sensibility—thus per-
mitting us to transcend momentarily the normal limits of consciousness and escape the ennui of routine awareness, the restrictive boundaries of the unitary ego.

Another way to say this is that we respond to sf even at its most
sophisticated, as we respond to fairy tales (at a level where, like
children, we have not ceased to feel at home with the marvelous), and
not as we do either to mimetic or self-reflexive formalist fiction. It is,
therefore, essentially for their mythopoeic power, their ability to
create or evoke the primordial images which trigger such ecstatic
release, that we prize the best-loved makers of science fiction, rather
than for their ethical import and metaphysical insight, their architectonic skill or linguistic subtlety. This is as true of those who happen to
possess the latter qualities, like H. G. Wells, Olaf Stapledon or Ursula
LeGuin, as of those who are notably lacking in them, like Heinlein,
Asimov or Doc Smith.

Both kinds of writer, whatever other satisfaction they may or may not give to the close and diligent reader, provide most of all, instant gratification—thus making us critic-pedagogues, initially at least, a little redundant. Pondering this fact confirms what surely any student of literary history suspects, that neither nobility of character, learning, or even good old true-blue Protestant hard work at their craft is necessary to mythopoeic writers. The sole absolute requirement is easy access to their own unconscious at the point where it meets the collective unconscious of us all. Clearly the reader is not made better in any sense of the word, not wiser, nor more pious, nor more sensitive, by the reading of sf. Like all popular literature, it affords pleasures more often than not disreputable, if not downright perverse. Consequently, to test the delightfully schlocky classics of the genre, any standards of elite criticism, ethical or aesthetic, are beside the point. When measured by traditional standards, it is not sf which fails the test, but those standards themselves, suggesting that it is high time to reject or revise the latter, not just for science fiction but for all literature which "pleases many and pleases long" So at least I am convinced. And that is why I am now engaged in writing a study of which these remarks are a part, an irreverent but loving look at the contemporary crisis in criticism which I am calling "What Was Literature?"

ERIC S. RABKIN

# The Descent of Fantasy

"All art," according to Oscar Wilde in his preface to *The Picture of Dorian Gray* (1891) "is quite useless." Indeed, all the qualities especially associated with verbal art are customarily dismissed as insignificant: specious arguments are just rhetoric, popular misconceptions are only myths, and impossible longings are mere fantasies. Nonetheless, we all acknowledge the universal occurrence of stories in general and of fantasies in particular: as the ancients knew, all leadership involves force of rhetoric; every culture founds itself on its own creation myth; and fantasies include both the socializing tales of insubstantial Faëry and the breathless visions of humankind's highest hopes. In the face of such ubiquity, I reaffirm the utility of art and wish to uncover at least part of what that utility might be. This subject, of course, is vast, as various as the forms of art and the myriad arenas of artistic production and consumption. And yet, if a phenomenon is universal, one supposes either parallel evolution of an extraordinary kind or descent from a common source or condition. This essay into what might be called semiobiology[1] is my initial attempt to sketch in the merest stages in the descent of fantasy. My speculations here are trials, attempts to lay out lines of inquiry and articulate areas of investigation without at this point marshaling the full data from those areas. Like Freud's primal myth, this cartoon is offered in the hope that it will draw forth debate and help in the posing of useful questions. I begin with the notion that if this fantastic story has use, as in eliciting useful questions, then other fantasies may have a use in common with it and that the telling of the story may suggest reasons why the story, and stories the world over, need to be told.

The first use of anything, or perhaps its last, is survival. The cacophony of modern biology opens every strain with random variations and ends each tune with a funeral dirge. Those of us who survive

14

dance to whatever tune the piper plays. In social beasts, such as we, the piper's music symbolizes our most powerful tool for survival: sociality. Bees find pollen by communicating with bees, deer protect their young from lions by grazing in herds, and men defend their safe territories by pledging allegiance to a flag. While the young of sea turtles hatch alone and march wobbly-legged to the sea, the offspring of primates cling to their parents and gaze into their eyes. Among the competing hordes of our ancestors, those races with the chance capacity to employ more signals more subtly held their territory best, hunted most efficiently, and beat or starved other hordes into extinction. The roaring lion coordinates the movements of his pride and holds sway over resources otherwise more easily run to ground by the swift but often solitary cheetah; the yapping canines flourish in far greater numbers—and biomass—than the stealthy felines; and the homo sapiens who teaches his offspring to wield a club and circle in on prey to the sound of a beating drum defeats them all. Men, in number and in biomass, overgrow every other single species. Our groups are the most efficient groups, the largest groups, the most stable and subtle and adaptable groups and we rule the world. The making of groups, the bringing of young into effective roles within groups, and the continual trimming of the life courses of individuals in groups, makes our potent sociality possible. The single most flexible tool for the creation, adjustment, and use of human groups is language. To be capable of language is to have a survival advantage; to be incapable of language is to abandon this particular field. The gorilla withdraws to ever smaller plots of Kenyan forest while our species hurls itself at the stars.

No human infant, dropped in the most equable clime, could survive alone. While this is true of some other animals, such as most primates, the interdependency of humans extends throughout life. Even the atavistic Natty Bumppo circulates about the fringes of society, tied to the rest of humanity by his need for shot and powder and, more important, his needs for companionship and sharing of values. To have been raised to human adulthood means to have been socialized, to have heard the stories of the sacrifice of one's own deity and the tales of origin of the plants one eats, to have acknowledged authority in the persons claiming your parentage, and to have chosen to take on your human mantle by speaking the formulaic words. The liar is cast out; the hypocrite is demoted; the tongue-tied are ignored; and the autistic do not reproduce at all. The greatest survival mechanism evolved by our species is sociality itself and the greatest tool evolved by our species for sociality is language.

Virtually all human functions necessary for survival are beyond much conscious control. Although we can choose one sort of food over another, few of us, in the presence of food, could or would starve to death; none of us could hold our breath to the point of death; almost all of us feel strong and frequent urges toward activity that results in tending the body and reproducing it. Most people, most of the time, succumb to these urges. In fact, human happiness seems to arise from the satisfaction of these urges to eat, to exercise, to rest, and even to tell and hear stories. I propose that such happiness is our reward for cooperating with the urges evolution has built into us. When we are tired, sleep feels good; when we are hungry, food feels good; when we are grappling with problems of understanding, storytelling and -listening feels good. I am glad to be able to tell this story to you.

In larger or smaller degree, those functions crucial to our group survival, which of course include functions that preserve the individual members of the group, all employ processes of exchange among members of the group. No human being could survive long, and certainly not reproduce and raise young, outside a functioning human economy. You feed the child while I gather the berries; you draw water while I hunt for meat; you stand guard while I sleep and in turn I will later guard you. Safety is not only in numbers but in communication used to organize the relations among those separate numbers. We will exchange your child-rearing services for my berry-gathering services, your water for my meat, our guardianship for each other's. Thus through exchange is sociality reinforced repeatedly and pleasurably in the daily necessities of human life.

In fairy tales, as Max Lüthi points out in *Once Upon a Time* (1970), no one ever says "I love you;" instead, food is given and taken. Lüthi was referring to mother love, as when Red Riding Hood's mother gives her cake and wine. But something is amiss in that story since the food is to be passed not to the child but by the child to the grandmother, that is, to the mother of the food provider. That social deformity manifests itself in Red Riding Hood's own desire to receive pleasure; she readily gives in to the wolf's suggestions that she stop and enjoy the woods. The girl's disobedience to her mother's instructions not to tarry compounds the social disorder. As the story proceeds, the consequences of this deformity grow: the girl is unsafe even in her own grandmother's house. Now the consequences of wishing oneself out of maternal control are traumatically clear; instead of eating the cakes and wine the mother gave her, the girl is in turn eaten. But social order is strong; the huntsman passes by and divines the difficulty. He slices open the wolf's belly and the girl gets the chance to be born again, this time much more obedient. In the Grimm brothers' version, "Little Red-cap said to herself that she would never stray about in the wood alone, but would mind what her mother told her."

This small story has much to tell us. Note first that it ends in obedience, that is, in the delineation of the exchange relations between parent and child: I give you food, you give me service. This obedience is established, or more properly reestablished, against expectable pressures. Mothers do sometimes show love to others than their children; children do sometimes have desires of their own. It is normal for some human affairs to tend against obedience. This is dangerous and wrong, the story seems to say to its little child listener, but, despite initial appearances, not necessarily fatal. One can easily imagine a grandmother lulling a granddaughter to sleep with this story, assuaging the child's guilt on a day that included some signal but understandable childish act of self-motivated desire. The story itself becomes a good for exchange: through the telling at the bedside, the grandmother is providing psychological pleasure in this story of heightened and then ameliorated fear; she is also providing the occasion to attend the child as sleep comes on, performing her grandmaternal guardianship. In return, the child is drawing the psychological sustenance that perhaps earlier it had been denied or feared it might lose as Red Riding Hood had to carry but not eat the cake and wine. In drawing this sustenance, the child listener is going to sleep as requested, being a good little child, and giving due obedience. By the telling of the story then the child is given one more opportunity at the end of the busy day to perform the required obedience. It can fall off to sleep now secure in the knowledge that it has been good and that the big people will therefore protect it. Society and its children rest secure on a base of known relationships.

This fairy tale is hardly unique. The relationship between mother love and food exchange is common. Witches are anti-mothers and known to be witches, as in "Hansel and Gretel," by their desire not to feed children but to eat them. When Snow White's evil stepmother can express her hate and envy no other way, she feeds the girl a poisoned apple. Cinderella's role in her stepmother's house is obviously topsy-turvy since it is the child who must do the cooking for the adult. Fortunately, the fairy godmother, doubtless the spirit of the dead true mother, provides help, just as other god figures in all cultures demonstrate their parental care by providing loaves and fishes or manna or cargo or, through their own ultimate sacrifices, the seasonal renewal that is life itself, a sacrifice we participate in by retelling the god's story, by performing again the rituals of painful initiation, by taking the host into our own mouths and consuming the god in obedience to him. By this exchange, performed often with the help of such powerful tale bearers as educated priests or epileptic shamans, human sociality is extended to the fullness of the awesome universe engulfing us and thus the realm of the overpowering is made the realm of our parents and our right relation to it is defined. Through the story, we become able to sleep in comparative peace.

There are other kinds of love than mother love. Cinderella dances in the embrace of the Prince; Sleeping Beauty is awakened with a kiss; Rapunzel bears her lover twins. Put bluntly but truly, the phrase "I love you" is omitted from these stories not to be replaced by an exchange of food but by an exchange of physical contact. Seen most oppressively, the exchange of genital contact defines, at least for Susan Brownmiller (*Against Our Will*, 1975), a social order dependent on constant rape. I will give you my daughter if you will give me her bride-price. Seen less oppressively, the ordering of allowable exchanges of genital contact is not only the concern of these stories but of marriage rites, law, and courtship rituals—including a young couple's self-revelation through presentation of autobiographical narratives. Exchange of genital contact, like the exchange of food and guardianship, is crucial for the survival of our species and is, in our species, accomplished with and through the employment of language in general and stories in particular.

Language can be used for many purposes. Each phrase made and attended to participates in the continual jostling within the web of sociality that maintains and develops our human groups. Aggressive competition, strongly suggestive of territorial posturing, plays out the social drama through the weapons of promise and threat. Promises and threats are made of language and are exchange items. Social relations may be revealed in part by discovering whose threats have sway with whom, whose promises are relied on by whom, the nature of the reciprocity or asymmetry of those relations and so on. The king's promise and threat are the law of the land; he need rely on no one's word. The serf extends all promises of loyalty if required to do so, including even acknowledgement of the droit du seigneur, relying on the promise of protection and believing the threat of dissociation from the human economy by sanction or by death. Thus the hierarchy of feudal society comes in focus. Tristan is bound by his oath. Nowadays the exchange of food that means "I love you" (or is it the other way round?) does not go only from female to male and the exchange of protection marked by the marriage ring does not go only from male to female. Women often pay for men at restaurants and men often wear wedding rings. Tristan and Isolde each drank the magic love potion and created a symmetrical social order between themselves that was insupportable in the inevitable and overwhelming network of the hierarchical society they both more generally inhabited. The result was death. Tristan had no offspring.

Language obviously has exchange value. It is worth much to some people to have the right person say "I dub thee knight," "He is my friend," or "You may now kiss the bride." Unlike money or cowrie shells, however, language does not have only exchange value. The exchanges of language may be used to warn, cajole, coordinate. All of these activities, done by us to each other, keep producing our social world.

What world do we inhabit? My world, to take an example with which I am acquainted, floats tiny in the emptiness of space. Yet this was true of no one's world until 1643, the year in which Evangelista Torricelli deduced by experiment that the air around us was a local phenomenon and that most of the distance to the moon must be truly empty. How did he deduce this? I can only say by telling you what he did: he took a tube, sealed at one end and filled with mercury, and inverted it into a bath of mercury. The mercury began to flow out of the tube but then stopped, producing in the top of the tube a partial vacuum and suggesting to the early physicist that air had weight. Given this hint, he quickly discerned that the weight of air necessary to hold up the column of mercury, what we now call barometric pressure, would be produced by a column no more than five miles tall if the air did not attentuate. And the moon was known to be a quarter of a million miles away. Suddenly, nature preferred a vacuum. Outer space was discovered.

This little story, like the tale of Red Riding Hood, also has, I think, much to tell us. First, it has a human interest, the happy conjunction of accident and genius, the satisfactory correction of error. Second, it must once have—in fact did—reshape people's beliefs about the nature of their world. Aristotle's assertion that nature abhors a vacuum was dealt a hard blow. This story is the current basis for my own belief in the vacuum of space although I did not know the story until many years after I had already been taught of the vacuum. I believed my teachers and they believed their teachers, or so I suppose, back to Torricelli. This story about Torricelli explains their belief, at least to my satisfaction, and thus my sense of the world conforms to the story. Yet I must admit that I have never felt or seen the vacuum of space nor have I ever seen Torricelli's experiment performed. My belief rests on the reliance I place on the tale and on the plausibility of the tale given all else I have come to accept. It is true that so-called scientific facts take their places within a web of observations and assertions which have implications for each other and so no single experiment need be personally experienced in order to assent to science. Yet it is equally true that the vast majority of what we know we know only by report, relying on a few tests having proved true and thus having established the probable believability of individuals. When scientists are found to have distorted their results, they are fired and ostracized. Believability is not simply a matter of the truth of one's assertions but of one's place in the social fabric, a place defined by one's own experience and attested to by one's own life story. When you apply for an academic job, you send your vita—the summary of your life—before you. I did a few experiments in school, and many of them worked out much as the books said they would, but my belief in outer space really rests on my belief in the social order, a continuous and evolving thing that extends back over three centuries to Torricelli and over the eons to our mute ancestors on the ancient plains.

All explanations, I would suggest, are at bottom narrative. Not only does scientific explanation require faith in the telling but all matters of human fact are established by testimony and history. Not only will the sun rise because it has always risen but the sacred symbol will lead us to victory because it has always done so. The most immutable narratives, the explanations for the most profound aspects of our world, are told in a time out of time, the time of ever-repeatable scientific experiment and the time of myth and fairy-land; the times, in short, of permanent reality and of untouchable fantasy. We learn by conditioning: once bitten, twice shy. For a social animal, there is an obvious survival advantage in being able to understand and believe someone else's experience. Events happen to us all. Language can report these events. Narrative is the exchange of the report of events. A full theory of narrative would clearly need to ask who exchanges what sorts of reports of what sorts of events with whom in what contexts for what purposes. That is a massive project; let us focus in this first effort on the story at hand.

My telling the story of Torricelli does have exchange value. It may, for example by its oddity perhaps or its satisfactory resolution, strike you as a good story and hence one you are glad to have heard.

That would make me, in consequence, a bit more of an individual whom you might credit, to whom you might extend believability. In addition to simple exchange value (I'll tell you a joke for five dollars) a storytelling performs other social functions. The telling may well help define the status of the teller and of the hearer in the sociality, the nature of the world beliefs they may share, and may give happiness or in some other way cooperate with some fundamental urge. The fundamental urges we might spot operating in the telling of this story are several: curiosity has survival value and so does its exercise; its assuagement by this narrative ought to give some pleasure. Order and regularity are well worth perceiving for they help us predict future conditions and hence prepare for them; stories with perceivable form assuage the desire for order. But once we have come to the idea of stories serving us by their very order, we have come to the point of suggesting that part of the true use of a story is its aesthetic value. I would suggest that the telling of proper tales, well made and rhetorically interesting tales, in a social world so dominated by language exchange as is ours, signals social success and the likelihood of social position. He who can produce good language has a constant supply of items for social exchange. Just as grebes delight potential mates with displays of plumage and acrobatics, we delight our potential mates, or curry our employers or dominate our inferiors, by displays of language. The development of an aesthetic sense has survival value and one ought to wonder little that, in varying degrees, all humans share it.

The most brutal narratives simply assert social order on the basis of that order: "Do this because I am your father" or "The law is the law." In other words, there are other words, older words that recount earlier events such as intercourse or legislation and these earlier events are to be taken to institute and explain our worlds. Yet it is not the events which institute our world but our belief in the report of the events. This belief comes in part from our experience in social exchange—we know teachers and doctors and parents are trustworthy by experience and by failure to disconfirm our earlier belief in them; this belief also comes in part from our capacity to test some of the reports against our own experience; and this belief finally comes in part from our aesthetic sense. To tell a well made story is to move up in the social scale. Priests and poets have often dominated soldiers and stonecutters. The pen, we have all said, is mightier than the sword. For a species for which the question of the well-madeness of language is and should be central to survival and reproduction, an aesthetic sense is a tool for survival. How shall we exercise that aesthetic sense?

Narratives are but one class of language as used that might be tested aesthetically, but they are a significant class. Some utterances are primarily adjunct to accomplishing physical deeds. We warn people to duck a flying object, command platoons into battle in the most deadly manner, and teach apprentices how to wield their tools. These utterances are judged in part by their well-madeness, but mostly they are judged by their effect. A vulgar, mispronounced order that nonetheless carries the day was a good order. In narratives, different sorts of events may be reported. Some of those events, like what happened when Torricelli did what to which, are testable and may be judged good or bad according to their accuracy. Such tales, however, fit less completely into the realm of physical consequence of military commands and more into the social fabric of believability. The tale might be better or worse told. Narratives that are the least susceptible to physical test must be judged most by their well-madeness. There is minimal specifiable content to the great assertions of religion, like "God is love," and there is minimal testable report in the great narratives of creation. The same is true of fairy tales. But these tales are great despite their untestability because they assuage, in a broad and powerful way, our aesthetic sense. While the theories of caloric and phlogiston are no more, the story of the Fall still touches us. In part this is so because the content accords with something in our own lives, of course, but in part because the story handles that something in ways to create potent order, aesthetic order. The more the particular, realistic content in a narrative, the more susceptible it is to disconfirmation; the less the particular, realistic content, the more its value rests on aesthetic considerations. Fantasies are special narratives made of unfalsifiable events in part so that the reports of these events can be exchanged long after particular reality changes. The exchanging of reports of fantastic events shapes the world of homo sapiens. And it is by well made fantasy that homo sapiens shapes the world. Put another way, displaced as they are from our time and our world, fantasies are the richest field for the growth and display of the human aesthetic urge, an urge inherited through the accidents of survival and competition and remaining with us as a crucial capacity for our group struggle on toward the future. The descent of fantasy mirrors the descent of man.

GERALD PRINCE

# How New Is New?

I am, rather appropriately, an alien: I have not read very much science fiction. I am, of course, acquainted with Plato's *Republic* and More's *Utopia*; I know *Brave New World*, *1984*, Cyrano, Voltaire, and most of Jules Verne; and I have read at least one work by such luminaries as Heinlein, Asimov, Philip K. Dick, and Ursula LeGuin. But I am not even an irregular reader of anthologies or magazines; nor do I consume, like some of my friends, an sf novel a day. I should add perhaps that, since familiarizing myself with some of the critical literature, I do not quite know whether my statement, so far, can be very meaningful for I am no longer entirely sure what science fiction is: one prominent critic, for instance, does not consider "the space adventure story . . . as science fiction at all"; and another one thinks that Ray Bradbury is a writer of pure fantasy;[1] conversely, it seems that not only Barth, Coover, and Pynchon but also Cervantes, Defoe, and Kafka are really writers of sf. Speaking very generally and approximately, and whether or not all of the great forerunners and pioneers are included, I suppose, however, that any assessment of science fiction ought not to disregard the production and achievements of what is referred to as mere space opera, of what is called the Golden Age, or of what has been dubbed the New Wave; in other words, it ought not to neglect what can be designated, with a touch of arbitrariness and snobbery, as lowbrow, middlebrow, or highbrow sf. Maybe I should also state explicitly that I do not particularly like science fiction (except for some of its titles) but that I also do not dislike it (except for character and place names which I don't even know how to pronounce). My main purpose here is therefore not to denounce the weaknesses of the genre or to extol its strengths, not to bury it or praise it. Rather, I intend to focus on the capacity of science fiction for newness. Naturally, I will

base my arguments on extrapolating from what little I have read, all
the while hoping for tolerance.

We all know that science fiction, especially when compared with
so-called mainstream fiction, has provided the occasion not only for
many crudely negative statements but also for some highly positive
ones. Of the latter, an entire set seems to me somewhat misguided. I
am not referring to the words of Judith Merrill for whom there was "no
adequate literature in existence" in 1966 except for some science
fiction; or to those of Samuel R. Delany, who said in 1976 that "just in
terms of Bradbury, Bester, and Sturgeon you have more exciting
language being done in science fiction in the fifties than you have in all
of the mainstream put together"; or to those of Robert Heinlein,
according to whom sf is the "most difficult of all prose forms," superior
to historical and contemporary-scene fiction and the only kind of work
"which stands even a chance of interpreting the spirit of our times."[2]
Nor am I thinking of the many representations of sf as a superb
predictive instrument since it is now widely recognized, I believe, that,
on the contrary, sf is not very successful at prophecy. No, I am talking
about those depictions of sf that put the accent on its capacity for
newness, presenting it as a particularly privileged form for capturing
the new and saluting it for being itself new. Critics too often praise sf
for creating a new human consciousness by producing fictions that are
newer than their mainstream counterparts. Thus, Boris Vian calls sf a
"nouvelle mystique"; David Ketterer believes that it "puts humanity
in a radically new perspective," destroying old assumptions and suggesting "a new, and often visionary, reality"; Edward De Bono finds
that it "tugs the mind into new frames of reference"; Alvin Toffler
thinks that, to avoid future shock, the shock of the new, we had better
arm ourselves with some sf; and several others feel that science fiction
constitutes a superb laboratory for testing new products or understanding the new man (shades of Zola's *Experimental Novel!*).[3]

Now, it is certainly true that, whether we consider lowbrow,
middlebrow, or highbrow science fiction, we will find much that could
be called new. *Frankenstein* was new; indeed, it was, in some sense,
inaugural. Jules Verne, with his remarkable enthusiasm for hardware,
was new. H. G. Wells was new and did invent the time machine. Such
fundamental themes of sf as time travel, robot construction, cosmic
invasion, or alternate time streams were new; and parables developed
around these themes and telling of an individual who is his own father
or describing an artist who, because he travels to the past, is able to

imitate his own material of twenty years later were also new. Even four-eyed aliens with indigo skin and sixteen fingers would have to be regarded as new, in some way; and, at least within science fiction, the New Wave, with its radicalism and self-consciousness, certainly deserved its name. Besides, didn't sf provide us with expressions like *robot, Big Brother, 1984,* and *brave new world*?

A lot of evidence seems to be there and it is overwhelming. Yet, when it comes to science fiction, I am a little bit like some of Ray Bradbury's astronauts. You will remember that, some time in the late twentieth or early twenty-first century, several astronauts from Earth (from Ohio, to be more specific) arrive on the planet Mars. Their ship lands on a lawn of green grass upon which stands an iron deer. Further up the lawn, there is a brown Victorian house, with hairy geraniums and an old swing on the porch. All around, there are other houses, white ones and red brick ones; there are church steeples with golden bells; there are elm trees and maples and horse chestnuts. Somebody, somewhere, is playing "Beautiful Dreamer" on the piano. Somewhere else, a phonograph is "hissing out a record of 'Roamin' in the Gloamin',' sung by Harry Lauder." The Martian site, it appears, is very much like earth towns around 1920 or 1925. Indeed, it is practically a replica of Green Bluff, Illinois, where the ship's captain was born.[4] Well, when I read science fiction, I do not see a strange universe; I see my own familiar world. I recognize the known rather than glimpsing the unknown. Instead of new problems, I discover age-old puzzles or fairly contemporary ones. I come upon myth and not, as some would have it, upon a form diametrically opposed to it. I do not feel anxious or disoriented but secure. I am not drawn into a space fostering Negative Capability but into a scene inclined to Certitude. I do not find the new but the old.

It may, of course, be simple ignorance on my part: like the tourist (or the anthropologist) who is condemned always to come up against what he is already acquainted with (for how could he see what he has never learned to see?), I perceive only that which is not unfamiliar. It may be sheer madness. In another Martian Chronicle, Captain Jonathan Williams, from New York City, lands on Mars with his crew. He knocks on the door of a stone house and a woman answers: "Well? . . . What do you want? . . . —We are from Earth. I'm Captain Williams . . . we are from earth . . . I don't think you *understand* . . . We're from *Earth*!—I haven't time . . . I have a lot of cooking today and there's cleaning and sewing and all."[5] Williams slowly realizes that he has come upon an insane asylum. It may also be blind prejudice, stubborn resistance to sf. But I don't think so. At least, I don't think it is only a matter of want of knowledge, insanity, or bias.

In the first place, there are innumerable examples I could use to account for my reactions, examples taken not only from the founding parents of science fiction, from space opera, or from sword and sorcery, but also from more recent mainstream sf and even from various New Wave products. Jules Verne's masterpieces are mainly old-fashioned fictional spaces brimming with technological hardware; H. G. Wells's wonderful *Time Machine* uses temporal distantiation to dramatize social problems in Victorian England; space opera transplants the western from Texas or Montana to Saturn or Mars; and sword and sorcery describes faraway planets and galaxies teeming with dukes, duchesses, and conjurers born in Medieval Europe. Important and very popular works from the Golden Age of sf and after are structured in terms of a spy story, a love story, a crime story, or some well-studied paradox about time and space. Villains are punished and heroes rewarded just like in fairy tales; behind most mutants stands a romantic figure; and, as Michel Butor once remarked, a spaceship is nothing other than a magic carpet in disguise.[6] More specifically, Isaac Asimov's *Foundation* trilogy, apart from offering a rather hackneyed and simplistic account of mankind's history, is a good thriller in which, as is well known, a teenager saves an entire galaxy; and the much-acclaimed *Canticle for Leibowitz* develops the ultraclassical theme of ignorance-cum-charity triumphant. Even New Wave works are not free from the grip of what is already quite old. For instance, J. G. Ballard, who is justly admired, often brings to mind surrealistic fiction.

I should add that nothing of what I have just said is idiosyncratic and that all of it is itself pretty old. Indeed, New Wave writing can perhaps be explained in part as a rebellion against science fiction's dependence on well-worn schemes. Moreover, many excellent critics, who probably love sf and certainly do not despise it, have repeatedly pointed out its attraction for conventional forms and contents. Mark Rose calls science fiction "the characteristic romance form of the scientific age"; Robert Scholes and Eric S. Rabkin show how it uses the discoveries of science "to motivate inquiry into age-old problems;" John Huntington argues vigorously that it portrays the present rather than the future and that it is quite conservative at heart; and Stanislaw Lem accuses sf writers of constructing their new worlds with clichés.[7]

I should also add that much if not all of what I have said applies to non–science fiction as well: not only is it very tricky (and perhaps futile) to talk of the new (new for whom? and for what?), it is also very hard to innovate and surprise. In the case of genres associated because of their very names with astonishment, it becomes even harder. As C. S. Lewis said: "Only the first visit to Mars . . . is . . . any good."[8] Furthermore, disregarding what is, at most, superficially new (the New Ajax or New Fab variety!), one might point out that, for the truly new to be felt as such, it must somehow incorporate the old. What is the *other* as strictly *other*? What is the *unknown* as *unknown*? Any representation, any utterance must, in order to be meaningful, be connected in some way to the known and no world or being can be constructed that is not somehow related to our experience.

Finally, I should add that, for every example of something relatively old in science fiction, one can come up with an example of something relatively new, even in the very works I have taken to be fossilized. But that is not the point. What I want to argue is that sf is inherently wedded to the familiar because of at least three constraints to which its very nature subjects it (three classes in which it can be included).

One constraint I have already touched upon. Science fiction is fiction and the materials of fiction are always old, to some extent. This is perhaps why novels are often dismissed by "serious" people: if you have read one, you have read them all; they are useless; at best, a luxury, an antique, for example. It is also why some avant-garde writers have rejected fiction to opt for "writing," *écriture*, and doggedly pursue nonrepresentational linguistic constructs. Obviously, for certain fictional modes, say, realistic ones, familiarity is a boon: this is indeed the world we know! For science fiction, on the other hand, unless it underlines its allegorical thrust or portrays a world very close to our own in spatiotemporal terms and avoids drastic changes in the conditions of life depicted, the consequences can be disappointing. What! Thirty thousand years from now and millions of miles away, in a universe ruled by giant butterflies and where teleportion is commonplace, money, love, and glory still rule! It is a little bit like watching a television series where, week after week, the protagonists go through harrowing new experiences yet, week after week, they go on behaving in exactly the same way. *Plus ça change, plus c'est la même chose* (which is, of course, an important theme in sf).

The second constraint, which is related to the first though by no means equivalent to it, is the constraint of narrative. Like much, not to say all, of fiction, sf is articulated narratively. Now, narrative is one of the most powerful modes of organizing experience, controlling disorder, eliminating disparities; it has even been called fascistic in Gallic or Gallic-inspired flights of lyricism. Narrative is also one of the oldest such modes; indeed, it must go back to the origins of language. Above all, it is one of the most predictable (at least for some of us), casting series of situations and events in one of ten, or twenty, or a hundred basic molds. It may seem, on the surface, that the variety of narrative forms is inexhaustible; but we should not forget that there are grammars of narrative, algorithms for generating all and only possible narratives with a finite set of rules. I could write a diary novel in the third person, avoid a chronological ordering of entries, and adopt a strictly predictive mode of narration. I do not believe that there now exists such a work and, in a sense, I would be innovating; on the other hand, of course, such an innovation is one of the possibilities described by narrative grammars. Because of its nature, because of its predilection for order and meaningfulness, narrative is the enemy of scandal and *difference*. This partly explains why realistic writers have often tried to downplay the narrative dimension of their productions: life is neither orderly nor meaningful. It also explains why more adventurous writers, in and out of science fiction, have attempted to move away from or go beyond the more traditional kind of narrative, by laying bare its procedures, subverting its believability, refusing its linear and totalizing schemes. A few novelists—I am thinking of someone like Philippe Sollers—have even abandoned narrative entirely. In the case of sf, this might prove to be difficult. When Samuel Delany, without discarding narrative, rejected traditional mimetic conventions in favor of a highly self-reflexive discourse, various readers wondered whether his *Dhalgren* was science fiction at all. Suppose now that an sf writer decided to eliminate narrative altogether from his work. Not only would he lose many of his readers (I imagine there are more grievous losses!); he would also discover that he was no longer producing science fiction but, rather, a semiphilosophical treatise, a poetic prose, or a kind of writing as yet unnamed.

The third constraint is, I think, the most important one and the one most specific to sf. It is the constraint of plausibility, credibility, rationality or, to put it more precisely, the constraint of scientific motivation. Science fiction is what it is (and not, say, "plain" fiction, or detective fiction, or fantasy) because it always makes a bow, however casual and quick, to science. By this, I do not simply mean that it shows the impact of scientific thought upon artistic endeavors: Zola was heavily influenced by Claude Bernard and his experimental method; countless parallels have been drawn between so-called postmodernis-

tic fiction and Heisenberg's uncertainty principle; and, in some way or
other, no literary production is unaffected by the scientific horizons of
its age. I mean that science fiction is articulated around some distortion
of reality as we know it and that it explicitly accounts for that distortion
with the help of some real or fictive scientific achievement or concept.
As Eric S. Rabkin put it, "a work belongs in the genre of *science fiction*
if its narrative world is at least somewhat different from our own, and if
that difference is apparent against the background of an organized
body of knowledge [read: 'science']."[9]

It is this explicit link to scientific or pseudoscientific achievements
and concepts which underlies whatever innovation sf can be credited
with in the realm of situation, incident, or character motivation:
human waste has become extremely valuable because scientists have
found a way to recycle it as a delicious and nutritious food; what John
saw was not really a human being but the latest in a long line of
scientifically tested androids; Shirley does not want to learn Peter's
language because she feels there is no need for it: her mind can
communicate with his directly thanks to recent advances in telepathy.
At the same time, and paradoxically, it is this very link which best
signifies and ensures science fiction's allegiance to certainty rather
than doubt, order rather than disorder, the familiar and understandable rather than the mysterious and incomprehensible. Everything
that is potentially disorienting, everything that could be unsettling,
uncanny, weird, is brought back into the fold and domesticated not so
much because fiction means safety (it is only fiction!) but because
scientific motivation rules. The unexpected is not only expectable but
explained; the unintelligible is elucidated; the wondrous is made
rational through scientific explication. Whereas a fantastic writer or an
absurdist one attempts to present the strange as such, an sf writer
explains it by having recourse to science. He makes the marvelous
plausible (it is no wonder that sf abounds in what Roland Barthes
called *effets de réel*, reality effects) and justifies whatever is different in
terms of scientific changes. Sf cannot be scandalous if by scandalous we
mean that which is unexplainable. Science is never very far. There is a
key for any mystery, a light for any darkness, a reason for any excess.
Even the New Wave, with its emphasis on non-linearity and its subver-
sion of the transparent language of *vraisemblance*, does not quite
escape the aura of science. Take *Dhalgren* for instance, which, I must
confess, I have not read in its entirety (it is 879 pages long!). *Dhalgren*
delights in relativity and destabilization; but the Bellonna it describes
is in a distinct space-time continuum from that of the rest of the world

and, for each individual in Bellonna, things happen in a different space-time continuum; in other words, even in this borderline case, the lack of a stable core finds itself somewhat motivated. It is not unlike the movie called *Images*, I think, and directed by Robert Altman, where strange happenings and disturbing situations turn out to come from the heroine's schizophrenic mind; and here we thought we had something irreducible to explanation! Of course, should sf do away entirely with scientific motivation or with motivation, period, it would become indistinguishable from avant-garde fiction, "plain" fiction, or fantasy. J. G. Ballard's "The Assassination of John Fitzgerald Kennedy Considered as a Downhill Motor Race" is a good case in point. Science fiction without some kind of science is like detective fiction without some kind of detection or a vertebrate without a backbone.

I have tried to argue that, because of its fictional, narrative, and science-bound nature, sf is not fundamentally newer than much of mainstream fiction and that it does not necessarily have more potential for newness than that fiction. This, of course, in no way constitutes a rebuke of sf. Rather, it might be taken to be a critique of the notion "new" as a measuring instrument. There is no compelling reason for valuing the new more than the old or for appreciating relatively unconstrained texts more than relatively constrained ones. In fact, it is through the very constraints that sf must respect that it acquires many of its strengths. Sf is fiction; as such, it can be concrete philosophy, allowing us to *recognize* our *self* rather than losing it, to understand better what we might already be aware of (basic symbolic processes, human nature, the order of things), to see more clearly what we can see (we could all use a good pair of glasses). Sf is narrative; as such, it can give us a sense of beginnings, ends, and the meaningfulness of temporal order and provide us with the thrills of repetitions and double takes; it can also be fun. Sf is linked to science; as such, and however fragile the link may be, it can furnish a privileged setting for the adventures of reason, its defeats, and its triumphs. In short, perhaps because sf is not so much about what will be as about what was and what is, perhaps because it is not so much about what we have never known as about what we are more or less familiar with, it constitutes a distinguished domain where our meditations, ruminations . . . and whimsies can breathe and stretch.

MARK ROSE

# Jules Verne: Journey to the Center of Science Fiction

Jules Verne's subject is nature.[1] The *voyages extraordinaires* explore worlds known and unknown: the interior of Africa, the interior of the earth, the deeps of the sea, the deeps of space. Verne's imagination projects itself in terms of "inside" and "outside." Characteristically, Verne's voyagers travel in vehicles that are themselves closed worlds, snug interiors from which the immensity of nature can be appreciated in upholstered comfort. The *Nautilus* is the most familiar of these comfortable, mobile worlds; inside all is cozy elegance, the epitome of the civilized and human, while outside the oceans gleam or rage in inhuman beauty or mystery. Roland Barthes finds the principle at the heart of Verne's fictions to be the "ceaseless action of secluding oneself." The known and enclosed space, the comfortable cave, is safe while "outside the storm, that is, the infinite, rages in vain." The basic activity in Verne is the construction of closed and safe spaces, the enslavement and appropriation of nature to make a place for man to live in comfort. "The enjoyment of being enclosed reaches its paroxysm when, from the bosom of this unbroken inwardness, it is possible to watch, through a large window-pane, the outside vagueness of the waters, and thus define, in a single act, the inside by means of its opposite."[2]

*Journey to the Center of the Earth* (1864), is of course just such an exploration of "insideness," except that here rather than being the place of enclosed safety, the interior world, a realm of subterranean galleries, caverns, and seas, becomes an immensity, a fearful abyss. Abysses dominate the novel. Even before Professor Lidenbrock and his nephew, Axel, begin their journey into the interior, Axel, the story's narrator, has nightmares in which he finds himself "hurtling

31

into bottomless abysses with the increasing velocity of bodies dropping through space."[3] The idea of the abyss is continually kept before us, and always the danger is as much psychic as physical. Standing on the edge of the first real chasm, Axel speaks of the "fascination of the void" taking hold of him. "I felt my centre of gravity moving, and vertigo rising to my head like intoxication. There is nothing more overwhelming than this attraction of the abyss" (p. 104). The danger, evidently, is of losing one's sense of self and of disappearing, intoxicated, into the infinite void.

The abyss in *Journey to the Center of the Earth* is a version of the cosmic void, but the geometry of the earthly chasm differs from that of the astronomical infinity, for the earth is round and therefore has both poles and a center. Poles and center are magical loci, the three still places on the turning globe. When the earth is conceived as a bounded world located in unbounded space, the poles are extremities, the furthest points on the globe. Indeed, imagined in this way, the poles are magical precisely because they are the earth's boundaries and thus partake of the numinous power associated with any boundary zone. They are the icy, uninhabitable regions in which human space—the habitable world—meets the nonhuman space of the infinite. To reach and explore the poles is to achieve the completion of the human sphere by defining the earth in its entirety. (This is the meaning that seems to generate the nineteenth- and early twentieth-century obsession with polar exploration.) To reach the center of the globe also means to achieve completion, except that now the earth itself has become the imagined immensity and the attainment of the center means the penetration of the essence, the achievement of the heart of the mystery. The liminal poles are frigid; the mystical center is generally imagined as hot, as the fluid, living core of the globe. The earthly chasm thus opens onto a different kind of imaginative space from the astronomical void; at the bottom of the bottomless abyss is the region not of transcendence but of immanence, the locus in which all knowledge, all being, all power are immediately present. To attain the center of the earth, then, means to penetrate the heart of nature, to possess nature absolutely. This is the object of Professor Lidenbrock and his nephew Axel's quest.

Extremes meet and magical opposites are always, in a sense, identical. At the time Verne was writing *Journey to the Center of the Earth* he was also writing *Captain Hatteras* in which an obsessed adventurer reaches the North Pole. The pole itself turns out to be an erupting volcano—magical heat in the center of the regions of cold—

and standing on the lip of the polar crater, the margin of the space in which heat and cold, life and death, inside and outside, immanence and transcendence interpenetrate, Hatteras goes mad.[4] Significantly, in *Journey to the Center of the Earth* Lidenbrock and Axel gain access to the interior by traveling north to the cold and barren arctic limits of the habitable world, Iceland, where they enter the subterranean regions through the cone of the extinct volcano Sneffels.

In traveling to Iceland Lidenbrock and Axel are following the directions given in a runic cryptogram that the professor has discovered in an ancient book. "Descend into the crater of Sneffels Yokul, over which the shadow of Scartaris falls before the kalends of July, bold traveller, and you will reach the centre of the earth. I have done this. Arne Saknussemm" (p. 32). Arne Saknussemm, Lidenbrock knows, was a sixteenth-century Icelandic alchemist. The deciphering of his coded message is the novel's first narrative concern and this initial action provides the paradigm for the fiction as a whole, for nature itself is conceived here as a kind of cryptogram to be decoded. The key to Saknussemm's message is that it must be read backward. Likewise, in their descent Lidenbrock and Axel must in effect read nature backward as they pass through the strata of successively earlier and earlier periods of natural history, eventually finding themselves in a marvelous underground world filled with plants from the era of the giant ferns. Here they discover long extinct animals and in one of the well-known Vernian set pieces witness a mortal battle between an ichthyosaur and a plesiosaur. Finally, and climactically, they have a brief glimpse of a giant prehistoric man guarding a herd of mastodons.

> *Immanis pecoris custos, immanior ipse.* . . . Yes, indeed, the shepherd was bigger than his flock. . . . He was over twelve feet tall. His head, which was as big as a buffalo's, was half hidden in the tangled growth of his unkempt hair—a positive mane, like that of the primitive elephant. In his hand he was brandishing an enormous bough, a crook worthy of this antediluvian shepherd. (P. 281)

Lidenbrock and Axel's journey to the earth's center is thus also a journey into the abyss of evolutionary time, and this fusion of the spatial and temporal modes is one of the fiction's sources of power. Temporally projected, the quest for the center, the heart of the mystery, becomes the pursuit of origins, the quest for an ulimate moment of beginning. Understanding this fusion of modes helps to explain why the prehistoric giant is presented in the language of pastoral, a language which activates a literary code of origin that in simultaneously spatial and temporal in mode, both "there" and "then." Understanding this also helps to explain why Lidenbrock and Axel's journey is presented as a repetition of Arne Saknussemm's journey, as a recovery of an original knowledge once possessed by science in its primeval past. The professor and his nephew in following the mysterious alchemist's footsteps are in effect restoring science to its center and origin.

The process of decoding, of learning to read nature, is in this fiction essentially an action of naming. Like many of Verne's protagonists—think, for instance, of Aronnax and Conseil in *Twenty Thousand Leagues Under the Sea*—Lidenbrock and Axel are obsessive categorizers concerned to find the exact name for each geological stratum, the exact botanical and zoological classification for each underground species of plant or animal. As they descend they are concerned, too, with being able to name their precise position in relation to the surface, the exact number of vertical and lateral feet that they have traveled at each point. Moreover, since they are penetrating an unknown world, Lidenbrock and Axel are obliged not only to discover but at times to create names: the "Hansback" for the underground stream that guides them part of their way, "Port Gräuben," "Axel Island," "Cape Saknussemm." The imposition of human names on the nonhuman world is obviously an act of appropriation and conquest, for to be able to decipher and read nature is here to possess it, to drain it of its mysterious otherness and make it part of the human world.

In characteristic moment Axel describes coming upon a dense subterranean forest composed of weird umbrellalike trees.

> I quickened my step, anxious to put a name to these strange objects. Were they outside the 200,000 species of vegetables already known, and had they to be accorded a special place among the lacustrian flora? No; when we arrived under their shade, my surprise turned to admiration. I found myself, in fact, confronted with products of the earth, but on a gigantic scale. My uncle promptly called them by their name.
>
> "It's just a forest of mushrooms," he said.
>
> And he was right. It may be imagined how big these plants which love heat and moisture had grown. I knew that the *Lycopodon giganteum*, according to Bulliard, attains a circumference of eight or nine feet, but here there were white mushrooms thirty or forty feet high, with heads of an equal diameter. There were thousands of them; the light could not manage to penetrate between them, and complete darkness reigned between those domes, crowded together as closely as the rounded roofs of an African city. (Pp. 166–67)

Notice how this passage enacts a conquest, an annexation of alien territory. It begins in tension with Axel unable to name the "strange objects." As the passage develops the objects become "just" mushrooms. Next they are associated with the *"Lycopodon giganteum"*—that is, with a scientific or exact name. Finally they are transformed metaphorically into "the rounded roofs of an African city" so that we are now viewing a primitive but specifically human landscape.

Appropriately, it is Professor Lidenbrock rather than Axel who in this passage first names the "strange objects." From the beginning Lidenbrock is a figure of heroic will engaged in mortal combat with the nonhuman world. Arriving at the base of Sneffels, he is described as "gesticulating as if he were challenging" the volcano. "So that is the giant I am going to defeat!" (p. 85) he announces in a phrase that sustains this aspect of the fiction. Nothing daunts the professor. Obsessively, he presses forward through every difficulty that lies in the way of the total conquest of nature. "The elements are in league against me!" he cries at a moment when the battle is particularly furious. "Air, fire, and water combine to block my way! Well, they are going to find out just how strong-willed I am! I won't give in, I won't move back an inch, and we shall see whether man or Nature will get the upper hand!" (p. 206).

The narrative establishes the professor's significance in part by placing him in opposition to Hans, the phlegmatic Icelandic peasant who acts as guide. By trade an eiderdown hunter, an occupation that signficantly involves no struggle with nature since the "hunter" merely collects the feathers from the elder's readily accessible nest, Hans is clever and resourceful but utterly without will. Indeed, Axel calls him "that man of the far West endowed with the fatalistic resignation of the East" (p. 236). The principal thing that Hans cares about is his salary; he insists upon having three rix-dollars doled out to him each Saturday evening no matter what the exploring party's situation or location. This mechanical action becomes a comic leitmotif in the novel, but it is also significant, suggesting the peasant's absolute unconcern about his surroundings, his obliviousness to nature's marvels. Curiously, Hans and Professor Lidenbrock, while in most respects opposed figures, are at one point seen as similar. Sailing across a magnificent underground sea, the professor expresses irritation that they are making no progress toward the center. Axel is delighted with the beautiful views, but Lidenbrock cuts his rapture short.

> "I don't give a damn for views. I set myself an object, and I mean to attain it. So don't talk to me about magnificent views. . . ."

> I took him at his word, and left the Professor to bite his lips with
> impatience. At six in the evening, Hans claimed his wages, and three
> rix-dollars were counted out to him. (P. 183)

Each imprisoned in his own form of obsession, Lidenbrock and Hans
are equally blind to the magic of their surroundings. Paradoxically, the
aggressive, passionately involved, Western attitude toward nature can
isolate one from nature no less effectively than the passive unconcern
of the East.

Both Hans's passivity and Lidenbrock's will to conquer nature are
opposed to Axel's romanticism. In a characteristic exchange, the
professor and his nephew discuss the fact that the subterranean sea has
tides like those of the surface. Axel is amazed and delighted; his uncle,
however, finds nothing marvelous in the discovery, pointing out that a
subterranean sea will be as subject to the sun and moon's gravitation as
any other.

> "You are right," I cried. "The tide is beginning to rise."
> "Yes, Axel, and judging by the ridges of foam I estimate that the sea
> will rise about ten feet."
> "That wonderful!"
> "No, it's perfectly natural.
> "You may say what you like, Uncle, but it all seems extraordinary to
> me, and I can scarcely believe my eyes. Who would ever have imagined
> that inside the earth's crust there was a real ocean, with ebbing and
> flowing tides, winds and storms?" (Pp. 170–71)

Axel and his uncle live in different mental universes, Axel embodying
the spiritualistic response to the nonhuman ("That's wonderful!"),
Lidenbrock embodying bourgeois materialism ("No, it's perfectly
natural.") Not surprisingly, each at various points in the story believes
that the other has gone mad.

Near the end of the novel, however, Axel undergoes a conversion. Confronted with what appears to be an insurmountable obstacle
to further descent—a huge boulder has sealed the gallery through
which they must pass—the youth is suddenly seized by his uncle's
demon of heroic conquest. Now it is Axel who is impatient with delay
and who insists that they must immediately blow up the rock with
explosive guncotton. "The Professor's soul had passed straight into
me, and the spirit of discovery inspired me. I forgot the past and
scorned the future" (p. 266). Nothing matters for him now except the
imperative of penetration to the center. Demonically possessed, Axel
has become, like his uncle, a "hero." His journey, then, has become
an initiation into the bourgeois-heroic attitude toward nature, a

"going in" in a social as well as a physical sense, and the story ultimately ratifies his new status as an adult male by granting him the hand of the professor's beautiful god-daughter, Gräuben. Nevertheless, as the comic ironies persistently directed against Professor Lidenbrock's limited vision suggest, in the youth's passage something has been lost as well as gained. Caring neither for past nor future, imprisoned in the narrow cage of his own will to dominate, Axel can no longer confront nature except as an antagonist, something utterly apart from himself. Demonically possessed, he is no longer a free agent.

Axel and his uncle never do reach the earth's mysterious center. The guncotton explosion triggers a volcanic eruption and, like an animal defending itself against an intrusion into its body, nature expels the explorers, vomits them out along a great volcanic shaft back into the air. Perhaps physical achievement of the center is impossible? Or perhaps reaching that magical locus would mean going mad like Captain Hatteras on the crater of the polar volcano? In any case, the point of furthest penetration, the journey's true climax, is reached, significantly, not by the professor but by his romantic nephew and not in literal reality but in a vision.

Before his conversion, Axel, reflecting upon "the wonderful hypotheses of paleontology," has an extended daydream in which, first, he supposes the subterranean world filling with long-extinct creatures: antediluvian tortoises, great early mammals, pterodactyls and other primeval birds. "The whole of this fossil world came to life again in my imagination." As his dream continues, however, the great animals disappear, the earth grows steadily warmer, and he finds himself in a still earlier age, the period of gigantic vegetation. Even here the dream does not end. Sweeping backward into the abyss of time in quest of the center, the point of origin, Axel finds the heat becoming more and more intense until the earth's granite liquifies and finally the planet itself dissolves into its original white-hot gaseous mass. "In the centre of this nebula, which was fourteen hundred thousand times as large as the globe it would one day form, I was carried through interplanetary space. My body was volatilized in its turn and mingled like an imponderable atom with these vast vapours tracing their flaming orbits through infinity" (pp. 179–80). Climactically, Axel himself disappears, becoming part of the cosmic infinity. At the ecstatic center, the boundary between man and nature, the human and the nonhuman, melts and the explorer merges with the world being explored.

Axel's dream represents, of course, both a romantic alternative to the professor's treatment of nature as an antagonist to be conquered and a fusion of spiritualistic and materialistic world views. Moreover, in Axel's dream, the text calls attention to its own status as a fiction, an imaginary voyage. This kind of fictive self-consciousness was perhaps implicit in such earlier passages as Axel's rhetorical question, "Who would ever have imagined that inside the earth's crust there was a real ocean, with ebbing and flowing tides, winds and storms?" Now, however, in the description of the fossil world coming to life in Axel's imagination—these events are shortly to occur in the narrative proper as the explorers begin to encounter extinct animals and plants—the text's play with its own fictionality is particularly emphatic and we can hardly miss seeing Axel as momentarily a version of Verne.

Expelled from the interior, the explorers emerge in an eruption of Mount Stromboli in Sicily.

> We had gone in by one volcano and come out by another, and this other was more than three thousand miles from Sneffels, from that barren country of Iceland at the far limits of the inhabited world! The chances of our expedition had carried us into the heart of the most beautiful part of the world! We had exchanged the region of perpetual snow for that of infinite verdure, and the gray fog of the icy north for the blue skies of Sicily! (P. 249)

Like the interior, the surface is a realm of infinities, but here the "infinity" is one of welcoming, protective vegetation. Since, in this novel, the interior space has become the void, the exterior world becomes the known and safe space. In reaching Sicily, Lidenbrock and Axel have, ironically, reached the earth's center, the primitive heart not of nature but of the human sphere. "We were in the middle of the Mediterranean," says Axel, "in the heart of the Aeolian archipelago of mythological memory, in that ancient Strongyle where Aeolus kept the winds and storms on a chain" (p. 249). Warm and nourishing in contrast with the icy polar verge, the Sicilian landscape is a paradise of olives, pomegranates, and vines hung with delicious fruit free for the taking, a landscape that recalls and fulfills the brief evocation of pastoral in the subterranean encounter with primeval man.

With the arrival in Sicily the narrative proper is over; in substituting one code of "centrality" for another, the text has achieved narrative closure. Nevertheless, a further detail remains to be treated in a coda. On the shore of the subterranean sea, after a fierce electrical storm, the explorers' compass seemed to indicate that they had been traveling for nearly 1,500 miles in the wrong direction. Had they really been going north when they thought they were going south? The mystery of the compass remains an unexplained phenomenon and a torment to Professor Lidenbrock since "for a scientist an unexplained phenomenon is a torture for the mind" (p. 253). One day, however, back in Hamburg, Axel notices that the compass needle points south instead of north and he realizes that the electrical storm in the earth's interior must have reversed the instrument's poles. The final mystery is explained, the puzzle is complete and, in a version of the lived-happily-ever-after formula, Axel tells us that "from that day onward, my uncle was the happiest of scientists" (p. 254).

This coda affirms the materialistic faith that the book of nature is readable to the last word, that nature is merely a cryptogram to be decoded, or, as Axel puts it, that "however great the wonders of Nature may be, they can always be explained by physical laws" (p. 208). And yet, despite this explicit positivistic affirmation, the narrative's romance structure suggests a more problematic view. Here "explaining nature" is represented by the idea of reaching the center, which, of course, the explorers never do attain. Did Arne Saknussemm ever in fact reach the center? Throughout the story, Axel and Lidenbrock debate the question of the earth's internal temperature. Is the earth's core molten or even gaseous with a temperature perhaps over two million degrees as Axel, the romantic, maintains? Or, as the positivistic Lidenbrock supposes, does the rise in temperature experienced as one descends into the earth reach a limit at a certain depth, leaving a core that can be explored by human beings? So far as the explorers descend the temperature remains comfortable, but the ultimate issue of whether the center itself is transcendently hot is never resolved, and in the narrative this debate becomes equivalent to the question of how nature can be known. Is the center literally reachable as Lidenbrock passionately believes? Or, as Axel's dream implies, is it in fact a magical place attainable only in dream or in vision or in fiction?

What I hope my analysis of Verne's novel has suggested is the way the narrative is built upon an unresolvable incompatibility between a fundamentally materialistic ideology and a literary form that projects the world as ultimately magical in nature. *Journey to the Center of the Earth* can be taken as representative of science fiction in general. Science fiction has typically asserted a materialistic point of view, and yet, at the same time, science fiction has typically expressed itself through the spiritualizing categories of romance. Most often, as in

Verne, the contradiction at the heart of the narrative remains more or less disguised. This formula is characteristic of hard-core science fiction. Asimov's *Foundation* series, for example, asserts both a deterministic view of history and a spiritualistic belief in the efficacy of individual free will. Alternatively, instead of suppressing the incompatiblity of spiritualism and materialism, a text may focus directly upon the contradiction, questioning its validity. Such narratives generally take the form of a progressive discovery of the interpenetration, or even of the identity, of matter and spirit. Olaf Stapledon's novels characteristically operate in this way, dissolving normally discrete categories of thought. At one point in *Last and First Men*, for example, the moon's orbit is found to be decaying faster than physical theory alone would predict, and the narrator explains that man had not yet discovered the "connexion between a planet's gravitation and its cultural development."[5] C. S. Lewis's *Out of the Silent Planet*, Walter Miller's *A Canticle for Leibowitz*, and many recent fictions operate in a similar manner. What is the difference between matter and spirit in a world such as that of Brian Aldiss's *Cryptozoic* in which one can travel in time by taking a mind-altering drug?

Alfred North Whitehead, among others, points out that a tension between spiritualistic and materialistic world views is fundamental in modern—that is, post-Renaissance—culture.[6] Oversimplifying, we might say that modern culture wishes to believe both in the priority of matter and of spirit, both in free will and in determinism. In the nineteenth century this tension generally took the form of fierce debates between the proponents of science, particularly evolution, and the proponents of religion and the dignity of man. At present we more often encounter the tension in displaced form, in, for example, the antipathy between humanistic and behavioristic psychology. (Curiously, Freudian psychology, which in the early part of the present century figured as another in the long series of deterministic threats to human dignity, now appears to have crossed a crucial semantic boundary and to figure as spiritualistic in opposition to properly "scientific" therapies. Psychoanalysis is regularly accused of being a religion rather than a science.) On the plane of popular culture, the tension is evident in recurrent waves of interest in such pseudo-sciences as astrology and parapsychology, and in oriental mysticism. In periods of social stress such as the 1960s in the United States, this tension is likely to become particularly evident as dissenters from the predominantly pragmatic and materialistic culture express their position by aligning themselves with various spiritualistic movements. Not surprisingly, dissent from the Vietnam War often manifested itself in such quasi-religious forms as "bearing witness."

What I am suggesting, then, is that science fiction characteristically operates within the space of a basic contradiction in modern culture. Indeed, as a genre, one of science fiction's functions appears to be to produce narratives that mediate between spiritualistic and materialistic world views. I realize of course that such a generalization requires a much fuller consideration of texts than I can possibly present here. I think, however, that it would be a relatively easy matter to illustrate the observation both from classic narratives such as those of Wells and from recent texts such as, say *The Left Hand of Darkness*.[7] For the present let me be content with remarking that understanding science fiction's role as mediator helps to explain the genre's interest in such quasi-scientific topics as telepathy, teleportation, telekinesis, matter transmission (which may be understood as a mechanized version of teleportation), and time travel. We can note in passing that the paradox at the heart of the notorious time loop in such stories as Heinlein's "All You Zombies" is that both free will and determinism are asserted simultaneously, for here free agents are nevertheless caught in cycles of determined repetition. Understanding science fiction's role as mediator also helps to explain the genre's interest in mechanical spirits such as robots, androids, intelligent computers, and cyborgs. (Interestingly, computer psychiatrists have become a popular motif in current science fiction.) All of these topics can be understood as points at which the spiritual and the material intersect.

Do we believe in free will or in determinism, in the priority of spirit or priority of matter? According to Whitehead the "radical inconsistency at the basis of modern thought accounts for much that is half-hearted and wavering in our civilization."[8] This may be true and yet in fiction contradiction is not necessarily a defect. Indeed, as Verne's *Journey to the Center of the Earth* perhaps suggests, the contradiction itself as embodied in narrative may be understood as a well of vitality, one of the sources from which science fiction as a genre draws its power.

*JOSEPH M. LENZ*

# Manifest Destiny: Science Fiction and Classical Form

The science fiction empire is in some ways anachronistic. An empire, after all, is constituted by a strong, centralized, often monarchical government backed by military power and religious sanction; a hierarchical, even feudal, social order; a capitalistic economy; and a chauvinism that seeks to expand the empire's borders ever outward, reducing diverse cultures to their lowest common denominator, their identity as parts of a whole. In short, an empire is a political, social, and economic dinosaur that (we think) belongs more to our past than to our future. Nonetheless, it remains an important and persistent icon—to borrow Gary Wolfe's term—in science fiction.

The reasons for its persistence are many. Imperialism is in part a holdover from science fiction's romance ancestry. The romance tale involves a knight's founding, defending, preserving, or sometimes replacing an earthly empire that is analogous to an otherworldly one. Redcrosse's service to Gloriana, Lancelot's to Arthur, Roland's to Charlemagne all exemplify this familiar pattern. *Star Wars* offers the most recent and recognizable science fiction illustration. True, Luke opposes the Empire, but like many another romance rebel, he wants to correct the Empire's errant ways, not to abolish it altogether. Another image of empire descends from our own geopolitical history. Many writers tend to view space, "the last frontier," as we heard so often on "Star Trek," in much the same way that the British viewed Africa and India and the Americans viewed the West: as territory not simply ready but rightfully to be won, to be civilized, and incorporated into the homeland. Conflict in projected galactic empires occurs not so much between human and alien as it does between the capital and the province, chiefly because man will have scattered his image across space. C. S. Lewis wrote *Out of the Silent Planet* partly to protest the vision of a homogeneous universe, although again he did not oppose the idea of empire, as his partiality to a divine order shows. Then again there is the mundane matter of expedience. The empire's unity, comprehensiveness, and capacity for analogy make it an attractive and powerful construct for the science fiction writer. Gary Wolfe notes that the empire-builders—Asimov, Herbert, LeGuin, Lewis, to name just a few—often write stories that describe their creations' history.[1] Here the empire provides not only a prefabricated secondary world to be mined and mined again, but occasionally a reflexive metaphor depicting science fiction's emergence as a legitimate literary form.

It is to this use of empire, specifically by Isaac Asimov and Frank Herbert, that I wish to call attention. In a very strict and limited way, the *Foundation* trilogy and the *Dune* books can be called classics. I do not mean that they are classic science fiction in the same sense in which we speak of classic cars or basketball tournaments—that they are qualitatively better or that they better represent others of their kind. Rather, I mean that they are classical, reminiscent of and belonging to a literary tradition that originates with Rome and *The Aeneid*.[2] Each is written to dedicate an empire, one foretold by prophecy and realized in time. Asimov and Herbert each tell the classic story, the founding of an empire, yet the manner in which each tells that story has special implications for science fiction, the empire being dedicated.

In his study called, appropriately, *The Classic*, Frank Kermode examines Rome's history as a symbol in Western thought, detailing how every major attempt to establish a new empire—whether political (Britain's descent from Brut), religious (the Reformation), or literary (neoclassicism)—has had, perforce, to reckon with Rome, either appealing to it for its blessing or renouncing it in favor of another model.[3] It is no accident, then, that science fiction empires are often peculiarly Roman. That Asimov uses Rome as a model for his Galactic Empire is both familiar and obvious. He himself has admitted that he had Gibbon's *Decline and Fall of the Roman Empire* in mind when he wrote the *Foundation* series.[4] And we see Roman remains everywhere in the stories, from Trantor, the monolithic city-planet at the Empire's heart, to the sun-and-spaceship emblem that, like the Roman eagle, signifies military power, to the corrupt court, to the Empire's slow dissolution, beginning with its weakened grasp on the periphery and ending with Trantor's repeated sacking by barbaric provincials. Herbert pays similar tribute unto Caesar. His empire portrays the much feared imperial legions through whom the emperor rules; the Landsraad, or senate of Great Houses that, in form, serves to balance the emperor's power; the gladitorial games that persecute slaves and prisoners for the entertainment and education of the populace; and the emperor himself, who plots against his own kin and who is brought to his knees by a tribe of religious fanatics.

In each case the author assigns the Roman characteristics to the empire that falls. Rome is an unfit model for the new epoch, so Asimov and Herbert, in a sense, deconstruct it. Yet, as Asimov's titles suggest, these books are about the foundations of empire, about its origins as well as its demise. It is paradoxical—but perhaps inevitable—that behind *Foundation* and *Dune* is the original classic written to inaugurate an empire. Just as the ideal of Rome symbolizes permanence and unity in a world of political change, so *The Aeneid* signifies permanent literary achievement amidst ever-changing critical values and judgments. At the same time that Asimov and Herbert reject the Roman model they rely on *The Aeneid*, the scripture that canonizes that model, to construct the new empire.

Asimov, especially, owes much to Virgil. To begin with, he expropriates the epic hero. In his essay "What is a Classic?", T. S. Eliot describes Aeneas as "from first to last, a 'man in fate,' . . . a man fulfilling his destiny, not under compulsion or arbitrary decree, and certainly from no stimulus to glory, but by surrendering his will to a higher power . . . he becomes an exile, and something greater and more significant than any exile."[5] Eliot could just as well be describing the First Foundation. It, too, is an exile, traveling through space and time from Trantor to Terminus, destined by its god, Hari Seldon (referred to once as a deus ex machina), to germinate a second and greater empire. The First Foundation is active, always mindful of its mission, always wary of stagnation, always questing, first for security, then for trade and territory, finally for the Second Foundation. As Aeneas is to Rome, so the First Foundation is to the new empire, from whose perspective we read the history of its genesis.

That the narrator presents the Second Empire as an accomplished fact does not mean its story is without conflict and tension. Like other epic heroes, including Aeneas, the most dangerous threat to the Foundation's destiny comes from a pastoral temptation. The Seldon Plan, the controlling prophecy for the new empire, calls for the contemporaneous but separate evolution of two foundations, one the mirror—that is, the reverse—image of the other. To fabricate the Second Foundation Seldon simply inverts the First. He publicly records the location and function of the First Foundation, but he hides those of the Second. He sends the First to Terminus, on the Galaxy's periphery; he keeps the Second on Trantor, at its center. The First Foundation is industrial, the Second agricultural. The First's science is technology, the Second's pyschology. The First acts, the Second contemplates. The First Foundation conquers outer space, the Second commands inner space. And if all this is not enough, Asimov follows precedent by typifying the pastoral in the figure of a young girl. Listen, for example, to the following description:

> Arcadia Darrell, dressed in borrowed clothes, standing on a borrowed planet in a borrowed situation of what seemed to be a borrowed life, wanted earnestly the safety of the womb. She didn't know that was what she wanted. She only knew that the very openness of the open world was a great danger. She wanted a closed spot somewhere—somewhere far— somewhere in an unexplored nook of the universe—where no one would ever look. (*SF*, II, 5)[6]

That nook turns out to be Trantor. Closed, safe, provincial, secret, meditative—these all mark the pastoral. Arcadia, says Mrs. Palver, wife of the Psychologists' First Speaker, "is a good Trantorian name."

The Second Foundation poses the same threat that pastoral always poses to epic. Knowledge of the Seldon Plan and the Psychologists' protection tempts the First Foundation into exchanging its dynamism for passivity, forsaking the impetus needed to achieve its destiny. Explains one Psychologist, "And that very abandonment of effort; that growing inertia; that lapse into softness and into a decadent and hedonistic culture, means the ruin of the Plan. They must be self-propelled" (*SF*, II, 10). The Second Foundation plays Dido to the First's Aeneas. Its mere existence lures the Foundationers into softness, decadence, and hedonism. Because epic must necessarily resist the temptation to leisure, the trilogy's final episode recounts how the Foundationers locate and destroy the Psychologists, opening the way to a destiny accomplished by free will, not under compulsion.

Or so they suppose. The last chapter reveals the truth: the Psychologists have staged an elaborate charade, tricking the Foundationers into a belief in their autonomy and freedom from Seldon's strings. This ironic ending dramatically alters the usual relationship between epic and pastoral and represents Asimov's most radical departure from formula. This change might imply that Asimov agrees with his mayor, Salvor Hardin, who claims that "Violence is the last resort of the incompetent." Where past empires may well have been achieved through violence and glorified for it, any future empire—including literary empires—must rely instead on its ability to mythologize. Throughout the *Foundation* series, duplicity—the facility to make credible fictions—defeats direct action. Yet Asimov dampens the Psychologists' victory with one last irony. I mentioned earlier that the story is told from the vantage of the new empire, a perspective that ought to verify Seldon's Plan in the same way that *The Aeneid* testifies to prophecy. And in a sense it does: we know the truth about the Plan's survival and its achievement. In effect, however, the Second Empire discredits prophecy. Because it believes the Plan defunct and the Psychologists defeated, the Second Foundation does not exist for the new empire. As keepers of the Plan, as perpetrators of fictions, as seers of future societies, the Second Foundation becomes an alien in the world of its own making.

Nowhere do we feel Asimov's ambivalence toward his craft, his "sense of burden from tradition" as Donald Hassler puts it, more than in his ironical treatment of the Second Foundation.[7] Asimov is on the cusp between the old and the new, between a literary tradition he chooses to practice and a genre that that tradition rejects. He invokes Virgil to legitimize his science fiction. As a result, he, like the Second Foundation, is lost in space, belonging wholly neither to the past, which he alters, nor to the future, though he helps to make that future.

Because Herbert succeeds Asimov and writes what seems another science fiction epic, he is faced with a more complex problem. He must accommodate both the epic tradition and his science fiction predecessor. And in general outline *Dune* does resemble its antecedents. Herbert uses Rome to characterize the old empire gone awry. His hero's career follows Aeneas' pattern. Paul Atriedes is a noble exile, fleeing the ruins of one dynasty and chosen to found another. Like Asimov, Herbert resorts to ironic plotting, the "feints within feints within feints," to counteract the predictability caused by formula and prophecy. Yet Herbert is not satisfied with mere imitation. He does not, for instance, develop his story along the expected epic/pastoral axis. Instead he conflates elements of the two, making the Fremen a provincial people who live in hidden caves, who herd animals, and who dream of an Arrakeen paradise, yet who are aggressive, violent, dynamic, and destined to rule. This kind of conflation evidences Herbert's willingness to reshape his inheritance. He is like the writer Eliot describes, "whose hope of the future is founded upon his attempt to renounce the past."[8] Although Herbert does not altogether reject the classic, he does re-form it.

John Milton offers a suggestive, if curious, parallel. Milton, claims Kermode, "cites Virgil and the other classics only to reject them."[9] In his writings, especially in the polemics, Milton renounces Rome in all its manifestations—because it is pagan, decadent, imperial, papistic, and perhaps not least because it already has its epic. To justify England's reformed government and enlightened religion Milton turns to the Bible. The English become the chosen people, the inheritors of God's word and the progenitors of a new epoch. Ironically, Milton had the misfortune to live to see that epoch last a mere twenty years, never to see it fully realized, and could only hope that it anticipated a millenium yet to come.

Herbert attempts a similar renunciation—with similar results. In his rejection of Rome he also elects a biblical model. *Dune* tells the story of a desert planet populated by a nomadic people who are destined to depose the emperor, replace him with their messiah, and propagate their faith through space. The story's hero thus combines two figures. As Duke Atriedes, Paul belongs to the old order, figuring Aeneas, the founder and father of empire. As Muab'Dib, he heralds the new order, figuring Moses, the prophet who delivers his people but who is himself denied entrance to the promised land.[10]

Besides increasing his story's density, Herbert's play with typology and his displacement of Virgil alters the kind of classic he writes. Herbert's science fiction differs from Asimov's to the extent that romance differs from epic. The epic achieves stasis. It attests to past deeds; it affirms an existing (or past) civilization. Thus, Asimov's story reaches a climax in which Hari Seldon's vision of the new galactic empire is an assumed fact. The romance is a state of flux. It presents a process, a state of becoming something. Herbert projects a story that has no end, one in which the goal is often promised but never reached. Each book in the series brings the new empire closer to realization, but the progress never comes to a full stop. *Dune* concludes with Paul enthroned, but worried about the inevitable Fremen jihad. *Dune Messiah* ends with the Bene Gesserit/Space Guild plot frustrated, but also with Paul exiled and the empire unsettled. Its cover advertises that *Children of Dune* is "the climax of the classic DUNE trilogy," yet another book, *God Emperor of Dune*, follows it. The following description of Paul's prescience aptly reflects the multiplicity of Herbert's visions. "And what he saw was a time nexus within this cave, a boiling of possibilities focused here, wherein the most minute action— the wink of an eye, a careless word, a misplaced grain of sand—moved a gigantic lever across the known universe. He saw violence with the outcome subject to so many variables that his slightest movement created vast shiftings in the pattern" (*Dune*, p. 305).[11] Herbert, like Paul, is caught in his own labyrinth. He returns again and again to Dune, almost as if he is determined to exhaust all its possibilities.

Asimov and Herbert represent two strains of science fiction and two kinds of classics. For Asimov, the future replicates the past, and this cyclical sense of history affects the way he tells and the way we read science fiction. Because civilization is a closed system in which man merely repeats himself, Asimov writes a story that repeats old stories. He asks only that we relocate Gibbon and Virgil in outer space, sometime in the future. The narrative develops along predicted and predictable lines, making few demands upon us. He does employ an ironic ending to upset expectation, but the irony serves to cement the plot line (the Plan), not to reverse it. To give his fiction credibility Asimov conforms to his literary inheritance, writing an epic that, like all epics, arrests development. His science fiction represents the old classic, the story frozen in time.

Herbert writes what Kermode would call a modern classic, a narrative that "poses a virtually infinite set of questions."[12] These questions do not pertain to the story's content—in Herbert's case, the matters of genetics, prescience, and reincarnation that comprise the extrapolated science—but rather to the way we read the story. For Herbert, the past determines the future, but the future does not mimic the past. He builds upon a variety of literary traditions. To read him, however, we cannot rely on our conventional expectations, for Herbert plays with those conventions. He conflates familiar genres, plots, and character types, changing the known into the unknown. Most significantly, he refuses to give his story a close, the one narrative moment when process stops. His is an open text, one that both invites and refutes interpretation.

MICHELLE MASSÉ

# "All you have to do is know what you want": Individual Expectations in *Triton*

In Samuel Delany's *Triton*, the subtitle, *An Ambiguous Heterotopia*, leads to a series of fictional expectations that we establish, question, and discard as we read. In trying to decide just what a "heterotopia" is, the first model we compare it to is a utopia, but we know from the first that a novel whose protagonist, Bron, is introduced wondering if he is "reasonably happy" is not one in which the good of the individual is the same as the good of society, as in More's *Utopia*, Bellamy's *Looking Backward*, or Huxley's *Island*. The apparent omnipresence of a centralized government, seen in "ego booths" and money tokens, as well as the combat zone-like "unlicensed sector" and the random violence of the Dumb Beasts, seem to promise a dystopia, in which the individual is subsumed by extreme social chaos or order, as in Orwell's *1984* or Huxley's *Brave New World*. However, the rapid transition from violence to aesthetics—from Bron's watching a woman being hit by a Dumb Beast to that same woman's bringing him as sole spectator to an intense, minute-long microtheater performance—precludes dystopia. The blue woman, man in the cage, Dumb Beast, mumblers, woman—the Spike, writer/producer/director extraordinaire of microtheater—and Bron himself in the first chapter demonstrate a richness and variety of experience that can make Triton only "an ambiguous heterotopia."

A brief comparison of Delany's "ambiguous heterotopia" to Le Guin's *The Dispossessed*, captioned "an ambiguous utopia," reveals that "utopia" and "heterotopia" multiplied by "ambiguous" yield very different results. The two novels serve as commentaries on each other in several interesting ways. Anarres's anarchy, developed in response to Urras's rigidity, begins to lose its flexibility when anarchy becomes institutionalized and bureaucratized. Odo's radical precepts become pious slogans; deviance from the group becomes treason. The two worlds partially define themselves through their differences. Each views the other as a satellite and its is only Shevek, moving between them, who recognizes the relativity of perspective involved. In disallowing similarities, the two worlds confine themselves to a mirror relationship. The leveling pressure for uniformity that is the means inevitably contaminates the end.

Delany's subtitle multiplies the possibilities by eschewing the monadic utopia for heterotopia. The relationship of protagonist to text is inverted: Shevek tries to achieve mobility in two stratified worlds; Bron tries to impose his own rigidity on the ever-changing world around him. *Triton*'s scale is that of the individual and, through Bron's own attempts to rubricize and reduce others to mirrors, the utopian drive is itself critiqued. Whereas in LeGuin's worlds the heterodox individual is suspect, in Delany's heterotopia there is not room for the orthodox. LeGuin's Shevek, like the protagonists of many of Delany's earlier novels, supports the notion of the heroic individual as a shaper of worlds; Bron's characterization dissects that heroic impulse. Bron's ostensible goal—knowing what he wants—is nullified through his means, the absorbing egocentricity that tries to reduce the multifariousness of his world to formula.

Triton, unlike Anarres, is, above all, *urban*. Dome living calls for population density, and there are no Triton versions of pastoral. As Georges Simmel notes, the city "grants to the individual a kind and an amount of personal freedom which has no analogy whatsoever under other conditions,"[1] and Triton's inhabitants fully demonstrate some possibilities of that freedom. On an Earth trip, the Spike speculates that it is the space available on planets that lets people avoid having to deal with one another, while the exigencies of living on Triton demand a response, even if that response is willed silence. Earth's order is much as we know it now; Triton's "order" is a combination of a generally stable and successful government that insures fulfillment of basic needs, and a heterotopic society that is the embodiment of what Richard Sennett, in *The Uses of Disorder*, calls "creative anarchy."[2] Sennett argues that rigid social mores are the equivalent of the adolescent longing for "purified identity," a desire to have clearly marked rights and wrongs, logic instead of metalogic, and urges an embracing of "the complexity of confrontation and conflict in the city." "These new anarchic cities promise to provide an outlet for what men now fear to express directly. In so doing, the structure of the city community will take on a kind of stability, a mode of ongoing expression, that will be sustaining to men because it offers them expressive outlets."[3] Ideally, the individual, like the Spike, is able to accept, reshape, and, to some extent, change the world, even if the actual reshaping only lasts as long as the microtheater's minute.

The multiple possibilities of the city call for selection, a narrowing of focus to a point where a cohesive identity can be claimed and acknowledged. The individual often will look for solidarity in a small group of similar interests (Triton's communes and male/female/gay/ straight co-ops). This process of identification can become inverted, however, so that the group *becomes* the identity and takes care of the need of self-expression (Triton's numerous cults). Bron's experience in briefly walking with the mumblers, a Moonie-like crew of zombies, is illustrative: "The feeling was of lightness, almost of joy, of reasons and responsibilities, explanation and expiation shrugged off, abandoned."[4] If recognition is needed by the individual or group, urban life calls for increasingly aberrant behavior. It's easy to be the village eccentric, but competition is fierce in the city. Simmel points out that the behavior chosen is as insignificant as whether the Dumb Beasts, one of Triton's cults, are eschewing meaningful or meaningless communication.

> Finally, man is tempted to adopt the most tendentious peculiarities, that is, the specifically metropolitan extravagances of mannerism, caprice, and preciousness. Now, the meaning of these extravagances does not at all lie in the contents of such behavior, but rather in its form of "being different," of standing out in a striking manner and thereby attracting attention.[5]

The urban dweller's identification does not have to be with a single group, unless a particularly strict cult is chosen: for example, Sam, who spends three days of every two weeks in Bron's nonspecific co-op, is also employed by the government and a member of a family commune. In addition, groupings can be into what Robert Park calls "moral regions," such as the unlicensed sector—groupings not determined by occupations, sex preference, or socioeconomic status.[6]

Triton's satellite status, social usages, urban organization, systems of government, employment, and living arrangements make it a perfect vehicle for the freedom Simmel and Sennett hold out as the strongest lure of metropolitan living. Given enough people—particularly when the population is as immigrant and here-and-now oriented as Triton's—everyone can find his/her own, can fulfill his/her expectations, as Park's sanguine comment indicates. "The attraction of the metropolis is due in part, however, to the fact that in the long run every individual finds somewhere the sort of environment in which he expands and feels at ease; finds, in short, the moral climate in which his peculiar nature obtains the stimulations that bring his innate dispositions to full and free expression."[7] While, as *Triton* shows, this does happen—and some "innate dispositions" can be very peculiar—what are we to make of the protagonist, in whom desire itself is atrophied? Bron's plea to the Spike is a counterpoint to Park's stance. "But the great lie those people hold out, whether they're in a commune or a co-op . . is: Anyone can have it, be a part of it . . . somewhere, someplace, it's waiting for you. . . . Somewhere, in your sector or in mine, in this unit or in that one, there it is: pleasure, community, respect—all you have to do is know the kind, and how much of it, and to what extent you want it. That's all" (p. 122).

Bron is the individual who can join no group, form no satisfactory "sexualizationship" or friendship, even in heterotopia. Bron's position as the protagonist of *Triton* is a large part of what makes the heterotopia ambiguous, for there is no deterministic answer to his malaise. Bron is neither the rebel nor the alienated man who points out the flaws of a given society. His development, the social structure of Triton, and the pressure of strong secondary characters thwart any attempt to find a source through an outward (environmental, situational) or backward (biographic) search. While his past, his present, and Triton can be seen as related to Bron's disaffection, no one of these demonstrates a causal relationship. There are no easy answers to the plight of the individual or of society, and any attempt to locate one is firmly checked by details in the text. Although single factors in Bron's past are sometimes suggested by him as the "reason" for his personality configuration, each is matched by the experience of other characters: upbringing (the Spike), prostitution (Windy), Mars (Brian). His complaints about social and economic mobility are refuted by the lives around him: for example, Audri and Phil, his "bosses" at work, show that both advancement and change are possible. Bron's suggestions that others are the causes of his problems lose credibility, for the three important secondary characters, the Spike, Sam, and Lawrence, a seventy-four-year-old man in Bron's co-op, show commendable patience in their dealings with him and are themselves admirable personalities.

In Triton's flux, Bron is a static character. His insistent "I" is not the breakthrough that we see with the Butcher in *Babel-17*, for he lacks a "you." He tries to establish a self by delimiting the not-self. His either/or structures lack the punning combination found in "Rydra Wong." He attempts to control others by rigid, omnipotent formulae, and is puzzled when the content he thinks he seeks always evades him. The shifting of time, point of view, and logic that Peter Alterman points out in Delany's work[8] operates here to support a central myth of the self, and the purpose of that myth is to avoid mutability. Bron wants to believe that the shape of the past is present and future also. He, like Let in *Out of the Dead City*, wants to block "the fabric of reality back into the shape of expectation" by conflating "suppose" and "is."[9]

In earlier novels by Delany, "should" often does become "is" for the exceptional protagonist. The characters are overreachers who succeed in part because of unusual powers. They are active: they reach out to others to help shape their worlds. Bron stands apart in his passivity: his aspirations are the same, but the attributes given to him are garden variety. The gap between expectation and reality, self and other, is emphasized and, because there is no magical bridging, Bron's expectations and *Triton* itself become a commentary on the extension of the earlier works, a painstaking examination of what seems now an impossible heroism. In his article "To Read *The Dispossessed*," Delany points out that, in science fiction, "there is no implicit limit on the distance from the self to the Other . . . to contour the fictive reality."[10] A parapsychological melding of minds has occasionally provided the means of collapsing that distance in works like *The Jewels of Aptor, The Fall of the Towers, Babel-17, The Einstein Intersection*, and *Nova*, where knowledge of self becomes knowledge of the other and sameness and difference conflate. But Bron has no special force of mind or personality that enables him to evaluate and decide between "the real and—the rest."[11] Triton is not made for the greater glory of Bron, and none of its technological wonders can make him extraordinary instead of ordinary.

There seems little science, then, in the central fiction of *Triton*, unless that science is psychology. Although Bron sometimes seems an anachronism from the twentieth century, his lack of adjustment is not ascribable to the time, situation, or world in which he is found. If a name has to be given for what ails Brons, we could call his problem a narcissistic personality disorder: the emphasis upon a grandiose self, which sees the self and others as they "should" be, a need to rubricize experience and others, a wish for acknowledgment of one's own uniqueness *and* superiority, the tendency to see others as figures in a private drama, the construction of a self-myth through unusually powerful introjections (good qualities) and projections (negative traits). Bron wants to be a planet with his own group of reflecting satellites. Despite the social structure which still exists on Earth in *Triton*, Bron's problems would be much the same there, but perhaps mitigated by commonly held beliefs that would more easily allow him to maintain the conviction of his own superiority. Triton's "creative anarchy" exposes Bron's expectations as idiosyncratic: there is no religious or cultural consensus which would allow him to define himself by comparison to an "inferior" race, sex, or class. The freedom of the city is, for Bron, chaos come to rule.

Bron attempts to superimpose a grid on all experience: the grid is not a training device for beginners, as is that on Lawrence's vlet game, but a need to compartmentalize people and things permanently so that he can assure himself that he is in control. His establishment of a me/them, black/white universe is ironic in view of his job as a metalogician or analyzer of the gray areas. It is doubly ironic when the result is a loss of any distinction between self and other. Bron does what Iimmi, in *The Jewels of Aptor*, says "a static mind always does. Everything bec[omes] equivocated with everything else."[12]

Bron's quickness at typing others is only matched by his resentment at others doing the same to him. From the first page of the novel, we see him classifying others to establish his own difference. His definition of different runs toward the statistical, and he often decides to act only after calculating the odds. He first decides *not* to be the type to use the ego-booster booths (for retrieval of individual government records), and is nonplussed to think, upon changing his mind, that his reversal too marks him as a type. He cannot understand Lawrence's, Sam's, and the Spike's acceptance of being types—nor their corrections of him when he speaks of people as *only* types. "He hated being a type. ('My dear young man,' Lawrence had said, '*everyone* is a type. The true mark of social intelligence is how unusual we can make our particular behavior for the particular type we are when we are put under particular pressure.')" (p. 6).

Bron's categorizing is an attempt to fit people and events into self-determined slots, and it is only he who has the right to do the sorting. He realizes no humor, truth, or point in the many exchanges like this one with Spike.

> "You're a pretty cold and inhuman type," he said suddenly. "You think you've got everything figured out from the start."
> The Spike laughed. "And who is it who has called me a type three times in ten minutes?" (P. 91)

Bron is the only character in the novel who frequently uses racist and sexist terms—"crazed lesbian," "obnoxious faggot," "nigger," "cocksucker," "whore," and "dyke" (pp. 76, 119, 120, 121, 193, 244, 254). There are only two other instances I noted, both indicating that the usage is no longer common or acceptable: an Earth guard uses "nigger" (p. 163), and Philip, baiting Bron, uses "dyke" so that Bron can respond, embarrassingly, "I like Audri, and she's . . ." (p. 104). Bron's tags set him apart from and above those so designated, just as his pleasure in the use of money while on Earth enables him to draw a class distinction through the humiliation of a "serving class." George Slusser, in his discussion of *Babel-17*, observes that "men can control what they name, but only if they can name themselves first,"[13] and this is the one thing Bron as namer has failed to do. The flesh does not become word at his mandate but continues independent existence.

On Earth, Bron's assertion of superiority succeeds in a limited way through the use of money: acknowledgment is guaranteed as he scatters bills. The wonderful evening on the town, reminiscent of Bron's prostitute days, also demonstrates the vulnerability of someone who has to depend on the ratification of others for self-worth. Bron is exquisitely sensitive to the nuances of social protocol (at least as he remembers them from fifteen years ago on Mars), and the purpose of the evening is to impress—the hostesses, waiters, maître d'hôtel, and the Spike. Enjoyment is not one of the evening's purposes in Bron's trip down memory lane at "Swan's Craw," and he spends his time agonizing over faux pas. He takes comfort and pride in the thought "But at least I know *what* to be mortified about." There is no content to the experience; the satisfaction is in following a series of forms. When Bron asks the Spike if anything is the matter, he continues to query "Are you sure? Are you positive? There's nothing about my manner, my bearing, my clothing that you disapprove of?" (p. 206).

Simmel observes that, "For many character types, ultimately the only means of saving for themselves some modicum of self-esteem and the sense of filling a position is indirect, through the awareness of others."[14] For Bron, that awareness is mandatory but in itself insufficient. Just as, on the first page, the follow-up to Bron's wondering if he is "reasonably happy" or "happily, reasonable" is to question "how different that made him from those around," so Bron in his miseries and mortifications needs to be the best. At the party at Philip's commune on the Ring, he throws up and is reassured that he's "not the only one." As he explains aggrievedly to Spike, "I mean, after a while, you *want* to be the only one—some way, some form, some how" (p. 120). Statistics *are* sometimes wrong, as the government discovers when 80 percent of its citizens go out to watch the sky during a gravity leak, but, for Bron, they are another form which could—but doesn't—validate his uniqueness. When, after having been laid off, he asks Sam about the political situation and Sam is surprised, Bron explains his sudden interest by claiming that "Well, maybe I'm just that odd and inexplicable point oh oh oh oh oh one percent they call an individual—" and is annoyed when Sam responds, "No. You're a type like the rest of us" (p. 143).

When others fail, as they almost inevitably do, to endorse Bron's "specialness," the response is an immediate denigration of their intelligence and/or sensitivity: Bron understands these types fully, but they cannot fathom someone as complex as he is. Alfred, a neighbor usually dismissed by Bron as a pimply cretin, can still be called a "friend" because *he* comes to Bron—a tacit acknowledgment of Bron's position. "I suppose, Bron thought. . . . I understand him, which has something to do with it" (p. 47). After unfairly firing a woman, Miriamne, Bron's self-justification even invests Alfred with a rationale that would help to excuse himself.

> They don't understand, he thought. . . . And Alfred probably understood least of all, though from another point of view Alfred probably understood the best; that is, Alfred certainly understood by first-hand experience the feeling of having nobody understand you. . . . And didn't . . . Alfred's complete refusal to offer anyone else any interpretation . . . of their own psychological state represent a kind of respect, or at least a behavior that was indistinguishable from it? (P. 109)

Bron's attitude toward others is hardly respect and not even indifference. It ultimately reveals a complete inability to know that those around him have discrete existences: to him they are typical and he is an individual, and the two terms are irreconcilable antitheses. What is more, the people whom he sees most he sees as inferior types, who show moreover no consciousness of their "lowly" status: the Spike is a woman, Sam a black, Lawrence old and gay. Bron finally bases his identity on a masculine mystique that asserts: "Women don't understand. Faggots don't understand either" (p. 254).

Any effort made by others to reach Bron he sees as an intrusion: his understanding is already complete. Nonetheless, he is miffed when others exhibit information not known to him and, again, makes no connection between his never having asked and lack of knowledge. He *should* know about Alfred's computer course if Lawrence does; he *should* know of Sam's sex change operation. And he does *not* know that his omissions and commissions affect others, that, as Spike says, "your confusion hurts other people." To him other people are simpler organisms, and their lives reducible to formulae. When Bron sets out to become better acquainted with the Spike, he ends by delivering a monologue on his unhappiness. At the end of his delivery, she makes an ironic comment, and he replies:

> "But I *do* know all about you," he said. "At least, a lot. . . . you're living the romantic life as a theatrical producer in the swinging, unlicensed sector of the big city, where you've gained fame, and, if not fortune, at least a government endowment. What else is there to know?" (P. 125)

For Bron, there is nothing else to know. More detail would only clutter his clear outline.

During their night on the town, Bron announces that he loves the Spike, and she tries to tell him about someone she did love. He interrupts to ask why no one is wearing shoes, and is reduced to misery over his bananas Foster when told it is the thing to do: "What she had been telling him was important to her, he realized. Probably very important. But it *had* been unclear. And, what's more, dull. There comes a point, Bron decided, where for your own safety you have to take that amount of dull for the same as dumb" (p. 212). And, when Bron goes for a walk with the Spike after his brief Earth captivity, he is as frustrated and petulant as a child at show and tell by the prohibition on discussing his jail stay:

> What *was* there, then, to talk to her about, tell her about, ask her support for, her sympathy in, her opinion of?
>
> It was the most important thing that had happened to him since he had known her; and Sam's crazed paranoia had put it outside conversational bounds. (P. 181)

That *she* might be an appropriate subject of conversation doesn't occur to him: her function is to absorb and reflect information about Bron. It is important, though, that Bron know in advance what the subjects of his conversations may be and what form his response should take.

Bron constructs his grandiose self-image through unusually strong introjection of good qualities and projection of negative ones. He needs to believe that he is the initiator and focus of action, and quickly devalues others if they show strengths he does not possess or indicate weaknesses on his part. As the above passages show, Bron's self-referentiality can be extraordinary. Yet, as they also show, he is dependent upon the responses of others to maintain his image. Although Bron can make outrageous claims upon others, in the main he is passive in his actions and relationships since that allows the responsibility for their maintenance and quality to fall upon others. "Several times in his life, people had pointed out to him that what friends he had tended to be people who had approached him for friendship rather than people he'd approached" (p. 43). To express desire is to voice a need or incompleteness Bron will not claim as his own. When Sam asks Bron to be a part of his Earth entourage, Bron's response is "Not with you"—in part, we can suppose, because Lawrence is asked first. Upon remembering that he is out of work for two weeks, "He wished Sam would ask again," but does not himself ask (p. 146).

Bron's devaluation of others is consistent, but Sam presents a particularly vexing problem. He can dismiss Lawrence (who, ironically, receives recognition as a musician at the novel's end) and the Spike's opinions often are depreciated because of her sex, but Sam, a young man, is a potential competitor through his very existence. It is important that he locate the flaw and lessen Sam's significance. His early hypothesis is a projection that he doesn't see as applicable to himself. "The fact that Sam chose to live in an all-male nonspecific probably meant that, underneath the friendliness, the intelligence, the power, he was probably rotten with neurosis; behind him would be a string of shattered communal attempts and failed sexualizationships— like most men in their thirties who would choose such a place to live" (p. 32). Behavior like his own frequently draws a negative response from Bron. When the woman he fires, Miriamne, first appears, he says that he knows nothing about cybralogs, her area of specialization. She responds that *she* knows nothing of metalogics, and he is as offended by her ignorance as if it were a personal slight. "While Bron laughed, inside the ghost [of belligerence] momentarily became real" (p. 55). Conversely, Sam's knowing too much about metalogics is an infringement of territorial imperative and equally offensive.

Behavior or views that are his own can get assigned to another, often the victim, who is then belittled. When it is suggested that he fired Miriamne because of her failure to respond to his overtures, he is as indignant as when it is hinted that he is sexually jealous—both no-nos on Triton. In both instances, the sexual motivation is the right one, but Bron makes it Miriamne's in self-righteously explaining the situation to the Spike. "As much as I dislike her, all the way over here I've been feeling sorry for her. But if she *is* the type who would do that to another person . . . hell, do it to *me*, I wonder if I have the *right* to feel sorry for her" (p. 124). Sexual harassment becomes physical at the end of his evening on the town with the Spike. Since she doesn't want to enact his idea of the appropriate ritual ending, she elbows him. Yet, upon finding a letter from her awaiting him on Triton, his first response is "An apology from the Spike? He smiled. Well, it was to be expected" (p. 225). His immediate response to her explication of his faults is a displaced fury which moves from what others think, through dismissal of her as a type and falsified focus upon a particular example, to emphasis upon himself. "What the hell *had* she been saying to them about him anyway? . . . Anger welled. The type of person *he* was? He knew *her* type! Where did she come off presuming he'd had anything personal to do with that crazed lesbian's dismissal. Everyone was being laid off. Even *him!*" (p. 230). The letter is the mark of her bizarre irrationality—"She *must* be crazy!" (p. 231)—and people who cross Bron are often labeled "crazed." He earns the rubric himself, at this point and after his sex change, for his ersatz love, the only kind he is able to extend. "I must be crazy . . . , completely crazy! What could possess me to want a woman like that?" (p. 293). A woman "like that," as he later tells Lawrence, is one whose main concern during a pleasurable outing is an analysis of how she impresses others and a ridiculous preoccupation with proper form—a woman whose responses are Bron's own at the "Swan's Craw."

Bron's tendency to see others as figures in a private drama demands that he be writer/producer/director—the Spike's role, without the Spike's sense of balance, since Bron is also the star of his productions. His wishes become claims that demand compliance. In Bron's account to Audri about the Spike, he makes her into a fantasist, unable to distinguish between illusion and reality—makes her, in fact, a copy of himself. "Whatever she feels, that's what *is*, as far as she's concerned. But then I suppose . . . that's the right we just fought a war to defend. But Audri, when someone abuses that right, it can make it pretty awful for the rest of us" (p. 322). He claims the love of the Spike and Sam as his rightful due, and cannot understand *why* they won't honor the claim. At dinner, he engagingly proposes to the Spike, "Throw up the theater. Join your life to mine. Become one with me. *Be* mine. Let me possess you,' " and is uncomprehending when she doesn't want to be merged or possessed. "*Why* not? I love you. . . . Isn't that enough?" (p. 209). "Love" is not enough, a point he still doesn't get when he meets the Spike as a woman. "You don't *believe* you're the only person I've ever felt like this about?" (p. 292). Bron sees belief in his need as all that is necessary to fulfill his demand, and cannot understand that the Spike, Lawrence, and Sam are autonomous beings. The Spike and Sam, Bron claims, don't "understand."

What is more, were he even to begin to understand their point of view, his own grandiose self-image would be destroyed. The Spike's letter and the outbreak of war precipitate a sudden decision: he will become the very woman who *can* understand him. In so doing, he becomes his own mirror image as well as incorporating at least the appearance of the Spike and of Sam before his sex change.

Bron's dramatic metamorphosis is the only major change he undergoes in the novel. He becomes increasingly rigid, and repudiates—or simply doesn't recognize—the opportunities for freedom offered by events, those around him, and Triton itself. After their first meeting, the Spike explains to Bron why he was a good audience: "You'd be surprised how many people *do* fight that moment of freedom" (p. 89). Bron's response is belated: he spends the whole novel fighting that moment, which returns at the novel's end. In *City of a Thousand Suns*, Vol's thought is left incomplete: "We are trapped in that bright moment where we learned our doom, but still we struggle, knowing, too, that freedom is implied the very moment when the trap springs."[15] In Bron's first moment, the trap springs open; in the second, it shuts. The trap built by himself is not fearsome but secure; freedom is what terrifies him and what he cannot escape. As he tells Lawrence after the microtheater, "It was as though, suddenly, I couldn't trust *anything*" (p. 27). The interfusing of form and content in microtheater is one end of a continuum that moves through the vlet game to the formulaic ice operas. Even mastery of the vlet game demands consideration of more options than he is able to handle, and he ends with a credo or self-fiction as flat as that of the ice operas he so enjoys.

At different times, Bron tries to assign responsibility for his own identity to the Spike and Sam but both wisely refuse. He asks the Spike to "Help me. Take me. Make me whole," and, this first time, she tries. She responds with an incantatory "Come with me. Follow close. Do what I do" (p. 126), and brings him to a microtheater performance in which he is a participant, not a spectator. What Bron gains is simply a new formula, for he repeats her words later in the evening to invite her to his own performance. He is inexplicably disappointed afterward, thinking of possible errors in scenario, cue, entrance, and prop, and wondering in what way she has contaminated his powers of belief. "And what had she done that he was able to see her less and less clearly, while he thought of her more and more in terms from her work, in words his own tongue had tasted in her mouth?" (p. 126). What Bron gets is a husk: he does not do as the Spike does, he *acts* as he thinks she does, and the imitation loses any sense that informs the original.

Lawrence, the Spike, and Sam stand as models of creativity and flexibility in the novel. Lesser characters, like Audri and Phil, also adapt to changing circumstances, and complexity of character is suggested. Even the "Dumb Beast" evolves into Fred and forms a "sexualizationship" with the Spike as complementary as the artist/criminal joining of Rydra Wong and the Butcher. Bron's opposition to the possibilities presented by the Lawrence/Sam/the Spike triad is as unalterable as that of the Lord of the Flames to the Triple Being in *The Fall of the Towers*. There is no possibility for the kind of tetrad we find at the end of that trilogy or at the close of *Tales of Nevèrÿon*. Bron is not capable of being the stabilizing fourth—or second or third—that Zwon and Madame Keynes discuss in *Tales*.[16] His world view accommodates less and less. He has to reconstruct events to make them fit his self-image, and the same projection and shifting of sequence seen early in the account of Miriamne's firing become more frequent. He inverts sequence when he tells Audri that his lowered efficiency rating came after—and because of—seeing the Spike again. In this same conversation, the Spike has now become the petitioner to him that he in reality was to her. Finally, in talking to Lawrence, his own reactions at the "Swan's Craw" are now attributed to the Spike and we can only assume that the dislike of homosexuals he ascribes to her is also his own.

Equally startling examples of Bron's mythologizing are the accounts of his incarceration on Earth and of his getting home during the gravity loss. In both instances, Bron in reality was passive and his actions the result of chance. Retrospectively, however, all these happenings have become the result of volition and daring. As part of Sam's entourage during a political mission about which Bron knew nothing, Bron was briefly jailed, struck, and subjected to a lie detector test. But in his account his ignorance of *why* is forgotten, and the episode becomes one in which he was tortured for secrets of state and reinforced in his belief in the male solidarity that he sees as incomprehensible to women and faggots. "Some of us didn't come back," he solemnly informs Lawrence, and Lawrence is supposed to acknowledge his own exclusion from that "us" and admire Bron's inclusion, if not his clichés.

Bron's unwitting falling in with a group of mumblers who get past the cordon guarding his section during the gravity shift and the ensuing "rescue" of Audri also become a tale of calculated derring-do. As

Bron explains to Lawrence in a line that could be Bo Ninepins's of the ice opera, "I wanted to come back here, to check out you, and Audri and the kids. . . ." And, further, "that ingenuity comes out of the aloneness, that particular male aloneness" (pp. 256, 257). Bron's inability to recognize another or to understand mutuality becomes a sterile virtue. What Slusser refers to as a "web of language" formed by the use of "we" is to Bron a noose that he tries to avoid by his insistent "I." Yet, as Slusser continues, "The quest for the absolute blinds and thus restricts, while acceptance of limits—the fact that the speech act is necessarily relative, that any utterance implies a specific 'point of view'—leads to expansion."[17] Bron tries to become his own absolute.

Bron's explicit idealization of his life as a man, a mishmash of John Wayne-, Hemingway-, and Malraux-like attributes and explanations, demands that he stop being a man, because he cannot live up to the retrospective standards he has claimed. His earnest explication of the "horrors of war" to Lawrence stands as his own eulogy, in spite of Lawrence's deflating interruption.

> "Lawrence, regardless of the human race, what gives the species the only value it has are men, and particularly those men who can do what I did."
> "Change sex?"
> "What I did *before* . . . before, when I *was* a man. I'm not a man any more, so I don't need to be modest about it. What I've been through in the war, and the torture and terror leading up to it, the bravery demanded there, because of it. That showed me what real manhood is." (P. 276)

That once-upon-a-time man is one who can only exist as an ideal frozen in the past. All Bron can do is to become the woman who will be to that man what no one was to him.

Becoming a woman "solves" all of Bron's problems. Remaking himself in his own image assures that, finally, he is a rarity—one in 5,000, by Lawrence's estimate. Work can "mean less to her than before . . . at the materialization of the proper man." She doesn't have to be responsible because she is "now more at the mercy of her emotions than she had been." She can wonder at the fact that "I never lied when I was a man" (pp. 286, 293, 329). She thinks that she can be possessed, but adored, passive, but fascinating. In short, she can be as anachronistic a woman as she was a man. Bron believes that she is no longer responsible for Bron. Jon, in *City of a Thousand Suns*, asks a question much like Bron's: "*What* am I free to do?"[18] He finds his own answer: he loves, and he discovers what his work is. Bron sees her female self as her own answer to the question—"nothing." In Sennett's terms, "the threat of being overwhelmed by difficult social interactions is dealt with by fixing a self-image *in advance*, by making oneself a fixed object rather than an open person liable to be touched by a social situation."[19] Bron as a woman is as frozen as her past self. No man "materializes" because of her metamorphosis, no kiss or tear brings the Ice Princess to life, and Bron's expectations for the woman she has become forbid her seeking out a man.

Bron, then, is still Bron, despite her telling the Spike "But I've changed!" (p. 288). As Philip comments, she "still doesn't like to be touched" (p. 283), and neither does she touch. Bron's female body is another form without content, a type and emblem she expects others to interpret on her terms. The new shape signifies nothing in itself to those around Bron, and her renewed offers to the Spike and Sam meet no different responses than the old ones. The face Bron presents to Sam when she asks to be taken away may be remolded, but behind it lies the same Bron, someone never interested enough to remember details about other people, who cannot make the connection between destroyed Lux and the family she wants to join. It is this same Bron who at the novel's end lies awake in the night wondering if dawn will come.

According to Frank Manuel, utopias rest "on a set of implicit psychological assumptions about the nature of man."[20] *Triton's* heterotopia holds out the hope of what Freud called "common unhappiness" through a more flexible and adaptive environment, but no panacea for the ills of the individual or of society. This realized hope makes *Triton's* social structure a resounding success to which Lawrence, Sam, and the Spike are testaments. As Bron states early in the novel, Triton "makes it so easy for you—all you have to do is know what you want." For those who know their own desires, Triton offers a myriad of possibilities. But Bron's dreadful clichés about "the horrors of war" and "the coming of the dawn," point to a heterotopic reality. War *is* still a horror, and dawn may *not* come for Bron or others like him. There is no easy assignment of blame in *Triton*: individuals like Bron are not the "reasons" for wars, nor is the society of Triton the "cause" of Bron's disaffection. Their relationship is in the gray area of metalogic: the dilemmas of individual and social identity are no more easily solved in future time than in present, and there is no final answer or solution to the questions he poses:

But what happens to those of us who *don't* know? What happens to those of us who have problems and don't know *why* we have the problems we do? What happens to the ones of us in whom even the part that wants has lost, through atropy, all connection with articulate reason? Decide what you like and go get it? Well, what about the ones of us who only know what we *don't* like? (P. 122)

GARY K. WOLFE

# Autoplastic and Alloplastic Adaptations in Science Fiction: "Waldo" and "Desertion"

At a recent gathering of science fiction fans—a "con," to use the jargon of the fans themselves—an acquaintance and I were watching the bizarrely dressed crowd milling about in the lobby of the hotel when he turned to me and asked, "Have you noticed how many *grossly overweight* people there are here?" In fact, there were a surprising number of rather large people present, but there were also quite a few fans who seemed to represent the more traditional stereotype of the science fiction fan as undernourished adolescent. There was even a sizable number of people of normal, undistinguished girth. But the person who called this to my attention assured me that a rather atypical distribution of body types was quite common at conventions of this sort, and that he had noted it often. Perhaps he was more acutely aware of bodily structures than I, for, himself a science fiction fan since childhood, he had recently published his second book on body building and weight control.

Later, in talking with others more generally familiar with the world of fandom than I, I found that many people had made observations similar to these. A few even offered theories about how science fiction conventions offered a safe arena for social intercourse among people who felt inept or awkward on the outside. Such a theory reminds one of the cliché that "science fiction is a crutch for people who can't handle reality" and of the retaliatory T-shirt slogan that was making the rounds of these conventions a couple of years ago: "Reality is a crutch for people who can't handle science fiction." Both suggest in different ways the often tribal nature of interactions among fans, but it was not solely this hard-core group of fans I was concerned with. I looked at a number of interviews, memoirs, and autobiographies of science fiction writers—including Isaac Asimov's remarkably detailed *In Memory Yet Green*—and found frequent confirmation of what had now become a growing suspicion: not that science fiction was necessarily fattening (or emaciating, for that matter), but that it seemed to address the needs of adolescents and even adults who, at some key stage in their lives, felt themselves to be unattractive or ill at ease in their own bodies. I am not suggesting that such an attitude is in any sense a prerequisite to the enjoyment of science fiction, or that it is even characteristic of a majority of readers, but I will attempt to demonstrate that in a genre which spent many of its formative years catering to a largely adolescent audience and responding to the needs and desires of that audience, this attitude has been reflected in the literature.

This pattern has been noted before. Joanna Russ, in a 1970 essay titled "The Image of Women in Science Fiction," declared that science fiction readers "are overwhelmingly likely to be nervous, shy, pleasant boys, sensitive, intelligent, and very awkward with people. They also talk too much."[1] But while science fiction did for a long time garner a predominantly male audience, such a feeling of social awkwardness was not confined to boys. An attractive woman science fiction reader in her late thirties reports that, as a teenager, she often felt ungainly, unattractive, and ostracized from the social life of her school—partly because of her appearance, but partly also because of her superior intelligence, which seemed to be regarded as inappropriate in a girl. She took solace in stories of mutants, particularly Henry Kuttner's "Baldy" stories (collected as *Mutant*, 1953), and in stories of bodily transformation, such as Clifford D. Simak's "Desertion" (collected in *City*, 1952). The mutant stories conveyed to her the promise of a world in which mind or intelligence could act directly on the environment through telepathy or telekinesis, without the mediation of socializing agencies such as schools and families. Furthermore, the mutants themselves, the holders of these secret powers, were often physically unattractive outcasts (hence their nickname "Baldies" in the Kuttner stories). The tales of bodily transformation were another matter, and perhaps reflect a deeper fantasy. These tales, which might include James Blish's "pantropy" series (collected in *The Seedling Stars*, 1957) as well as the Simak title, concerned the fantasy of achieving a near-perfect match between a body and an alien environment, made possible by a liberation from earthly form altogether.

The point of all this is not just that science fiction is a genre principally concerned with mind-body dualism—though it does often address that issue—but that one of the uses of science fiction is to provide its readers with alternate models for relating to one's environment, and for gaining rewards from that environment. Generally, these models are of two kinds, and in describing them we might borrow an opposition originally suggested by Géza Róheim in discussing the differences between primitive and technological societies. One such difference, Róheim suggested, is that the former tend to be autoplastic while the latter are alloplastic; that is, the primitive seeks a more hospitable relationship with the environment through manipulation of his or her own body (as in surgical rites of passage), while a technological society such as ours manipulates the environment itself through such means as engineering and architecture.[2] The opposition takes on added meaning when one remembers that Róheim sought to establish a psychoanalytical model for anthropology which would permit parallels between ontogenetic and cultural development—an idea later developed and extended by Bruno Bettelheim and Norman O. Brown.[3] While later anthropologists have persuasively disputed any such one-to-one correspondence, the autoplastic-alloplastic antinomy remains in use in both cultural anthropology and developmental psychology.

What I want to explore in this essay, then, is the manner in which science fiction attempts to resolve the opposition of self and environment through both autoplastic and alloplastic fantasies, with some sidelong speculations on how this may in part account for the appeal of certain science fiction works to their readers. For this I would like to borrow another unusual term, this time from science fiction itself. "Instrumentality" is a useful word in discussing the means by which ends are achieved in science fiction, but it is a term that came into the genre through an odd route, probably originating in a novel that is not science fiction at all and that is almost never read today. Science fiction readers will recognize the word from its usage to describe the intergalactic government, the "Instrumentality of Mankind," in the stories published under the name Cordwainer Smith. It has been suggested that Smith (Paul Linebarger) intended a spiritual meaning for this term, borrowing it from references in Roman Catholic and Episcopalian theology to the priest becoming the "instrumentality" of God while performing the sacraments.[4] Without disputing this, I suggest that Linebarger may have had a broader meaning in mind as well. His earlier, non–science fiction novel *Ria* (published under the name Felix Forrest, 1947) ends with the protagonist undergoing a kind of mystical vision on a beach in North Carolina. "She felt that she stood somewhere in the lower part of her own tremendous skull, and that she listened to the fluent deep roar of a resounding bronze instrument of some kind—something metallic, something which sounded like the instrumentality of man, not like the unplanned noises of nature and the sea."[5] The echo of Wallace Stevens may be deliberate, for the clear implication in this passage is that instrumentality includes the whole project of imposed human order, a project that in Smith's science fiction would be extended to the entire universe. But in Smith's science fiction, the instrumentality of man expresses itself through both autoplastic and alloplastic means; the predictable alloplastic fantasies of vast cities and controlled environments, common to nearly all galactic-federation stories, are balanced by stories in which the limits of human form itself are questioned by making humans partly into machines or animals partly into humans.[6] Smith's first published story, for example, "Scanners Live in Vain" (1950), concerns humans surgically restructured to survive in the hostile environment of space, cut off from all knowledge of their own bodies save through special "scanning" instruments. In keeping the Róheim's model of cultural development, the scanners are phased out once the instrumentality discovers alloplastic means of dealing with this problem—namely, building better spaceships.

Science fiction, then, offers its readers the promise of greater and more satisfactory integration with the environment in two ways. In the first, the environment itself becomes the instrumentality of integration through its appropriation and alteration to humanity's will. This is the focus of the bulk of imaginative fiction which extrapolates trends in a direct line from an already highly alloplastic culture such as ours, and it leads eventually to fantasies of completely remaking environments to meet cultural needs: "terraforming" alien worlds in many novels, but also custom-building new worlds in novels such as Larry Niven's *Ringworld* (1970), Bob Shaw's *Orbitsville* (1975), or, on a smaller scale, Arthur C. Clarke's *Rendezvous with Rama* (1973). (It is interesting to note that, even though physicist Freeman Dyson has seriously suggested the eventual possibility of constructing an *Orbitsville*-type artificial world, science fiction writers have often shied away from making humans responsible for such a wholesale alloplastic fantasy, and all three of the novels I mentioned present the artificial world as an alien artifact.)

Thematically opposed to such instrumentalities of the environment is a smaller but distinct tradition of science fiction stories which deal with what we might call instrumentalities of the body. In these stories, the human form itself is altered through artificial means in order to achieve greater integration with an environment that would otherwise be hostile. This tradition includes the Simak, Blish, and Smith stories mentioned above, as well as Bernard Wolfe's remarkable novel *Limbo* (1952) and any number of "cyborg" stories, including most recently and notably Frederik Pohl's *Man Plus* (1976). A still more recent story which gives evidence of the tradition's continuing appeal is Vonda McIntyre's "Aztecs" (1977). Although this tradition has antecedents as diverse as H. G. Wells's *The Island of Dr. Moreau* (1896) and Olaf Stapledon's *Last and First Men* (1930), I would like, for purposes of this essay, to explore its impact in a single period of science fiction history, at the height of the so-called Golden Age of magazine science fiction, and to contrast it with a more conventionally alloplastic treatment of the same theme of self and environment from the same period.

More specifically, I would like to examine two stories which appeared only two years apart in *Astounding Science Fiction* in the early forties. Both stories subsequently gained reputations as minor classics of the genre, and both deal in almost archetypal terms with the problem of integration between body and environment. But their approaches to this problem differ considerably: Robert Heinlein's "Waldo" (August 1942) is for most of its length a conventional alloplastic fantasy, albeit reduced to the most primal terms in a tale concerning a weak and ungainly individual's attempts to create a hospitable environment. Clifford D. Simak's "Desertion" (November 1944), on the other hand, is an equally simplified version of the autoplastic fantasy in which the body itself becomes the instrument of integration through bodily transformation, again in a tale focusing on a single individual's experience.

Heinlein's "Waldo" is a story which is remembered primarily for a relatively trivial reason: the fact that the term "waldoes," used in the story to describe the mechanical hands that Waldo uses to overcome his own weakness, later entered the jargon of nuclear technology to describe similar artificial hands used to handle radioactive or other dangerous material. But the story itself is far more interesting for other reasons, not the least of which is the portrayal of the world-saving genius as isolated weakling. As H. Bruce Franklin points out, "Waldo has something in common with many of the readers of *Astounding*, as we find out if we turn to the last page of this August 1942 issue."[7] What is on that last page, Franklin notes, is an ad for Charles Atlas's "dynamic tension" method of body building—a method not too different from that discovered by Waldo during the course of the narrative. Is Waldo a fantasy projection of the typical science fiction reader, then, and are we back to the body-image problem which I mentioned at the beginning of this essay? Perhaps that is carrying things a bit far, but there is much evidence within the story itself to suggest that it indeed addresses a number of concerns that were likely shared by its readers in 1942 and, for that matter, by many science fiction fans even today. Furthermore, the story exhibits clearly an ideological tension that characterized not only much of Heinlein's work, but the entire field of science fiction as it grew and developed under John W. Campbell, Jr.'s guidance during his years as editor of *Astounding*. The early signs of this tension were already apparent in 1939 with the launching of *Unknown* as a fantasy companion to *Astounding*, but the tension would continue to be apparent throughout the next decade, leading to such works as Jack Williamson's *The Humanoids* (1947–48 in *Astounding*) and culminating, perhaps, in the involvement of Campbell with the Dianetics movement in the early fifties. This tension, I believe, was not merely an opposition between fantasy and science fiction, but something more fundamental, arising, perhaps, out of a growing need to find a place for human mind and will in the mechanistic vision of the universe projected by much science fiction of this period. One might loosely characterize this, then, as a tension between free will and determinism, or between the individual and technology (using technology in a sense similar to that which Jacques Ellul describes in *The Technological Society* [1954], but for our purposes, both of these may be subsumed into the opposition between self and environment of which we spoke earlier. Put in more purely psychological terms, the question becomes: does one alter one's environment to conform to the needs of the self, or can one alter oneself in order to function in the environment? Does one seek integration through alloplastic or autoplastic means? This, it seems to me, is one of the central issues in "Waldo."

Near the beginning of "Waldo," a number of oppositions are quickly established which serve to separate the protagonist, Waldo Farthingwaite-Jones, from the mainstream of the future society in which the story takes place. Foremost among these is Waldo's physical condition, which alone would serve to isolate him from society: suffering from myasthenia gravis since birth, he is abnormally weak and "softly fat, with double chin, dimples, smooth skin; he looked like a great, pink cherub, floating attendance on a saint."[8] Waldo's prepubescent, babylike features are significant, and certainly might have served to promote identification among many of the adolescent readers of the magazine. His condition also accounts for his lack of sexual experience, which will become a motivating factor later in the story. Add to this a brilliant mind and an arrogant, somewhat paranoid personality, and the result is a fair portrayal of the boy genius as social outcast.

But Waldo is set in opposition to society in more symbolic ways, too. In an age when most people have taken to living and working in underground structures according to something called "the London Plan" (p. 20), Waldo instead lives in a gravity-free orbiting space station which puts fewer strains on his weakened body. He calls this station "Freehold," suggesting liberation, but earthlings call it "Wheelchair," suggesting quite the opposite—dependence. An opposition between the individual and the corporation is also established: while most earthlings are dependent on a conglomerate called North American Power-Air for their energy (the corporation holds a virtual monopoly on the "broadcast power" that runs the cities and transportation systems), Waldo has declared a vendetta against this company for allegedly cheating him on some patents. In all, there are three principal levels of oppositions established to differentiate Waldo from the rest of the society. On what we might call the mythic level, there is the opposition of the sky and the underground (with the surface of the earth virtually abandoned by both Waldo and society, as evidenced by the crumbling roads left to deteriorate because "90 percent of the traffic is in the air" [p. 45]). On the social level, this becomes the opposition between the individual (Waldo, who lives in the sky) and the corporate state (North American Power-Air, which literally runs the underground society). Finally, on a level which is both psychological and philosophical, the opposition is between freedom (Freehold) and dependence (Wheelchair). The problem thus set up, the basic movement of the story is toward resolving these oppositions and getting Waldo back down to earth. From a psychological perspective, this becomes a problem in integrating the individual with his social and physical environment.

Initially, Waldo seeks to achieve this integration through purely alloplastic means, by creating an environment suitable to his bodily infirmity and surrounding himself with mechanical extensions of himself (the famous "waldoes"). But this solution clearly takes its emotional toll on him, and his resulting loneliness is evidenced not only by his arrogant misanthropy but by his sentimental attachment to a pet dog and canary. Yet Waldo's genius remains wholly mechanical; like Edison (the model of many early technologist-heroes in science fiction), he is more the inventor than the theorist. It seems never to have occurred to him to have turned to medicine or physiology to seek solutions to his problem; instead he manipulates the environment to reduce the dimensions of the problem. To this extent, Waldo's Freehold is a microcosm of the technological society of earth, a purely alloplastic adaptation. At this early point in the story, the only figure warning of the limits of possible dangers of such adaptation is Waldo's mentor and uncle, Doc Grimes, who also serves as mediator between Waldo and earth society. Grimes is concerned that long-term exposure to broadcast energy on earth is having a debilitating effect on the human nervous system (p. 15)—eventually turning the whole country into a nation of Waldoes. To protect himself from these effects, Grimes introduces one of the few autoplastic adaptations in this part of the narrative: the lead-shielded clothing which he wears to protect himself (p. 14). Grimes is also a doctor, a profession logically associated with autoplastic adaptations, and at one point in the narrative he recalls delivering the baby Waldo with "the necessary 'laying on of hands' " (p. 17). Grimes is clearly Waldo's father figure throughout the narrative, and is the only one whom Waldo will turn to for advice.

The narrative of "Waldo" begins by introducing a technological problem that will eventually force Waldo to reassess his own dependence on technology by calling into question the very reliability of alloplastic adaptations. Broadcast power receivers on earth have begun to fail for no apparent reason, and the power company is forced to turn to Waldo for assistance in solving the problem. Already, through this collaboration, the individual/corporation antinomy begins to resolve itself, with Grimes the mediating agent. The only one so far able to repair an affected receiver is not a scientist, but an aging "hex-doctor" named Schneider, whose repair involves a mystic ritual and results in the receiver antennas wiggling like worms. Thematically, Schneider is set in opposition to a corporation scientist named Rambeau, who is devoted to a wholly deterministic view of the universe—a view underlined by the point made early in the story that an earlier "reformulation of the General Field Theory did away with Heisenberg's Uncertainty Principle" (p. 13). To Rambeau, physics is an exact science, and Schneider's repair of the broken receivers using power drawn from "the Other World" drives Rambeau crazy. The mad

Rambeau's ravings give Waldo the clue to solving the problem, but Waldo must visit Schneider (who refuses to leave the earth or communicate via technology) in order to learn the actual solution. Significantly, Schneider chooses to live on the surface of the earth, and when Waldo, decending from orbit, and corporate representatives, rising from their underground cities, meet at Schneider's home, the opposition of sky/underground is symbolically resolved.

Schneider, then, supplants Grimes as the symbolic mediator of the earth/Waldo antinomy; and in a sense he also temporarily supplants Grimes as Waldo's father figure: it is through another "laying on of hands"—Schneider's massage of his weak arms (p. 67)—that Waldo begins to learn how to tap the sources of inner strength that will result in his eventual rebirth. But Schneider also becomes one pole of another set of antinomies, with Rambeau representing his opposite, and Waldo himself must provide the synthesis for this level of the dialectic. The Schneider/Rambeau opposition can be expressed in a number of ways; Waldo's own formulations of it progress from magic/science (p. 76) to mind/world (p. 88) to will/determinism (p. 89). But it might also be expressed as autoplastic/alloplastic, for while Rambeau insisted that the problems with the mechanical environment could only be solved through reference to that environment itself, Schneider insists that the solution lay within the individual. And that, incredibly enough, turns out to be precisely the reason the receivers began to fail. The operators, indeed weakened by the radiation effects Doc Grimes had feared all along, permitted the machines to fail by losing faith in them, by being "run-down, tired out, worried about something" (p. 73).[9]

By adopting Schneider's methods; that is, by learning to focus on himself rather than on his environment, Waldo is able to gain the strength necessary to enable him to function successfully in the gravity of earth. Heinlein also strongly implies that Waldo manages to achieve a dialectical synthesis of the magic/science antinomy by means of a new, comprehensive view of the universe that encompasses both mind and matter, but as is commonly the case when a science fiction story extrapolates itself into this particular corner, the details of the new synthesis are necessarily vague.[10] What is important to the emotional impact of the story, however, is not that Heinlein should manage to construct a comprehensive synthesis of physics and mysticism, but that he should find a means by which Waldo can be integrated into society, and that this means can be drawn from Waldo's own mind and body. In a sense, the story becomes a cautionary tale about depending too

heavily on alloplastic adaptations. Like many fairy tales, including
"Rapunzel," the story indicates that the body may provide solutions to
problems, rather than simply being itself a problem.[11] As Waldo gains
strength, he also develops an interest in social relations that is new to
him. He learns how to use his body in relation to others—not belching
in their presence, defending himself when challenged—very much in
the manner of a child moving into adolescence. It seems appropriate
that his first request of his newfound friend Stevens (one of the
corporate representatives who had been his nemesis) should be
"Could you teach me how to behave with girls?" (p. 103). Later he
comments, "I'm just beginning to find out how much fun it is to be a
man!" (p. 103). By the end of the story, Waldo has become almost a
parody compilation of adolescent fantasies—a world-famous ballet
dancer, brain surgeon, and scientist, sought after by reporters, business managers, and beautiful women.

    "Waldo" begins by positing an extreme condition of alloplastic
adaptation and ends by showing the limits and dangers of such adaptations. In Clifford D. Simak's "Desertion," these limits of mechanical
adaptation provide the basic premise of the story. "Desertion" is a
much shorter story than "Waldo," but together with its sequel "Paradise" (*Astounding*, June 1946) it provides what may be the pivotal
element in Simak's remarkable chronicle-narrative *City* (1952). Furthermore, as Thomas D. Clareson points out, " 'Desertion' provides a
classic example of one of the basic sf structural patterns: the solution of
a specific problem."[12] This in itself is unusual for a story as exclusively
concerned with autoplastic adaptation as "Desertion" is; what is more
remarkable is the manner in which Simak elides the technical dimensions of the problem in order to present the tale purely as myth (and it
is, more than any other tale in *City*, presented as "entirely myth" by
the anonymous dog-narrator of the frame-tale). Within the sequence
of *City* stories, "Desertion" and "Paradise" provide the account of
how most of humanity abandons the earth, clearing the way for the
tales of intelligent dogs, robots, and ants that make up the bulk of the
rest of the narrative. But "Desertion" also has a power uniquely its
own. It may be in part, as Eric S. Rabkin and Robert Scholes suggest, a
fable of environmental determinism,[13] but I suspect this is not enough
to account for the peculiar fondness with which many science fiction
readers remember the tale. Many readers I have met can even quote
the closing lines of the narrative, when the protagonist Fowler and his
dog Towser, converted into Jovian life forms to explore the hostile

environment of Jupiter, refuse to return: " 'They would turn me back into a dog,' said Towser. 'And me,' said Fowler, 'back into a man.' "[14]

The narrative begins in a society that has already given itself over to autoplastic adaptations to aid in the exploration of alien planets. Simak does not bother to explain why technology failed in conquering these environments with more conventionally alloplastic solutions; he only mentions that "converters," machines which transform humans into native extraterrestrial life forms, have been in use on "most of the other planets" (p. 106). Jupiter, however, presents a special problem: not only is its tremendous pressure and corrosive atmosphere more than usually destructive of machinery, but the four men who have so far been "converted" into the native life form known as "Lopers" have failed to return to report on their findings. Humanity's reasons for wanting to explore Jupiter are described in terms of the classic manifest destiny theme of much technological science fiction: "Man would take over Jupiter as he already had taken over the other smaller planets." For this appropriation to succeed, however, it is important that humanity not be "forced to work with clumsy tools and mechanisms or through the medium of robots that themselves were clumsy" (p. 106). Two important, if somewhat contradictory, points are made here: first, that the autoplastic adaptations used to explore the other planets had not been geniune; that is, they were undertaken in the service of the larger alloplastic fantasy of acquiring resources to feed a burgeoning interplanetary technology. The idea, apparently, was never that humanity would permanently adapt to these alien life forms. Second, there is evidence that this technology itself is already beginning to prove inadequate; the "clumsy tools and mechanisms" have begun to frustrate humanity in its attempts to truly know other worlds. The story begins, then, at a point at which the limits of alloplastic adaptations are already making themselves apparent.

When a fifth man who has been converted into a Loper fails to return, Fowler, the project director, decides that he and his dog Towser will undergo the conversion themselves. (Fowler's attachment to his dog, although taking on added meaning in the larger context of the *City* narrative that describes the rise of a dog civilization, also recalls Waldo's attachment to *his* dog; in both cases the relationship serves to reassure us that these characters are not after all heartless technophiles and to prepare us for the emotional changes they will undergo later in the story.) The converter itself is one of those delightful pieces of science fiction business that seem totally impossible; we are not given a clue as to how it works or what is involved in the process, but in the context of the narrative, we tend not to question it, either.

Instead of the conversion process, what we get is a bold, dramatic transition in the story, something akin to the shock cut of motion pictures. In one scene, Fowler is announcing that he will take Towser with him into the converter; in the next, he is on the surface of Jupiter.

> It was not the Jupiter he had known through the televisor. He had expected it to be different, but not like this. He had expected a hell of ammonia rain and stinking fumes and the deafening, thundering tumult of the storm. He had expected swirling clouds and fog and the snarling flicker of monstrous thunderbolts.
>
> He had not expected the lashing downpour would be reduced to drifting purple mist that moved like fleeing shadows over a red and purple sward. He had not even guessed the snaking bolts of lightning would be flares of pure ecstasy across a painted sky. (P. 113)

Through the Loper's eyes, Jupiter is paradise. But there is more: the "smooth, sleek strength" of the Jovian body, the gift of telepathy that enables him to communicate for the first time with Towser, the suddenly increased intelligence and clarity of thought that results from being able to use the brain "down to the last hidden corner" (p. 116). One of the first insights that comes to Fowler from his new, improved brain is a formula "for a process that would make metal to withstand the pressure of Jupiter" (p. 116). There is, after all, an alloplastic solution to the problem of living on Jupiter and mining its resources. But to the reborn Fowler, this information is trivial when compared to the superiority of a life fully integrated to the environment. He decides he cannot return. "Back to the fuzzy brain. Back to muddled thinking. Back to the flapping mouths that formed signals others understood. Back to eyes that now would be worse than no sight at all. Back to squalor, back to crawling, back to ignorance" (p. 118). Fowler does go back, five years later, in the story "Paradise," but only to spread the word of the wonders of Jovian existence and ultimately contribute to the virtual abandonment of earth by humans seeking a better life. But "Desertion" itself ends with the classic lines I quoted earlier, emphasizing the near-impossibility of returning to an earlier state of existence once one has achieved a total integration with one's environment. It is important to remember that the Lopers are not merely integrated to the environment of Jupiter, but that the quality of that integration is far superior to the integration of humans even to an earth environment.

Thomas Clareson argues that "Desertion" and "Paradise" "emphasize Simak's denunciation of the human condition more than did any of his previous fiction."[15] Simak himself has written, in regard to the whole of *City*, "Perhaps, deep inside myself, I was trying to create a world in which I and other disillusioned people could, for a moment take refuge from the world in which we lived."[16] But readership studies of *Astounding* suggest that Simak's original audience was perhaps a little young to be genuinely disillusioned. Instead, I believe, "Desertion" presents a fantasy of what might be called "super-integration," radically different in form but similar in structure to the integration which Waldo achieves at the end of Heinlein's story. In "Desertion," it is only the dog Towser who speaks to the issue of dissatisfaction with the old bodily form. "Lately I've been feeling pretty punk. Legs stiffening up on me and teeth wearing down to almost nothing" (p. 114). Displacing this speech to the dog prevents too close reader identification with a situation that might appear threatening—the inability of the body to fulfill the goals of the mind—but it keeps the issue from being lost in what might otherwise appear a fantasy of pure escapism. Like "Waldo," "Desertion" holds out the promise that bodily changes can be rewarding, that one can find in one's own body a superior means of achieving integration with the environment, that a threatening environment can be made rewarding through autoplastic adaptation, and that the most awkward, unpromising body can achieve grace and agility in the proper environment (Fowler "grimaced at remembering how he had pitied the Lopers when he glimpsed them through the television screen" [p. 113]).

I believe that this issue of autoplastic versus alloplastic adaptations is a more fundamental one in science fiction than it might at first appear, and that it is related directly to the appeal the genre holds for many of its readers. Many other examples come to mind; in the remainder of *City* itself, the autoplastic/alloplastic antinomy takes the form of the contrasting civilizations of the dogs and the ants, with the dogs making use of only the minimal alloplastic adaptations of tiny robots to serve as hands and eventually achieving a pastoral community of all living things; while the ants choose purely alloplastic means of adaptation to construct eventually a great metallic dome which covers most of the earth. But to demonstrate the variety of ways in which this theme imbues itself even in mass-audience science fiction, I might conclude by mentioning the role it plays in a few recent science fiction films. In the *Star Wars* movies, for example, the villainous Empire is consistently associated with alloplastic adaptations huge

spaceships, superweapons, even an entirely artificial planet called the
"Death Star." In contrast to this are the desert, ice, and jungle planets
where the rebels live and are forced to adapt themselves to unpromising environments. The extreme of such autoplastic adaptation is the
jungle planet in *The Empire Strikes Back* where the ancient Yoda
survives by drawing on an inner power called "the Force" and where
the hero Luke Skywalker trains himself to adapt to any environment
using this Force. Near the end of *Star Wars*, Luke, who in that film had
only begun to learn the power of the Force, rejects technology in order
to use this inner force from his own body to destroy the Death Star. I
mention this scene in particular because it contains almost a direct
echo of Heinlein's "Waldo": Luke is persuaded to trust in the Force by
the calm, disembodied voice of his previous mentor, Obi-Wan Ke-
nobi, who had been earlier eliminated by the villain Darth Vader. The
similar scene in "Waldo" occurs when the myasthenic Waldo, at-
tacked by the insane Rambeau, hears the words of Schneider:
"Gramps Schneider said in his ear, in a voice that was calm and strong,
'Reach out for the power, my son. Feel it in your fingers'" (p. 96).

Even more direct autoplastic fantasies are contained in the recent
films *Altered States* and *Scanners*. *Scanners* is more traditionally a
horror film based on the common mutant theme of psychokinesis, but
*Altered States* literally concerns the alteration of the body through
liberation of "inner forces." Based on a 1978 Paddy Chayefsky novel,
the Ken Russell film is in part an inadvertent remake of a 1958
B-picture called *Monster on the Campus*, which concerned a scientist
whose experiments on himself transformed him into a Neanderthal.
*Altered States* not only re-creates that fantasy, but goes beyond it in a
tale of a scientist who combines isolation-tank experiments with hallucinogenic drugs to turn himself into a variety of amorphous primal
shapes which quickly get out of his control. In the film's climactic
scene, the scientist is able to overcome these transformations through
love for his wife, which he has never been able to declare before. But
before we dismiss this as a sentimental cliché common to films of this
sort, we should pause to consider the cliché's significance: it reassures
us that bodily changes, even when exaggerated to the level of the
biazarre special effects of a film like this, can indeed serve to promote
greater integration and a better relationship with others. Through the
transformations, the scientist Jessup in *Altered States* learns the value
of his own natural bodily form and gains the motivation needed to save
his failing marriage.

Such autoplastic themes as I have discussed suggest a number of things about science fiction that might easily be overlooked: that it is not exclusively a literature about mechanization and technological appropriation of the universe, that its roots do not necessarily lie in fantasies of power and subjugation, that it does not serve its readers wholly as a means of escape or as a device for intellectual game-playing, that it is not antihuman. The works I have discussed gain their power not from the technological marvels they introduce, but from the structural models of integration they provide. In this manner, science fiction can provide for an older, somewhat intellectual audience some of the same functions that fantasies and fairy tales serve for younger children. This is not to suggest that fantasy cannot do the same thing science fiction does—that is a matter for another essay altogether—but merely that the science fiction, grounded in a framework of intellectuality that many of its readers value, can use that framework to construct positive and highly affective models of integration and maturation.

ROBERT HUNT

# Science Fiction for the Age of Inflation: Reading *Atlas Shrugged* in the 1980s

Ayn Rand is a prophet whose time has come, gone, and come again. *Atlas Shrugged*—the enormous novel that served as the bible of Rand's Objectivist movement—enjoyed a great vogue in the late 1950s and early 1960s. In many high schools and colleges, one had to read Rand (as one later had to read Golding, Vonnegut, or Brautigan) in order to stay intellectually *au courant*. It is no coincidence that, like the other three authors, Rand writes an idiosyncratic science fiction. In recent decades, young readers have been drawn most fiercely to authors who can dismantle and reassemble the known universe.

Rand's vogue faded during the 1960s. The vogue novels of that decade (*Siddhartha*, for example, or *Stranger in a Strange Land*) elevated feeling and intuition at the expense of reason. All Rand's works have a notional commitment to *reason* and *objectivity*, at least as code words. Although (as I will show) her fictional presentation of both concepts is largely sleight of hand, Rand's work was far too earthbound, polemical, and uptight for most sixties readers—even if they had not found her ideas disreputable.

Inflation and recession, however, have put Americans in the mood for emotional as well as economic belt-tightening. Self-interest is *in*, in the eighties. Sensitive people who a decade ago were following Thoreau's admonition to "simplify, simplify!" are now buying personal computers to stay on top of their cash flow. In the political sphere, too, Randites now walk the corridors of power. The Republican triumph in the 1980 elections represents a real apotheosis for Rand's attitudes, if not for her programs. (For example, Budget Director David Stockman's 1981 pronouncement that nobody has a *right* to receive anything from the government is pure Rand.) The growing bunker complex of the middle class, the widening gap between the landed and the unlanded, the obsession with gold, guns, and real estate, the elevation of the MBA degree to a kind of beatification—all these phenomena are both causes and symptoms of the triumph of the American Right. The "Me Generation" has become, in Donald Katz's clever phrase, the "Gimme Generation."[1] Yet Rand, I believe, was in no significant way the author of this change. Her doctrine of self-interest above all has become part of the new American middle-class catechism, yet she remains an esoteric author; one now preaching, I suspect, only to the converted.

Because Rand's work is so alien to an academic audience, I will begin this essay by briefly examining her philosophy and showing how this philosophy is reflected in the form and style of *Atlas Shrugged*. I will show why *Atlas Shrugged* is science fiction—indeed, why any novel of its type must inevitably become science fiction. In doing so, I will be telling the story twice—once as a romantic best seller, and once as an example of structure controlled by genre. I will discuss what I see as the novel's sources, its underlying patterns, and its powerful appeal to many readers. I will close with some reflections on the novel's genuine strengths, and on the odd relationship between this artifact and what we sometimes call the real world.

Rand's philosophy is based on a single simple idea: that the goal of all life, culture, and government ought to be absolute individual freedom. The universe exists so that each man (Rand's usual term) can realize his dreams and ideals, restrained only by his respect for the freedom of others. All human or economic claims on a person's life, love, time, or property are invalid, unless he has entered into them voluntarily. The claims of the weak and the sentimental are lies invented by inferior people to exploit the truly creative.

Capitalism—an ideal most nearly realized in the nineteenth-century United States—is the ultimate expression of this individual freedom. A person's creativity is symbolized by the wealth and property he has earned and the businesses he has created. All governmental restraints—taxation, regulation, subsidies, guidelines, appeals to charity or social equity—are a form of theft, the *looting* (to use a key word) by the incompetent of what superior people have created. Political and economic freedom entails the freedom to fail without calling on others for help. The only "generous" acts that have any integrity are those based on self-interest.

The bane of civilization, in Rand's scheme, is altruism—the belief that valid personal claims exist outside the realm of contracts. In private life, altruism leads to neurosis and misery, as parasitic relatives and lovers drain the spiritual vigor of creative men. In public life, altruism leads to bankruptcy, depressions, and collectivism—that is, to slavery. Rand's principles are uncompromising, her style humorless, her contempt for the weak unbounded. *Atlas Shrugged* is, among other things, a mechanism for freeing the reader from all philosophies, religions, and other forms of sentimentality and self-deception, from 3,000 years of misguided thinking and feeling. Every principle of life, Rand holds, can be derived a priori from objective observation and the laws of cause and effect. Any system that is not based on reason is self-contradictory, absurd, unstable, doomed; and modern civilization, she believes, is almost totally divorced from reason.

Even this summary should suggest that there is much more to Rand's philosophy than the sanctity of profit, and more to her novels than the sermons on capitalism.[2] *Atlas Shrugged* is a novel, a monument, an artifact, a shibboleth. It both uses and suffers from many of the conventions of science fiction. It violently polarizes its readers, and moves and even converts thousands of them in ways that the usual assumptions of literary criticism seem inadequate to account for. It is also a paradigm of ideological fiction, the most powerful and influential work to emerge from the American Right. Understanding this novel is an important—perhaps essential—step in understanding the effect of literature on modern life.

*Atlas Shrugged*, which was published in 1957, is set in an America on the verge of collapse: factories are closing, manufactured goods are falling apart, unemployed workers roam the streets. The rest of the world has degenerated into starving, socialist "people's states"; capitalism survives only in the United States, and here it is near death. As factory after factory goes under, the federal bureaucracy becomes ever more rapacious, confiscating entire industries in order to keep the country running—and to line the pockets of the bureaucrats. But one by one the ablest engineers and entrepreneurs mysteriously disappear, leaving their factories in ruins, their technology unusable.

Formally, *Atlas Shrugged* draws on the expectations of several genres. First, and superficially, it is a detective story—at 1,200 pages, the longest, slowest detective story ever published. Dagny Taggart, heiress and de facto manager of the Taggart Transcontinental Railroad, tries to stop the attrition of talent and to discover what sinister force could induce the heads of corporations to abandon the businesses they have built. Of course, as we learn, there is no real culprit. The creative people—principally male engineers, but with token representation of doctors, judges, writers, musicians, and women—have resigned voluntarily from a world that does not appreciate them. Their inspiration, the mysterious John Galt, turns out to embody all the qualities Dagny has ever desired in a man: clearmindedness, unswerving individualism, and devotion to the sanctity of profit. His intellectual potency and physical potency are equivalent, and Dagny's acceptance of his ideas progresses with her acceptance of him as a lover.

For *Atlas Shrugged* participates in the formal and psychological characteristics of a second genre: the *Bildungsroman*, or chronicle of intellectual and spiritual development. Dagny's growth into an uncompromising individualist overshadows her role as investigator of the novel's central mystery. For the reader, indeed, the real mystery of Dagny's quest is why she did not recognize what was going on much sooner. The answer is that she had to be reeducated, and the novel traces this education in terms of her lovers, each of whom seems more ruggedly individualistic than his predecessor: first the brilliant (but apparently profligate) Francisco D'Anconia, then the determined (but sexually troubled) Hank Rearden, and finally Galt—who by the novel's end has fully realized all his ideals and about whom as a person almost nothing interesting can be said. In the reader's experience, Dagny's lovers represent a progression from flesh to mind to spirit; in Rand's scheme, however, all three men are stern and eloquent advocates of the capitalist ideal—and by page 1,200 all three sound exactly alike. (The ideological similarity of all the main characters is reinforced by the proponderance of velar and alveolar stops—*k, g, t, d*—in their names: hard sounds for intellectually tough people.)

This convergence of character in *Atlas Shrugged* would fatally weaken a conventional mimetic novel. An ideological work, however, has a purpose that supersedes all considerations of genre. Mystery and *Bildung* can be interpreted as formal devices (rather than generic strictures) designed to keep the reader turning the pages; and indeed many readers remember Dagny's economic struggles and amorous quests far more vividly than they do the code she finally adopts. But *Atlas Shrugged* is, after all, an apologue, an argument for an intellectual and moral position which happens to take the form of a novel. The test of any apologue is how thoroughly plot, setting, and characters are integrated with the underlying theme; whether they could be changed without blunting the effect of the ideas the author is expressing. Most of us would agree, I think, that Johnson's *Rasselas* could be refitted with new characters and incidents and yet express the same truths about human experience; *Candide*, on the other hand, is more than the sum of its literary machinery, and far more than simply an attack on Panglossianism. Rand's novels, weighed by this standard, are closer to the *Rasselas* mold: the ideas exert all formal control; the characters—provided they are the right types in the right positions—could be endlessly substituted for by other characters, as could the settings and the details of the plot.

Interestingly, however, Rand rejects the foregoing model of her literary method in all her critical writings. "I'm not a propagandist, believe it or not," she writes.[3] "My purpose is *not* the philosophical enlightenment of my readers, it is *not* the beneficial influence which my novels may have on people. . . . My purpose, first cause and prime mover is the portrayal of . . . John Galt or Hank Rearden or Francisco D'Anconia *as an end in himself*—not as a means to any further end."[4] "First cause" and "prime mover" are Aristotelian terms, wrenched from context in order to describe not God, but Rand, the godlike creator of a fictional universe. Her aesthetic, too, is that of Aristotle's *Poetics*: "My purpose," writes Rand, "is the presentation of an ideal man. . . . History represents things only as they are, while fiction represents them 'as they *might be* and *ought to be*.'"[5]

Once the ideal fictional hero has been created (a process based, according to Rand, on the author's act of observation, analysis, generalization, and re-creation—in short, a quasi-scientific synthesis), it is up to the reader to respond appropriately to the literary object. Rand believes (or professes to believe) that this response will be fundamentally intellectual, that the reader's emotions, when they are engaged, will be evoked by the power of ideas, not by the passions and conflicts on the printed page. "Emotions," she maintains, "are a result of your value judgments; they are caused by your basic premises, which you may hold consciously or unconsciously. . . . A rational man knows . . . the source of his emotions, the basic premises from which they come; if the premises are wrong, he corrects them."[6] Critical response, then, is a dialectic or reason and feeling, a process of self-correction and self-adjustment, leading to self-knowledge.

How well does Rand's professed aim square with the reality of *Atlas Shrugged*? As I hope to show, the novel works astoundingly well to fulfil the author's purposes, but it works almost entirely by manipulating the reader's unconscious. We will see this fundamental contradiction between theory and practice everywhere we look in *Atlas Shrugged*. The novel shouts at us on one level and whispers to us on another, but we pay more real attention to the whisper. To understand its powerful appeal, we must also examine the novel's relation to the science fiction genre, and probe the psychodynamics of Rand's imagery.

The first thing that strikes any reader is the physical dimension of *Atlas Shrugged*. The hardbound edition is an artifact of biblical length and heft; the paperback a thousand-page maze of eight-point type, its reading a pilgrimage of faith enacted on buses, subways, and park benches, a few pages at a time. The novel's bulk, which tends to subvert its value as entertainment, is actually an asset to its function as apologue. The reader is impressed, oppressed, and finally overwhelmed by the sheer weight of the world according to Rand. As with the much shorter *Dune*, readers must remain so long within the novel's fictive universe that the time expended becomes an emotional investment; only conviction (or at least openness) to the author's ideas can justify the effort. The act of reading is also a kind of sensory deprivation; *Atlas Shrugged* effectively shuts out all other literary and intellectual influences for a period of weeks or months. The reader, by the end, may acquiesce to Rand's world view because all others have grown dim and distant.

What exactly is the universe of Rand's novel? *Atlas Shrugged* is clearly science fiction, yet its setting is not simply a *future* America. The country's economy is extrapolated from the America of the 1920s and 1930s, rather than from the 1950s.[7] Railroads are still the arteries of the nation, and steel its most important industry. Airplanes are exotic, propeller-driven, and untrustworthy. Computers and complex electronics are—except as science-fictional inventions—completely absent. There is no foreign competition or need for imported petroleum; the United States is economically isolated (except for the copper from Francisco D'Anconia's Chilean mines) and responsible for its own misfortunes. (The crumbling economy of *Atlas Shrugged*, clearly inspired by the Depression of the 1930s, is startlingly prophetic of the falling productivity of the 1970s and 1980s; in 1957, however, Rand's vision must have seemed absurdly pessimistic.)[8]

Implausible as it may strike us, the isolation of America is aesthetically essential to the novel; the existence of foreign trade or competition on a significant scale would derail Rand's plot, and for the reader to put any more than a notional credence in the three billion or so people starving under socialism would open emotional and fictional dimensions the novel is not equipped to deal with.

America's isolation is far more than an economic one. Rand's America is cut off from its past—*our* past. She has rewritten American history to fit her vision of the apotheosis of capital. In *Atlas Shrugged*, the first transcontinental railroad—the Taggart Transcontinental—was the work of a single nineteenth-century genius, opposed by nearly everyone, financed only by his stockholders, rejecting all government aid. In historic fact, the transcontinental railroad was supported by presidents and Congress, involved the founding of two vast corporations (Central Pacific and Union Pacific), received millions of dollars in federal subsidies and rights-of-way, and was expedited by extensive graft.[9] To Rand the novelist, such history never took place—because it should not have taken place. In her universe, every successful corporation is the *creation*—a highly significant word—of an individual, independent genius. There is no arguing with the author; this massive simplification of history must be taken on faith.

The isolation of the narrative universe goes much further than the cancellation of history. *Atlas Shrugged* does not contain the name of a single real corporation, past or present (although D'Anconia Copper echoes, perhaps unconsciously, Anaconda); nor the name of any businessman, engineer, president, statesman, or inventor who ever lived; nor of any historical figure—neither Jesus nor Marx nor Adam Smith nor Stalin nor Hitler nor Napoleon—nor (with a minute exception) of any author, artist, or composer; nor of any invention, movement, system, or theory—including communism, fascism, evolution, or relativity—that can be attributed to one person; nor World War I, nor World War II, nor any other event of the twentieth century or of any preceding century.

Has any novel, professedly set in the real world, ever excluded human history and culture on so vast a scale? The only shred of contact is one contemptuous reference to Plato and a respectful one to Aristotle, whose *Metaphysics* provides the titles of each of the novel's three parts.[10]

No doubt this massive simplification reflects the author's own cultural isolation (her literary pantheon begins with Victor Hugo, ends with Mickey Spillane, and excludes almost everyone else). But it also augments the novel's claustrophobic effect, and accurately reflects the single-mindedness of the principal characters. Despite their geographical ties to the factual United States, Rand's people actually live in a version of that familiar science-fictional setting, the alternate universe. The author—unconsciously, I suspect—has rewritten history to exclude every factor that might weaken her apologue. Genre sf writers also have a passion for simplification; quite apart from their value as satire, the alternate universes of Aldiss, Amis, Moorcock,

Roberts, and others purge history of those complicating factors (science, rationalism, the Protestant Reformation, progress, the wheel) that have taken the fun out of the mimetic novel. The worlds that remain are simpler, slower, more brightly colored, and far more manageable than ours. Rand, likewise, has stripped her universe to a few monolithic shapes, throwing into the sharpest possible focus the black/white dialectic of altruist versus capitalist. Unlike the other sf writers, however, Rand does not invent a complex civilization to replace the one she has canceled. In its grimness of affect, *Atlas Shrugged* often suggests the solipsistic universe of Dick's *Eye in the Sky*, whose schizophrenic characters can eliminate all offending objects, one by one, until delusion and reality match.

Rand obviously had some familiarity with magazine sf (her short science fiction novel *Anthem*, originally published in 1938, appeared in *Famous Fantastic Mysteries* in June 1953). In its crudeness of characterization, indeed, *Atlas Shrugged* recalls the pulp sf of the 1920s and 1930s. Steel manufacturer Hank Rearden, whose personal and economic battles dominate the novel's first half, is cast in the same heroic mold as Garth Hammond, the planet-smashing entrepreneur of Jack Williamson's 1939 *Astounding* novella, *Crucible of Power*.[11] Indeed, all the novel's industrialists—oil king Ellis Wyatt, auto manufacturer Lawrence Hammond, and (before his conversion to apparent hedonism) copper magnate Francisco D'Anconia—fit squarely into the pulp tradition of the tight-lipped, two-fisted engineer/research scientist/capitalist/adventurer that dominated sf until and beyond World War II. Rand's heroes are tall, lean, and generally blond, with piercing blue eyes and hawklike features. Dagny Taggart, similarly, is first described as long-legged, casually elegant, with a "slender, nervous body," an angular face, and "a sensual mouth held closed with inflexible precision"[12]—a description that links her to the strong male characters while hinting at the powerful feminine sexuality held in check. Dagny assesses men's bodies with an appetite rare in fiction of the 1940s and 1950s. D'Anconia, Rearden, and Galt all have strong legs and "slender" waistlines, emphasized by matching slacks and shirts.[13] Dagny's lovers look neither like real businessmen nor like the beefy heroes of pulp fiction; they resemble the male models in *Gentlemen's Quarterly*, and project sex, money, and self-confidence simultaneously. The symbols of earned wealth, in *Atlas Shrugged*, are invested with an erotic aura.

With a Platonic correspondence of body and spirit, Rand's villains are invariably flabby and pudgy, with ill-matched features and shifty piglike eyes. The eyes, in Rand, are literally windows on the soul. Paul Larkin, Hank Rearden's sponging brother-in-law, has "gentle, pleading, . . . wistful eyes" and a "lost, helpless, appealing smile . . . like that of a boy who throws himself at the mercy of an incomprehensible universe"; Larkin, the narrative voice adds cuttingly, "was fifty-three years old."[14] Rearden's glamorous wife falls short of beauty for a similar reason: "The eyes were the flaw: they were vaguely pale, neither quite gray nor brown, lifelessly empty of expression";[15] and the muscles of her face have "an odd slackness, like the limbs of an animal lying in the road, intact but dead."[16] Dagny's weak brother, James Taggart, has "eyes [that] were pale and veiled, with a glance that moved slowly, never quite stopping, gliding off and past things in eternal resentment of their existence."[17] Contrast these dismissive descriptions of unfocused weakness with (for example) that of Hank Rearden, gaunt, ash-blond, whose eyes have "the color and quality of pale blue ice."[18]

We are dealing, of course, with characters conceived in the crudest emblematic terms. The names (Cuffy Meigs, Lester Tuck, Wesley Mouch, Tinky Holloway) and the physical descriptions of Rand's slouching, flabby villains makes it impossible for the reader to feel anything but revulsion towards them. Good people and bad may inhabit the same landscape, but they belong to different universes. The ambiguity that sophisticated readers so admire in novels is in Rand's aesthetic a symptom of moral rot; the closest she comes to it is the agonizing a superior being such as Dagny must undergo during the process of self-discovery. The casting-off of delusory ties seems painful, yet the weak must be not merely rejected but wiped from one's mind—a feat which their pallor and amoeboid vagueness make morally imperative. Behind this dualism, I suspect, lurk the cardboard villains of pulp fiction and the cookie-cutter aliens of prewar sf.

A second and much more significant debt to pulp sf is the use of science-fictional inventions as controlling plot devices. The novel's action is propelled by a series of four inventions. Three of these—the creative inventions that further the higher morality of production—are the work of individuals; the fourth invention is destructive, and is the work of a committee.

Rearden Metal, the first invention, motivates Part I of *Atlas Shrugged*. This miracle alloy, harder than conventional steel, is of course the product of Hank Rearden's mind and capital; only Rearden Metal can save America's decaying railroads and industries, but every customer fears to order it. Dagny Taggart alone has faith in Rearden, and she becomes his ally in laying Rearden-Metal rails on the Taggart line across the Rocky Mountains. Their struggles climax in a triumphant, hundred-mile-an-hour ride across the new line; immediately afterward, they become lovers. The train ride is described in transcendently ecstatic language, as Dagny realizes the profound identity of creative mind and machine. (Rand's aesthetic rejects "mystical" imagery; in practice, she reserves it almost exclusively for paeans to technology.) Their lovemaking is presented in the sadomasochistic imagery of ripped-bodice romances. Sex, for Rand, is an act both of tribute and of possession; blood, blows, and bruises are presumably meant as outward signs of violent—hence authentic—emotion.

Immediately after this consummation, Rearden and Dagny come across a second invention: a model of an electric motor, sitting in an abandoned factory together with a sheaf of decaying notes. With a phenomenal (but appropriate) intuition, Dagny recognizes the model as a "self-generator," a motor that could "draw static electricity from the atmosphere, convert it [into current, presumably] and create its own power as it went along."[19] (Readers of early-1940s sf will recognize parallels with the cheap, clean "broadcast power" that obsessed John W. Campbell and many of *Astounding*'s regular contributors.)[20] The model has been abandoned by its inventor, and Dagny, convinced that only this new technology can save industrial America, resolves to find him.

The inventor was the mysterious John Galt, who now visits harrassed industrialists ripe for defection from the looters' society. Her pursuit of Galt leads Dagny to a hidden valley in the Rockies, and to a third invention: a screen of powerful broadcast rays that projects the image of distant mountains onto the air layers above the valley, rendering it invisible from the air. The screen is Galt's invention; powered by his miraculous motor, it protects the society of defecting rationalists from the outside world. After Dagny's plane crashes in the valley, she is given a tour of this utopia. (Such tours, a common subgenre at the turn of the century, had come to seem old-fashioned even by the 1920s; Rand's imperviousness to irony, however, and her depiction of Dagny's growing desire for Galt, invest these chapters with great intensity.) Within the valley, the chosen few are making revolutionary discoveries in physics, medicine, and engineering—discoveries they have resolved to deny to an unworthy world. They work in isolation, without the need for research assistants or advanced facilities; they are, in short, not realistic scientists or inventors, but versions of the stock 1930s scientist-as-wizard, the genius who steps into the lab to cook up a solution to the latest plot crisis. Rand, it appears, accepts this stereotype of the scientist as authentic; indeed, she must, for her philosophy demands that every significant creation be the work of an individual.

Dagny is free to remain in the valley, but she declines, resolved to fight the last battle on behalf of her corporation in the outside world. Suddenly, with no preparation, the corrupt scientific establishment unveils the novel's fourth invention: "Project X," a "sound ray" generator capable of leveling all buildings and destroying all life within a range of 100 miles. The generator, described in organic terms, is quite unlike the sleek metallic avatars of productive technology.

> It was a small, squat structure of unknown purpose, with massive stone walls, no windows except a few slits protected by stout iron bars, and a large dome, grotesquely too heavy for the rest, that seemed to press the structure down into the soil. A few outlets protruded from the base of the dome, in loose irregular shapes, resembling badly poured clay funnels; they did not seem to belong to an industrial age or to any known usage. The building had an air of silent malevolence, like a puffed, venomous mushroom; it was obviously modern, but its sloppy, rounded, ineptly unspecific lines made it look like a primitive structure unearthed in the heart of the jungle, devoted to some secret rites of savagery.[21]

The "sloppy" and "unspecific" generator, of course, is emblematic of the flabby villains who developed it. Its appearance reflects its nature as much as any haunted wood or allegorical castle in the *Faerie Queene* figures forth the tempters and heretics lurking within. Despite its appearance, the generator works. Building it, we are told, was "easy"; once renegade scientist Robert Stadler had done his "invaluable research into the nature of cosmic rays and of the spatial transmission of energy," it took only "a few third-raters" to complete the infernal machine.[22]

But the villains never have a chance to use the death ray purposefully on the American public. Stadler attempts to restrain a drunken bureaucrat who has seized the generator in an attempted coup ("Don't touch those levers, you fool!"),[23] and generator, bureaucrat, and scientist all go up in smoke. The last representatives of the federal government appeal to Galt for help; when he rebuffs their offers, they kidnap and torture him. The torture device, a kind of footnote to the sound-ray generator, does no more than deliver calculated electric shocks, but Rand presents it as a major invention, with its own squat laboratory and hulking, brainless attendants. The machine breaks down (as misapplied technology, in this novel, always does), and Galt must regain consciousness to tell his torturers how to fix it. They flee in terror before Galt's Olympian laughter, and Dagny and her allies rescue him.

The holocaust for which the novel's last 300 pages seem to have prepared us never comes to pass. American civilization dies with a whimper, in the dark, as the panicking millions, cut off from food and power, crowd the roads and bridges out of New York. It is a marginally more sophisticated version of the pulp apocalypse: the easy triumph of four people over a scrambling horde, whether human or alien.[24]

Those millions, to be sure, have no more reality for the reader of *Atlas Shrugged* than do the starving billions overseas.As Dagny's plane soars above the darkened city, she reflects that now "the earth would be as empty as the space where their propeller was cutting an unobstructed path—as empty and as free."[25] "Empty," in Rand's context, means "free of opposition"; the human beings on the ground are an impotent, invisible mass waiting to be molded into meaning. When, on the novel's final page,the creative handful—having rewritten the Constitution and relaid the foundations for their banks, industries, and railroads—resolve to return to the world, Galt is cast as the Judeo-Christian God hovering over the *prima materia*: "He raised his hand and over the desolate earth he traced in space the sign of the dollar."[26]

The earth is "desolate" because the creative ego has been withdrawn from it. In a sense, Rand has exceeded the visions of the planet-smashing sf writers; anyone can destroy a planet on paper, but it takes an unusual talent to convince the reader that the world he or she knows has been effectively destroyed, deprived of all meaning for reasons that are essentially abstract.

How is Rand able to move her readers so thoroughly with such crude materials? For one thing, she has made potent use of the feeling we all have to some degree, of being unappreciated and exploited by others—whether parents, lovers, employers, or governments—the sense that *we were meant for something better*. Rand has objectified this instinct, reified that "something better" as the artifacts and emblems of industrial America, and raised the individual's struggle for recognition and self-esteem[27] to a cosmic scale. Reader indentification—that critically maligned lure of the popular novel—is Rand's great strength. The reader's ego soars amid the skyscrapers, penthouses, airplanes, and eyries of the creative elite; their chrome-and-leather furniture, platinum cigarette cases, blue fox stoles, and severe, expensively tailored clothes carry infinitely more emotional weight than Rand's token factory workers and switchmen, whose gruff eloquence is as unconvincing as that of Sholokhov's socialist peasants. (It is worth remembering that Rand's first years in the United States were spent as a movie extra and continuity writer at the Cecil B. DeMille Studio, where such films as *King of Kings, The Road to Yesterday, The Volga Boatman,* and *Madame Satan* were in production or preparation. DeMille's most memorable imagery—roiling mobs, hulking muzhiks, spectacular train wrecks, and art deco orgies in a zeppelin moored over Manhattan—can all be traced in Rand's fiction.)[28]

On a profounder level of technique, Rand has used imagery that casts the reader back to the confusions and struggles of early childhood; a time when the world of others—whether human or objects—is perceived as dark, mysterious, and disorganized, more susceptible to the manipulations of magic—that is, to the action of the unmediated will—than it is to the laws of cause and effect. When the will triumphs in *Atlas Shrugged* (as it inevitably does despite all opposition), the effect is of a creative light bringing order to a dark primal chaos. Repeated images reinforce this association: lighted corporate offices towering above darkened, doomed New York; lighted Taggart trains cutting across the blackened prairies; Hank Rearden's blast furnaces glowing in the night; "Wyatt's Torch," a burning plume of natural gas, flaming amid the dark wasteland of his abandoned oil fields; the spark of Galt's or Dagny's cigarette shining in a dark room or tunnel, a symbol that creative thought is taking place (in this novel, only the heroes smoke).[29]

Rand's set pieces of trains and factories have an eloquence and power that is missing from her descriptions of human beings; her machines seem alive, not only because of her frequent personification, but because they are endowed with the personalities of their creators. Nature, by contrast, is drab at best and hideously vacant at worst; in one of the novel's most significant passages, Dagny and Rearden realize that a landscape is truly barren because it contains no billboards.[30] Nature, Dagny reflects in a moment of crisis, is essentially futile.

> A circle, she thought, is the movement proper to physical nature, they say that there's nothing but circular motion in the inanimate universe around us, but the straight line is the badge of man, the straight line of a geometrical abstraction that makes roads, rails and bridges, the straight line that cuts the curving aimlessness of nature by a purposeful motion from a start to an end. . . . It is not proper for man's life to be a circle, she

thought, or a string of circles dropping off like zeros behind him—man's life must be a straight line of motion from goal to farther goal, each leading to the next and to a single growing sum.[31]

Modern man's nausea when confronted by the circles and loops of nature (successors to the vast spaces that so terrified Pascal) underlies an enormous amount of twentieth-century, and particularly postwar, science fiction, not all of it literature or even necessarily literate; Rand's thrusting tracks, tunnels, and vectors symbolize the rightmost boundary of a dozen thematic areas where sf attempts to grapple with the modern sense of life.[32]

Much of *Atlas Shrugged*, too, is powerfully mythic. The novel's eponymous titan and the myths of Prometheus and Phaethon link the action with the cosmic struggles of classic Greek theogony.[33] The Golden Age, another vital element of creation myths (and an expression of human nostalgia for the happy childhood no one ever quite had), is identified with nineteenth-century American capitalism. Gold itself, the medium of exchange among the elite in the valley, bears the associations of fairy tales, alchemy, and enchanted hoards before and above those of Coolidge/Hoover economics; Rand's imagery transfers gold's numinous qualities to the hair and features of her heroes.[34]

For the reader, the hidden valley becomes the archetypal goal of heroic quests, as well as a private symbol of escape and security. (In 1962, Rand unself-consciously told an interviewer that the first work of art that impressed her "was an adventure story in a French children's magazine called 'The Mysterious Valley.'" Rand herself, in a rejuvenated self-portrait, appears in the valley as a dark-haired, large-eyed young writer who gazes longingly and vainly after John Galt.)[35] It is a place of rebirth where one reencounters the friends and heroes who have died in—in *Atlas Shrugged*, disappeared from—the outer world. In the valley, Dagny meets again all the men she has admired, and she meets them transformed into their true selves. Rand identifies the valley metaphorically with Atlantis, the Isles of the Blessed, Elysium, and early America—all places "where hero-spirits lived in a happiness unknown to the rest of the earth."[36] The valley, by preserving and purifying the personality, serves to deny death—and appropriately, although death strikes several confused but sympathetic characters, the true elite seem invulnerable.

With each type of structure—the imagery, the man/nature dialectic, the mythic patterns—Rand is true to the reader's profoundest needs and perceptions. These controlling forms, not the novel's intellectual shape, are the true source of its power and the extraordinary

response it evokes. Rand's aesthetic, of course, rejects all such responses as "mysticism"; only assent earned through reason, she maintains, is fairly earned.

Yet even at the "rational," mimetic level Rand works almost
exclusively upon the reader's emotions. One important example can
stand for many: a large number of intelligent young women, feminist
by conviction and not conventionally right-wing, have read Rand
closely and remember her works in detail (though their memories
often conflate individual scenes from *The Fountainhead* and *Atlas
Shrugged*). Why such attention by independent women towards an
author who believes that "the essence of femininity is hero-worship—
the desire to look up to man"[37] and whose heroine finds her greatest
triumph in sexual surrender, in willingness "to accept anything" her
lovers wish?[38] Rand's reactionary sexual dynamics, I suspect, are re-
deemed for female readers by the exhilarating ease with which her
heroic characters renounce the emotional claims of parasitic friends
and relatives. This renunciation is unaccompanied by the beating
hearts and sopping handkerchiefs of ladies' magazine fiction; it is as
calm as Hank Rearden's acknowledgment of the utter indifference he
feels towards his family:

> "Henry, don't you understand us?" his mother was pleading.
>
> "I do," he said quietly.
>
> She looked away, avoiding the clarity of his eyes. "Don't you care what
> becomes of us?"
>
> "I don't."
>
> "Aren't you human?" Her voice grew shrill with anger. "Aren't you
> capable of any love at all? It's your heart I'm trying to reach, not your
> mind! Love is not something to argue and reason and bargain about! It's
> something to give! To feel! Oh God, Henry, can't you feel without
> thinking!"
>
> "I never have."[39]

The freedom not to give a damn is a heady concept even in the 1980s;
but in the midst of the Eisenhower years Rearden's calm contempt
must have been a delightful shock for the millions of women (and men)
who read *Atlas Shrugged*. Conventional literary history of the 1950s
focuses on the explosions of the angry left (Norman Mailer being
perhaps its most enduring example); Rand's denunciation of compla-
cent liberal America is equally radical, equally a warning that the years
of seeming peace and plenty were a dangerous illusion.

That illusion, it appears, has been irreparably shattered. We
return to the problem with which I began this essay: the role of a work

of ideological science fiction in a dangerous world of narrowing opportunities. Can a romantic artifact like *Atlas Shrugged* ever be—or could it ever have been—the force for social change that the author intended?

Certainly the nay-saying Rand, with her fierce absolutes and sweeping contempt for the inferior, suits the temper of our time alarmingly well. Polls and elections show, if nothing else, that Americans are feeling fed up with cultural relativism, of being told that the ungrateful beneficiaries of our wealth and technology enjoy a "spiritual" dimension that makes them our superiors. As Rand, speaking through John Galt, asks, "*Which* is the monument to the triumph of the human spirit over matter: the germ-eaten hovels on the shorelines of the Ganges or the Atlantic skyline of New York?"[40]

Five years ago, perhaps, most educated Americans would have denounced such a challenge as "fascistic." Rand is no fascist, but passages such as that sometimes foreshadow the xenophobia of Jean Raspail's extraordinary neofascist science-fiction novel, *The Camp of the Saints*.[41] The cult of supermen and the "hero spirits" in their hidden valley also evoke queasy memories of the Nazi racial elite in their mountain eyries. Certainly a fascist could draw comfort from isolated passages of *Atlas Shrugged*. But Rand is ultimately closer to Doc Savage than to Doctor Goebbels; authentic fascism, mystical and collectivist, is alien both to American society and to the radical individualism she evokes so effectively.

Much more to the point, Rand is the acknowledged inspiration of Heinlein's *The Moon Is a Harsh Mistress* and other libertarian sf.[42] Her most lasting influence, however, may be in the works of the gold-brick-and-bomb-shelter survivalists and in the screw-everybody inspirational books of Robert J. Ringer, Howard Ruff, and a small army of similar writers.[43] From *Crisis Investing* to *Restoring the American Dream*, disconnected ideological fragments of *Atlas Shrugged* have dominated nonfiction best-seller lists since the late seventies. Rand has indirectly helped create a genre, and through that genre has shaped the thinking of middle-class America.

But if Rand's ideas give aid and comfort to many 1980s rightists, she withholds it from the majority of them. Her system, like her narrative universe, is radically atheistic, and Rand reserves her harshest attacks for the *National Review* and its high-church, old-money brand of ancien-régime conservatism.[44] Dozens of barely compatible conservatisms worked in temporary alliance to elect Ronald Reagan. That alliance is now breaking up, and none of its components seems in the least inclined to embrace the full implications of *Atlas Shrugged*. This is hardly surprising; the novel demands the fervent elitism of late adolescence in order to be read with conviction. A taste for Rand must be acquired early or not at all, and of her youthful converts only Alan Greenspan (economic advisor in the Ford administration) attained a position of real influence.[45]

To be sure, scenes from *Atlas Shrugged* are being acted out in public life as well as in the national consciousness. But is it really life imitating art? It is far more likely to be coincidence of means aiming at drastically different ends. Rand's attitude toward nature, for example (that is, factory smoke is better than clean air; billboards are more beautiful than trees) is now being put into execution by Interior Secretary James Watt. Watt's vandalistic instincts, however, seem conditioned more by millenarianism (if the Lord is going to purge the earth with fire anyway, why not get the shale oil out first?)[46] than by the all-consuming egoism that drives Rand's godless supermen. As I write this, Budget Director David Stockman, the youngest and ideologically purest of Reagan's appointees, is the most eager to promote Rand's ideal of laissez-faire capitalism; he is also the least likely to persuade bureaucrats, congressmen, or business leaders to join such a crusade. As I remarked at the beginning of this essay, Rand had to dismantle and reassemble the universe in order to make *Atlas Shrugged* work. Only in the realms of myth and science fiction can human beings exhibit the purity demanded by ideological fiction. To critics, that is its fatal flaw; to thousands of readers, it is an irresistible attraction.

Books that are very much of an age tend to die with that age. *Atlas Shrugged*, compounded of Greek myth and classical economics, of fairy tales and nineteenth-century finance, of silent films and Depression pulps, certainly belongs to no single era. It is easy to make fun of this novel—and I have done so frequently while discussing it. Its style is lurid, its pace glacial, its rhetoric shrill, its view of the world humorless, impractical, and grotesquely oversimplified. Yet even a scornful critic must concede that Rand has confronted the questions that American readers are really asking, and that most artists and intellectuals refuse to acknowledge. Somewhere within her leviathan of a novel, Rand provides at least one answer for every potential reader.

Until recently, the premises of *Atlas Shrugged* seemed too materialistic to be taken seriously; suddenly, they are part of the mainstream. If readers are willing to grant those premises, it is difficult to resist Rand's conclusions. As I have shown, the novel's imagery, its characterization, its confident projection of a "universal calculus"[47] to resolve human conflicts by quasi-scientific means are all rooted in the 1930s and 1940s. Yet the mood of those decades has been assimilated into the national style of the 1980s. Rand's first vogue may have faded, but I think that—in one incarnation or another—she will be with us for a long time.

### Afterword

This essay was begun during August 1980 in anticipation of a Republican triumph in the November elections. That predictable victory had one unpredictable consequence among many traditional liberals: a mood of embarrassed elation, as though the ascendancy of the right had fulfilled a long-standing but rather shameful desire. During the spring of 1981, Americans with hitherto incompatible political prejudices were seen responding enthusiastically to homilies, symbols, and gestures they would have disdained a few months earlier.

For me, this response to public political fictions cast new light on readers' response to ideological fiction in general; as a result, my reflections on *Atlas Shrugged* draw extensively on the historical dynamics of 1980–81, and can be most fully understood from that perspective. I later had the opportunity to revise the essay and could have purged it of topical references; after much thought, I chose not to. Like the other essays in this volume, it attempts to "place" works of science fiction in their cultural context, and its insights should be no more true or false because that context can be narrowly defined.

Ayn Rand's death in 1982 has also turned her work into history. Although far less in the public eye during her last years (except for an occasional fulminatory letter to the *New York Times*), she remained a vivid presence to a minority on the American right. Since her death, the fundamental anachronism of her novels seems much clearer. She was a writer of the 1930s and 1940s whose continued popularity owed more to narrative drive, skillful use of myth, and a deep understanding of readers' needs than to a pure ideology. Her long-promised magnum opus, the work that was to have reestablished all philosophy on the basis of Aristotle's three postulates, was never completed—nor could it ever have been. Like Coleridge's unwritten commentary on St. John, Rand's project was an unrealizable ideal: the rational foundation for an irrational system of belief.

Although near-future, politically oriented science fiction—often as conservative in its assumptions as Sir John Hackett's *Third World War* or Allen Drury's *Throne of Saturn*—remains conspicuous on

best-seller lists and paperback racks, it attracts no more critical attention today than it did two years ago. Clearly, our understanding of
modern culture becomes distorted when critics ignore the books people *want* to read in favor of those they *ought* to read. This study of *Atlas
Shrugged* points out some of the remarkable stuff we've been missing.

GEORGE R. GUFFEY

# *Fahrenheit 451* and the "Cubby-Hole Editors" of Ballantine Books

In April 1975 on the campus of the University of California at Santa Barbara, Ray Bradbury delighted an assembled audience with an uninhibited speech entitled "How Not to Burn a Book; or, 1984 Will Not Arrive." At one point in his wide-ranging presentation he reflected on the emotions which have typically impelled his fiction. "Sometimes I get angry and write a story about my anger. Sometimes I'm delighted and I write a story about that delight. Back in the Joseph McCarthy period a lot of things were going on in my country that I didn't like. I was angry. So I wrote a whole series of short stories" (*Soundings*, 7, no. 1 [1975], 18).

One of those short stories, "Usher II," was first published in 1950. The hero of "Usher II" is William Stendahl, a wealthy lover of fantastic literature and an embittered enemy of censorship and book burning. At one time on Earth, Stendahl had been the proud owner of fifty thousand books, but the Bureau of Moral Climates, in league with the Society for Prevention of Fantasy, had destroyed his beloved library. Amongst the works burned were those of Edgar Allan Poe. "All of his books," Stendahl tells the architect he has hired to re-create the House of Usher, "were burned in the Great Fire. That's thirty years ago— 1975. . . . They passed a law. Oh, it started very small. In 1950 and '60 it was a grain of sand. They began by controlling books of cartoons and then detective books . . . , one way or another, one group or another, political bias, religious prejudice, union pressures; there was always a minority afraid of something, and a great majority afraid of the dark. . . . Afraid of the word 'politics' (which eventually became a synonym for Communism among the more reactionary elements . . . and it was worth your life to use the word!), and . . . the print presses trickled down from a great Niagara of reading matter to a mere innocuous dripping of 'pure material'" (*The Martian Chronicles* [1950; rpt. New York: Bantam Books, 1975], p. 105).

To gain a measure of revenge against the psychologists, sociologists, politicians, and moralists responsible for the burning of his books, Stendahl has built on Mars a letter-perfect imitation of Poe's original House of Usher and has invited many of his own persecutors to a very special kind of housewarming. Over the course of the story, Stendahl lures his antagonists one by one into traps inspired by Poe's macabre stories. One miscreant is killed by a robot ape and stuffed up a chimney; one is beheaded by an enormous razor-sharp pendulum; one is prematurely buried; and, in the climactic scene, the worst of the lot is mortared-up forever in a cellar beneath that melancholy and dreary house. His revenge complete, a jubilant Stendahl helicopters away from Usher II, as the great house breaks apart and sinks slowly into the dark tarn surrounding it.

Approximately a year after the publication of "Usher II," Bradbury broadened his attack on censorship. In a novella entitled "The Fireman" (*Galaxy*, 1 [1951], 4–61), he depicted a future society in which most kinds of books had been banned. The hero of this story is Guy Montag, a fireman. Ironically, in this heavily regimented world of the future, firemen no longer extinguish fires. Their primary duty is to start them. More specifically, their main occupation is the burning of books. At one point in the story, Leahy, a fire chief, delivers a short lecture on the recent history of expurgation and censorship.

> Picture it. The 19th Century man with his horses, dogs, and slow living. You might call him a slow motion man. Then in the 20th Century you speed up the camera. . . . Books get shorter. Condensations appear. Digests. Tabloids. Radio programs simplify. . . . Great classics are cut to fit fifteen minute shows, then two minute book columns, then two line digest resumes. Magazines become picture books. . . . Technology, mass exploitation, and censorship from frightened officials did the trick. Today, thanks to them, you can read comics, confessions, or trade journals, nothing else. All the rest is dangerous. . . . Colored people don't like *Little Black Sambo*. We burn it. White people don't like *Uncle Tom's Cabin*. Burn it, too. Anything for serenity. (Pp. 18, 19, 20, 21)

In spite of repeated warnings from Leahy, Montag becomes more and more fascinated by books and by reading. Eventually he is found out, and his small collection of books is burned. Angry and frustrated, he kills Leahy and flees to the open countryside. There, in a hobo camp, he meets a band of fugitives who have devoted their lives to the judicious memorization and communication of uncensored versions of the great classics. For years these "living books" have patiently awaited an inevitable, cataclysmic world war which will destroy all the oppressive bureaucracies inhibiting the free flow of ideas. At the end of the story, this long-awaited war comes, leveling the seats of government and, presumably, thereby making the world again safe for the dissemination of uncensored books.

Bradbury's rage against censorship and book burning reached its fullest and most eloquent expression in 1953 when he expanded "The Fireman" to novel length and published it under the new title *Fahrenheit 451*. During the following quarter of a century, *Fahrenheit 451* was reprinted at least forty-eight times by Ballantine. In 1979 Bradbury discovered for the first time that, ironically, *Fahrenheit 451* had in the past itself been systematically censored by its publisher.

At his insistence, the novel has recently been reset and republished, with a spirited Author's Afterword. In that afterword Bradbury emphasizes his continuing problems with publishers wishing both to reprint his popular stories and at the same time edit them for young readers. For example, his frequently anthologized story "The Fog Horn" was, he says, recently the proposed object of such treatment: "Two weeks ago my mountain of mail delivered forth a pipsqueak mouse of a letter from a well-known publishing house that wanted to reprint my story 'The Fog Horn' in a high school reader. In my story, I had described a lighthouse as having, late at night, an illumination coming from it that was a 'God-Light.' Looking up at it from the view-point of any sea-creature one would have felt that one was in 'the Presence.' The editors had deleted 'God-Light' and 'in the Presence'" (Author's Afterword, *Fahrenheit 451* [New York: Ballantine Books, 1979], p. 181). But worst of all was what Ballantine had in the past, without permission, actually done to *Fahrenheit 451*: "Over the years, some cubby-hole editors at Ballantine Books, fearful of contaminating the young, had, bit by bit, censored some 75 separate sections from the novel. Students, reading the novel which, after all, deals with censorship and book-burning in the future, wrote to tell me of this exquisite irony. Judy-Lynn Del Rey, one of the new Ballantine editors, is having the entire book reset and republished . . . with all the damns and hells back in place" (pp. 182–83).

Collation of a copy from the first printing of the novel in October 1953 with a copy from the forty-fourth printing in August 1977 reveals that by that date fifty-two pages of *Fahrenheit 451* had been completely reset and that, in the process, ninety-eight nonauthoritative, substantive changes had been made in the text. Most of those changes, as Bradbury in his afterword suggests, simply involved the deletion of expletives or oaths. For example, the Ballantine editors at one place in the book altered "'Jesus God,' said Montag. 'Every hour so many damn things in the sky! How in hell did those bombers get up there!'" to "'Every hour so many things in the sky!' said Montag. 'How did those bombers get up there!'" (p. 65).

But many of the changes made by the Ballantine editors fall into other categories. Nudity in the boudoir, no matter how abstractly described, troubled them. "His wife stretched on the bed, uncovered and cold" became merely "His wife stretched on the bed" (p. 11). And parts of the body, particularly that innocuous depression we call "the navel," seem also to have offended them. They altered "All the minor minor minorities with their navels to be kept clean" to "All the minor minor minorities with their ears to be kept clean" (p. 52). Wherever possible, references to the consumption of alcohol were muted. For example, the passage "Did we have a wild party or something? Feel like I've a hangover. God, I'm hungry" was altered to read: "Did we have a party or something? Feel like I've a headache. I'm hungry" (p. 17). In another instance, "Are you drunk?" became "Are you ill?" (p. 37).

Space will not permit an exhaustive account of the kinds of changes *Fahrenheit 451* suffered at the hands of the Ballantine editors, but I must, before moving on, call attention to at least two other examples. At one point in the book, Montag angrily says to his wife's superficial, narcissistic friend: "Go home and . . . think of the dozen abortions you've had, go home and think of that and your damn Caesarian sections, too." The Ballantine editors removed from the passage both the word "damn" and the reference to abortion, leaving only "Go home and . . . think of that and your Caesarian sections, too" (p. 91). Finally, at another point in the action, a vigorously delivered speech culminates in an emphatic, effective vulgarism. "'To hell with that,' he said, 'shake the tree and knock the great sloth down on his ass.'" Under the scalpel of the Ballantine editors, the passage died, leaving behind this poor, shriveled carcass. "He said, 'shake the tree and knock the great sloth down'" (p. 141).

Although in the afterword to the 1979 corrected edition of *Fahrenheit 451* Bradbury indicated that his novel had, "over the years," been censored "bit by bit," my own research suggests that the excisions and revisions we have been examining were the result of more concentrated efforts. Evidently, Bradbury is unaware (or has forgotten) that, in January 1967, *Fahrenheit 451* was for the first time published in the Ballantine Bal-Hi series. Comparison of my copy from the fifth Bal-hi printing of October 1968 with my copy of the first Ballantine printing of October 1953 demonstrates that all the variants we have been considering were in actuality the result of revisions made for this special high school paperback series. In addition, comparison of the texts of the fourth printing of October 1963, the seventh printing of September 1966, and the thirtieth printing of July 1972 with the first printing of October 1953 indicates that, although Ballantine was publishing a revised version of the book in its Bal-Hi series, from 1967 to 1973 an uncensored version of the novel was simultaneously being sold to the general public.

According to the copyright page of the corrected 1979 edition, the tenth and last printing of the Bal-Hi version of the novel occurred in October 1973. After 1973, instead of continuing to publish the unexpurgated and unrevised text of the first printing of October 1953, Ballantine, with no warning whatever to potential readers, published, until taken to task by Bradbury himself in 1979, only the revised text prepared for the Bal-Hi series. The text of my own copy from the fortieth printing of December 1975, although in no way labeled so, is identical to the bowdlerized text of my copy from the fifth Bal-Hi printing (as is the text of my copy from the forty-fourth printing of August 1977).

To understand Ballantine's treatment of *Fahrenheit 451* during the latter half of the 1960s, we must be conscious of the intense social and political pressures brought to bear on publishers of textbooks during the late 1950s and the early 1960s. In 1958, for example, E. Merrill Root published his *Brainwashing in the High Schools*, an assault on eleven textbooks, which, in his view "parallel[ed] the Communist line." Inspired by Root's opening thrust, the Daughters of the American Revolution in 1958 began to compile a list of "unsatisfactory" texts, and a year later, in 1959, began to distribute it. By 1963, the advocates of censorship had widened their offensive. In that year in their influential book, *The Censors and the Schools*, Jack Nelson and Gene Roberts, Jr., wrote: "A vice-president of McGraw-Hill says all publishers must be wary in their treatment of birth control, evolution . . . , sex education, and minority groups." "In some parts of the United States," Nelson and Roberts added, "it is worth a teacher's job to put modern novels such as J. D. Salinger's *The Catcher in the Rye* or George Orwell's *1984* on a classroom reading list" (Boston: Little, Brown, pp. 181, 182).

Although librarians and teachers fought back, the pressure for censorship increased. "The pressure of censorship is a growing part of school life today," wrote Professor Lee A. Burress, Jr., in 1965, the year the first book in the Ballantine Bal-Hi series was evidently published. "If articles on censorship in education journals," he continued, "constitute a reliable index, teachers are much more concerned today than thirty years ago. When *Education Index* commenced publication in 1929, one article a year on censorship was published. In the most recent issues of *Education Index*, there are lengthy bibliographies on censorship" ("Censorship and the Public Schools," *American Library Association Bulletin*, 59 [1965], 491). Burress cites numerous recent examples of capricious and ridiculous censorship in his own state of Wisconsin, including actions against Dostoevski's *Crime and Punishment*, for allegedly containing "too much profanity," and the magazine *Today's Health*, for dealing with "the birth of a baby" (p. 494).

Although self-appointed censors presented real problems for publishers of school texts during the 1960s, the rewards were great for those who managed to produce "acceptable" books. Especially lucrative, according to article after article in *Senior Scholastic* and *The Library Journal* during that period, was the growing market for paperbacks (See, for example, Hillel Schiller, "Panel Urges Schools to Incorporate Paperbacks: Striking Cases Cited," *Library Journal*, 88 [1963], 844–45). It was for this increasingly lucrative market that the Bal-Hi series was apparently designed.

A number of important questions now naturally come to mind: What were the titles of the other books published in the Bal-Hi series? (The following Appendix lists, along with their Ballantine numbers, those I have thus far been able to identify.) Were the other books in the Bal-Hi series, like Bradbury's *Fahrenheit 451*, bowdlerized in order to assure their marketability? And, if bowdlerized, did they, as in the case of *Fahrenheit 451*, eventually replace uncensored versions of the same titles in the regular Ballantine line? All these questions are, I think, well worth answering.

### Appendix:  Books Published in the Ballantine Bal-Hi Series

U2801    General Robert L. Scott, *God Is My Co-pilot*

U2802    Science Services, *Science Projects Handbook*

U2803    Robert C. Merriam, *The Battle of the Bulge*

U2804    Gore Vidal, ed., *Best TV Plays*

U2849   Sarban, *The Doll Maker*

U2852   Michael & Don Congdon, ed., *Alone by Night*

U2853   William Golding, John Wyndham, & Mervyn Peake, *Sometime, Never*

U2855   Robert Sheckley, *Untouched by Human Hands*

U2857   Chad Oliver, *Shadows in the Sun*

U2859   Henry Kuttner, *Mutant*

U2862   Robert Sheckley, *Citizen in Space*

U2866   James White, *Star Surgeon*

U5800   Edward H. Sims, *Greatest Fighter Missions*

## H. BRUCE FRANKLIN

# America as Science Fiction: 1939

It was the spring of 1939, and the World of Tomorrow was about to go on exhibit. The conflagration later to be known as World War II had in fact already ignited in parts of Asia, Africa, and Europe. Japan had occupied Manchuria, had overrun much of coastal China, had been repulsed in its 1938 invasion of the U.S.S.R., and was about to suffer a massive defeat in its new war on Mongolia and the Soviet Union. Fascist Italy had invaded Ethiopia and just occupied Albania in early April. Nazi Germany had seized Austria, and was in the process of dismembering Czechoslovakia, with the agreement of Britain and France. The government of Spain was on the verge of defeat by the united forces of European fascism. And back in 1936, in Berlin, the atom had been split.

America itself was still wallowing in the depths of the international Depression, with over nine and a half million people unemployed. But it was also bounding ahead technologically. Radio broadcasting had now been around for almost two decades. One could fly coast-to-coast on a commercial DC-3 in just twenty-four hours. The future seemed both thrilling and chilling. Amidst this interplay of economic crisis and technological progress, a crucial role was being played by science fiction.

We usually think of pre–World War II American science fiction as primarily a ghetto inhabited by *Astounding*, a few other science fiction magazines, and the fanzines. But actually science fiction had already moved close to the center of American culture. We might note in passing that in 1938 two radically diverse forms of alien beings from other planets had intruded into American mass culture. While the Axis armies were carrying out invasions on three continents, the United States was being invaded by technologically advanced beings from Mars, landing in New Jersey, courtesy of H. G. Wells, Orson

Welles, and that latest mode of communication, the national radio broadcast network. The very same year, Superman, a beneficient alien, had appeared from a far distant planet, and in 1939 Superman, the all-American analog of the Nazi *Übermensch*, was to have his very own comic book, in which he could fight "for truth, justice, and the American way."

But these popular cultural phenomena were relatively peripheral to what I regard as the principal form of science fiction in 1939—the New York World's Fair, boldly named the World of Tomorrow. Looking backward from the early 1980s, we can see that the 1939 New York World's Fair was a cultural projection that would indeed have a shaping effect on the future.

Alongside the World of Tomorrow projected by the World's Fair I should like to place the images of the near future projected in a classic repository of American science fiction, the 1939 volume of *Astounding Science Fiction*. Containing the first science fiction story by Theodore Sturgeon, Isaac Asimov's second, and the very first published works by A. E. Van Vogt and Robert Heinlein, this 1939 volume is now generally regarded as the first of the so-called Golden Age. Let us look briefly at each image of the near future to be found in the 1939 *Astounding* before we shift our view to the World of Tomorrow built on a garbage dump in Queens.

The 1939 *Astounding* actually offers very few detailed visions of the near future on Earth, and most of these are rather bleak. Technology does not bring any greater happiness to the masses of humanity, and often produces the opposite. What technology does bring is the opportunity for some people—mostly male scientists, engineers, businessmen, and adventurers—to escape from Earth's society altogether, to find high adventures in the aptly named *space*, that is, anywhere *but* on Earth.

The imagined worlds of space are of course a varied lot. But it is safe to say that the dominating vision projects far into time and space standard American male character types of the 1930s, cruising around in an environment shaped by corporate capitalism, and confronting aliens who, no matter what their physical form, psychologically resemble types commonplace in American culture in the 1930s. The space stories containing views of the near future are of course those describing the early stages, that is the colonization and exploitation of the solar system.

In John Berryman's "Special Flight" (May), space shuttles routinely ferry precious ores from mines on the Moon; the action consists of a crew of one ship heroically flying through the Perseid meteor shower to help rescue men trapped in a lunar mine accident.

"Nothing Ever Happens on the Moon" (February) by Paul Ernst describes a bizarre adventure that interrupts the lonely life of a man stationed on a lunar relay station. "Interplanetary travel was less than seventy years old," and our hero's station is an outpost of United Spaceways, "an efficient corporation."

"Mill of the Gods" (January) by Malcolm Jameson (like Heinlein a career naval officer disabled by health) is especially revealing in its enthusiasm for unbridled free-enterprise capitalism and exploitation of the mineral resources of the solar system. On Titan, a grizzled old heroic rugged individualist, a "mining trillionaire," runs his Saturnine Metals Corporation with tight fists and a hard head. This "hard-boiled, self-made" old capitalist, whose bark is of course worse than his bite, is stumped by how to extract the core of Saturn's moon Phoebe, which consists of a single gigantic diamond, before his rights run out. His would-be son-in-law, an up-and-coming young man on the make who has built up his own fleet of space tugs, ingeniously captures the moon, strips away its iron crust, and delivers the giant diamond core to the old man, thus winning his daughter.

Kent Casey's "Melody and Moons" (May) starts off near "the mine fields and ore-reduction plants of the Interplanetary Co. of Terra on Mars" which had been one of "the first points of attack by the Uranian raiders," who turn out to be just another bunch of alien guys with their own commercial and military interests.

Perhaps the least capitalistic near future in these tales of solar-system exploration is the one glimpsed in Robert Heinlein's second published story, "Misfit" (November), in which twenty-second-century boys are recruited into a Cosmic Construction Corps, obviously extrapolated from the New Deal's Civilian Conservation Corps. Set up "for the purpose of conserving and improving our interplanetary resources," the corps sends the boys out "as pioneers to fix up the solar system so that human beings can make better use of it," and "equally important" it offers these boys "a chance to build yourselves into useful and happy citizens of the Federation." These boys previously had been misfits who had either lost their jobs to "new inventions" or who simply didn't know what to do with "modern leisure."

Relatively few of the stories in the 1939 *Astounding* are set on Earth in the near future. I count fewer than a dozen terrestrial tales taking place any time in the next several centuries.

Conspicuously absent from any of these tales is the Wow! Gosh!

attitude of the science fiction dime novel and some of the earlier pulps. In fact, as we shall see, this attitude, with its uncritical enthusiasm for technological progress is far more integral to the futuristic visions found in something not usually considered to be science fiction, the verbal and model worlds projected by the large corporations. If anything, the stories about Earth's future found in the 1939 *Astounding* challenged this uncritical enthusiasm.

We obtain an especially revealing insight into the context of these extrapolations as we turn to the very first page of the January 1939 issue, a full-page ad for International Correspondence Schools featuring a news story about three thousand applicants turning up for six advertised jobs.

Some of the stories see little or no large significant changes in the near future. The one set in the closest future is "Employment" (May) by "Lyman R. Lyon" (L. Sprague de Camp), which takes place in 1960, three years into a new Depression; it merely describes the revivification of prehistoric animals and their bizarre adventures. Other than this amazing discovery, there is no hint of any technological, economic, political, or social change from the world of 1939. The characters, like the prehistoric critters they bring back to life, might just as well be living any old time.

Harl Vincent's "Power Plant" (November) describes a technological breakthrough but this also occurs in a society apparently unchanged from 1939. Vincent has a melodrama set in the first commercial atomic power plant, date unspecified. Though International Electric is fiercely competing with the Atlas Corporation for contracts, the presidents of the two big companies join to back up our hero as he thwarts the sabotage of a demented genius.

Theodore Sturgeon's first science fiction story, "Ether Breather" (September), presents another technological breakthrough, the advent of color television in the twenty-second century (!), when giant corporations control broadcasting as well as atomic power and antigravity. Other than the technological changes, and the amusing ethereal creatures who disrupt the first shows, life seems much like that in 1939.

Nat Schachner's "When the Future Dies" (June) is set in 1982, after World War III. We see practically nothing of this society, which is wiped out by alien invaders. Its last hope is a lone genius who builds a time machine in order to obtain a superweapon from the presumably advanced technological future, only to discover that there is no future at all for human beings.

Despite the fact, which should have been obvious by 1939, that scientific and technological advances are large collective efforts, many of these stories show the big breakthroughs as isolated acts carried out by lone geniuses right out of the pages of nineteenth-century science fiction.

Isaac Asimov's "Trends," his second published story and the first to appear in *Astounding*, exalts the individual genius above all else in modern society. Asimov's genius is also a conventional figure in later science fiction, the audacious capitalist who single-handedly brings about the Space Age, a type to be developed most memorably by Heinlein in "Requiem" (1940) and "The Man Who Sold the Moon" (1950). Asimov's tale is set in 1973, when antiscientific religious conformism is in total control of American society. The leading revivalist has convinced "the masses" that "it was science that brought about the horrors of the Second World War." So here is the forecast of the 1970s: Everybody goes to church on Sunday; "we have prohibition; smoking for women is outlawed; cosmetics are forbidden; low dresses and short skirts are unheard of; divorce is frowned upon." The story seriously suggests that religious revivalism could actually control the political and economic structure. Space travel is denounced by the churches, the press, and "the masses" as "defiance of God." Our lone hero has personally "spent a fortune" building the rocketship *Prometheus*, which is sabotaged by a religious zealot as it is about to launch for the Moon. Immediately an antirocketry bill passes both houses of Congress by unanimous vote, making any experiments in rocketry crimes punishable by death. (In this Congress, apparently no influence is wielded by the aerospace industry.) By 1974, Congress establishes the Federal Scientific Research Investigatory Bureau, which is so successful in strangling science that "once more colleges found themselves forced to reinstate philosophy and the classics as the chief studies." When reminded that "The '20s and '30s were years of anarchy, decadence, and misrule," as well as world wars, our heroic capitalist replies that "Men were not afraid then; somehow they dreamed and dared" and "science *flourished*." Finally a new group of entrepreneurs secretly finances the building of the *New Prometheus*, in which the lone genius streaks around the Moon, returning to launch the age of space travel, forcing the reversal of all the dominant trends in his society.

Jack Williamson's "Crucible of Power" (February) has "the brilliant scientific advance of the twentieth century" stopped dead by a viral plague that breaks out in 1998, inaugurating "a hundred years of stagnation, dread, and decay" as well as "endless wars." This not uncommon science fiction maneuver allows Williamson to detach his fantasied future from the processes and forces of actual human history. That is, an arbitrary event such as a plague, a natural cataclysm, or an alien invasion puts an end to *our* history, and the author is able to construct a new history out of his own fantasy. This might even be considered a reversion from the uniformitarianism dominant in scientific thought throughout the nineteenth and twentieth centuries to the catastrophic theories holding sway prior to Lyell, Darwin, and Marx. In this story, it permits the construction of world history revolving around the exploits of a single capitalist; like the entrepreneur in Asimov's "Trends," he is also a scientific genius who eventually singlehandedly discovers a cure for the plague and thus saves all intelligent life in the entire solar system. This superhuman figure is known as "the daring explorer of space, the stalwart captain of industry, the dashing Don Juan, the heartless capitalist, the greatest philanthropist, the dictator of the solar system and the conqueror of the Sun." Motivated by "ruthless ambition," he is actually a figure not out of the twenty-second-century future but out of the dime novels of the nineteenth-century past. "The penniless boot-boy, who rose to be financial dictator of nine worlds," literally becomes "the demigod of the whole creed of Success." This godlike figure builds and flies a spaceship to Mars, conquers the arthropodlike inhabitants, extorts from them the secret of unlimited power to be obtained from "sundust" and "sunstones," builds a sun station to bring this power to Earth, becomes head of the solar-system-wide monopoly he names the Sun Power Corporation, brings the solar system to the brink of destruction, and then saves it. Clearly we are here dealing not with the extrapolation of history but a mythic escape from it.

In contrast, Ray Cummings's "An Ultimatum from Mars" (August), set in the twenty-first or twenty-second century, makes an effort to show the future as a sequel to the present. New York has become a vast metropolitan region known as Great New York, the world's economy seems to be dominated by giant multinational corporations, and the political structure is formed under the World Federation of Earth. When Earth is threatened by a Martian invasion and colonization, it is one of the multinationals that saves the day: the Anglo-American Co. manages to get the needed strategic metal by a new process directly from the fourth dimension.

C. L. Moore's "Greater Than Gods" (July), set in the twenty-third century, presents an historical crux leading to alternative futures. The hero is a scientist working on a process to control the sex of human offspring. He is trying to make a choice between the two women he loves, and through a desk-top device is miraculously able to establish direct contact with the two alternate futures that would develop from his choice. If he marries pretty little Sallie, she will discourage his scientific work and the future will be dominated by women, ending in an indolent and decadent Eden. If he marries the scientist Marta, she will push him into premature application of his process, and the future will be dominated by men, ending in a universal fascism, complete with Nazi-like helmets and superweapons. Clearly we have here a parable about the relations between science and society, represented by the incarnate principles of feminity and masculinity. (By the way, the scientist escapes from his quandary by marrying Miss Brown, his secretary whose pulchritude is of course concealed by her eyeglasses.)

"Sculptors of Life" (December) by Wallace West shows a more serious commitment to extrapolating a social, economic, and technological context than most of the stories we have examined. The main characters are Marion Onethreenine and Frank Sixtwofour, a couple of unionized workers who clone replacement bodies for capitalists and aristocrats. In this story, unlike most, technological advances have integral relationships with both the details of everyday life and the larger social structure. Frank and Marion, whose last names suggest a technological dystopia, commute from their jobs via a superspeed overhead train which takes them to their auto in which they drive to their little cabin in a canyon deep in the Adirondacks. "Carefully censored news" is beamed out at the population on television, "strikes have been forbidden," and Britain is ruled by a dictator controlled by Henry Wharton,the richest man in the world, an ex-Yale football star of 1940 who gets his new body every seventy years. Wharton is not the beneficent genius or Promethean creator embodied by the capitalist in "The Crucible of Power," "Trends," and "Mill of the Gods." In fact, his history suggests the fallacy in the notion that a man of colossal wealth could represent a beneficent force in the actual world of the twentieth-century or later industrial society. Although originally he had believed "that his father's fortune, if rightly used," could "bring order out of the chaos which resulted from the second world war," he soon becomes "fascinated by the complexities of international finance" and is seduced by the power of his own money. By the time we see him, he is surrounded by bodyguards, steeped in corruption, and totally committed to preserving and extending his wealth and power, at the expense of the freedom of the common people. Somewhat taken in by Wharton, Frank expresses the view of the big capitalist we have found in other tales in the 1939 *Astounding*: although admitting that "half the productive capacity of America pays tribute" to this "hard-fisted slave-driver," Frank also calls him "an economic genius who has at last discovered how to eliminate recessions." But Marion, in strikingly prophetic words, quickly sets him straight. "Yeah, Frank. He spreads recessions and recoveries out thin, like butter on bread, and expects us to worship him because we can no longer tell the difference between them. You talk like a twentieth-century liberal."

Although the World of Tomorrow projected by the New York World's Fair may have been in the minds of many of *Astounding*'s authors, only one story focuses directly on that vision, "Rope Trick" (April) by "Eando Binder" (pseudonym for the Binder Brothers). On his way to visit the World's Fair, Breckenridge Wacker, a Texas cowboy, is bamboozled by a lone genius, Doctor Amos Meade, into undergoing suspended animation with him for a hundred years. Doctor Meade has been captivated by that vision of the World of Tomorrow: "think of the thrill, Breck, of being in the world of the future"; "just think, Breck, what a century of advancement over our times means. This will be a wonder-age!" So here we have the undiluted Wow! Gosh! attitude attributed to science fiction, but actually found in the World's Fair.

When they wake up in 2039, the first sign of progress they find is a ten-lane highway: "'Look at that!' cries Doc Meade. 'A hundred years of advancement in highway travel right before our eyes. These are the superhighways they vaguely planned in 1939.'" We shall return to this vision when we visit the General Motor Futurama at the World's Fair. Next they encounter the all-electric farm, as it appears in the Electrified Farm exhibit put on by the Electric Utilities Exhibit Corporation at the fair, to which we shall also return. As in the electrified Farm exhibit, the farm of the future is not part of a giant agribusiness, but an automated family farm, complete with farmer, farmer's wife, and eight kids. Life is not quite as idyllic as it might appear in the 1939 model farm from the World of Tomorrow, however. As Doc Meade oohs and aahs about the farmer's electric robot, air conditioning, and television, the farmer moans and groans about the payments he owes on these to the finance company.

The cowboy and the scientist hitchhike their way to New York, with their driver having to pay the huge toll of a dollar on the way. There they find the city of the future, just as they would have glimpsed it in 1939 at the fair. "'Elevated traffic spans!' says Doc, ecstatic like. 'And pedestrian-walks in the air. And look there, Breck, a regular sky-harbor for aircraft.'" Here there are atomic power generators, medicine that has wiped out most diseases, banks filled with fountains, shrubs, pretty pictures, and soft music, police armed with stun guns, women with short skirts, and continued threats of a war in Europe, far away from peaceful America. "'The wonder-city of the future—our future,' exclaims Doc. 'It's magnificent, glorious, breath-taking—'" The ultimate tribute Doc can articulate is his rapturous cry, "All the things we dreamed of in 1939 have come true!" But Breck, that man from America's mythic frontier past, remains unimpressed, and at the end even Doc is bored, apparently ready to move on further into the future.

Doc's enthusiasm is only a slight exaggeration of the official rhetoric of the New York World's Fair, the World of Tomorrow. Perhaps the slogan that best captures the spirit of the fair, and some of its ironies, is that of the Long Island Railroad, which promised to take you swiftly into the future from midtown Manhattan: "From the World of Today to the World of Tomorrow in ten minutes for ten cents."

Industrial capitalism had long since transformed the old trade fairs of medieval Europe into exhibitions emphasizing technological progress. Beginning with the London Crystal Palace Exhibition of 1851 and the 1853 Palace of Crystal in New York, there was a growing tendency to display the marvels of science and technology as harbingers of even greater wonders to come. But the 1939 New York World of Tomorrow was "The first fair in history ever to focus entirely on the future": "For months before the opening, the slogan 'Dawn of a New Day' had been the theme of parties and money-raising celebrations. Electric signs flashed Dawn of a New Day messages while bands played Gershwin's song of the same name."[1]

On March fifth, almost two months before the fair was to open, the *New York Times* published a special section celebrating and defining the event. The lead article, entitled "World of Tomorrow," written by H. G. Wells, "Historian and Novelist," maintained that "we are in the darkness before the dawn of a vast educational thrust. Steadily in the near Tomorrow a collective human intelligence will be appearing and organizing itself in a collective human will." Wells's extrapolations about material change contrast with those dominating the 1939 *Astounding*. For example he predicts that new modes of transportation will obviate the necessity of the concentration of people in cities, leading to a dispersal so rapid that the "difference of town and country will vanish altogether." Unlike Eando Binder's vision of the gigantic wonder city of New York in 2039, Wells declares that New York City "already has nearly outlived the forces that gathered it together."

Wells's emphasis on growing collectivism is echoed by Nobel-prize-winning physicist Arthur H. Compton, who identifies the present "machine age" as an epoch of growing mutual interdependence: "man is undergoing a remarkably rapid evolution from an individualistic to a social organism."

Two members of the New Deal cabinet call for immediate application of cooperation to America's economic problems. Henry Wallace, secretary of agriculture, in an article somewhat misleadingly entitled "A New Day for the Farm," argues that "we need to discover the social machinery" that will make the vast agricultural production a blessing rather than a curse. And Frances Perkins, secretary of labor, insists that workers and employers must together work out labor policy.

The representatives of industry writing in this *New York Times* World of Tomorrow section share all the optimism and none of the worries of Wells and Compton, Wallace and Perkins. "Might of the Spreading Word," by David Sarnoff, president of RCA, "Wheels, Keels and Wings" by Charles F. Kettering, vice president in charge of research of General Motors, and "Machines as Ministers to Man" by Henry Ford all wax eloquent and enthusiastic about the unmixed blessings to be brought by technology in the near future. Henry Ford not only maintains that machines invariably make life "easier, simpler and richer." He tells the readers they "should visit the World Fair to learn at first hand how every scientific advance in the production of goods and services contributes something to the general good and adds to their own personal well-being." Seemingly unaware of the nine-and-a-half million unemployed Americans, and of the millions more being driven off the land and into the city by new farming machinery, Ford actually declares that machines always reduce unemployment: "in the not-distant future . . . there will be more jobs in industry than there will be men to do them." "Technological unemployment," he blandly proclaims, "is now a disappearing term." This is just two months after the first page of the 1939 *Astounding* featured that clipping about three thousand people answering an ad for six jobs.

The most thoughtful vision of the near future to be found in this special section is an article by William Ogburn, the sociologist from the University of Chicago. In fact, Ogburn's extrapolation is arguably better science fiction than most of what we found in the 1939 *Astound-*

*ing*. He sees the city changing into a vast "metropolitan community," while subsistence farming gives way to commercial agriculture, creating a large "rural proletariat." He labels steam as the enemy of the home, electricity as the friend. The steam boiler created the factory, "to which the household occupations migrated, taking men, women, and children with them. The home became the parking place for people who spent much of their time in factories, schools," and other activities. "Electricity, with hundreds of new gadgets trailing in its wake, makes the home much more attractive and comfortable." But this is not an unalloyed blessing. "The new media of communication will increase our knowledge, but there will be special-interest groups, advertisers, and followers of creeds and cults who will try to control our thoughts with them." "The consumer," he declares prophetically, "will need protection." He sees new methods of birth control limiting the size of families. "In the future there will be more childless marriages. This means more marital instability, and further search for happiness." Women will tend to seek employment outside the home. Casting a different light for us on the question of bussing children to school, he reminds us that it was the "auto-bus" that by 1939 was allowing two out of three children to go to high school and predicts that in thirty-five years nine out of ten or more will be going.

Unlike Wells and Compton, Ogburn sees a more ambiguous stage coming between the people of 1939 and a collective consciousness. With the new modes of communication and transportation, and "the weakening of the family, church and local community," he predicts that inevitably "Government will surely become a bigger force in our lives." "The central government in Washington will expand greatly, whether we like it or not." And the growth of the central government, together with the expansion of corporations, leads to an ominous threat. "Some kind of closer union between government and business is certain. If war comes, or if the preparations for war are prolonged and thorough, we shall have the totalitarian state, for a time, at least, in effect if not in form. Modern war is the best device known for increasing the control of the State over industry."

The fair was a monumental display of all the contradictions we have seen so far. And to our eyes the fair reveals much more, for we have also seen the actual world of tomorrow that was being shaped by the same forces that created both the New York World's Fair and *Astounding Science Fiction* in 1939.

The two main themes of the World of Tomorrow were blazoned forth as peace and democracy, created through modern technology.

Not least in celebrating these themes was the pavilion of Fascist Italy, a nation that was now occupying Ethiopia and Albania. Italy announced that "it builds for the future," showed the wonder of its "mechanical and textile industries besides the naval, aeronautical and electro-technical exhibits," and capped it all with a towering statue. "Outside the Pavilion, in the Hall of Nations, is the 'Salone d'Onore,' dedicated to Benito Mussolini and containing an imposing statute of the Italian leader. Huge maps of gilded copper on black and green marble outline the Italian Empire, while beautiful frescoes depicting the social accomplishments of the Regime complete the decorative and informative series of exhibits."[2] Portugal bragged that it now "ranks very high among the great colonial powers of the world," and displayed how it was "about to accomplish in Africa one of the most ambitious colonial undertakings ever attempted" while building a modern future at home "under the brilliant leadership of Dr. Oliveira Salazar, youthful prime minister and one-man 'brain trust.'"[3] So Italy and Portugal actually had examples of those great geniuses celebrated in some 1939 science fiction. On the other hand, the most prominent exhibit in the pavilion of Japan was an ornate replica of the Liberty Bell of the United States, fashioned out of silver and cultured pearls.

Even on the most mundane level, there were deep historical ironies. Take, for example, that exhibit of the Electrified Farm. At this very moment modern technology and galloping agribusiness were tossing the family farm into the trashbin of history, with millions of small landowners and tenant farmers driven from the land to be turned into a rural proletariat in California, a marginally employed industrial proletariat in Detroit and Chicago, and creators of a new urban culture based on a subproletarian existence in Harlem, just a few miles from the fair. Yet here we get this idyllic fantasy of the Electrified Farm, showing how "the private electric utilities 'have brought the city to the farmer,'" providing him "increased revenue, less drudgery, more leisure and generally better living."[4]

### Electrified Farm

... a practical working farm, with a completely equipped farm house and buildings, cattle, horses, chickens—everything you normally expect to find on a farm, even the flower and vegetable garden. Here electricity does all the work efficiently and economically, and more than a hundred of its practical applications are demonstrated. The farm house—an attractive two-story frame structure, with a tile terrace—is set amid apple trees and elms; in the pasture nearby, maples furnish adequate shade for cattle. Grouped for convenience and efficiency are the silo and barn, with a bull exerciser, the milking parlor, dairy room, workshop and horseshed; at the other end of the plot you will find the poultry house, brooder house, greenhouse, hotbeds, community packing house, and the orchard.[5]

A fair billing itself as the World of Tomorrow may be considered just as much a work of science fiction as a short story or a novel, a comic book or a movie. The exhibits of working television, and the forecasts of broadcast television networks in the near future, were as popular at the fair as the predictions about television were in the 1939 *Astounding*. In the Transportation Zone, the "Focal Exhibit" in the Chrysler Motors Building featured the "Rocketport," described in the official *Guidebook* as "a display that seizes upon your imagination and projects it into the future."

> What of transportation in the "World of Tomorrow?" As the airplane finishes its flight across the screen, lines shoot out and harness the earth with other planets. Twinkling signal lights, the hum of gigantic motors and the warning sound of sirens indicate that the Rocketship is loading passengers for London. You see futuristic liners unloading at nearby docks; sleek trains glide to a stop, automobiles whisk voyagers to the spot, high-speed elevators rise and descend as the Rocketship is serviced for the coming journey. The moment for departure arrives. A great steel crane moves, a magnet picks up the Rocketship and deposits it into the breach of the rocketgun. A moment of awesome silence. A flash, a muffled explosion, and the ship vanishes into the night.[6]

This science fiction created by Chrysler is timid compared to the space fiction presented in the Theatre of Time and Space by the Longines-Wittnauer Watch Company and Hayden Planetarium, where "a make-believe rocket ship . . . annihilates distance at the fantastic speed of 480,000,000,000,000,000,000,000 miles per hour.[7]

There were two complete models of what a typical segment of America would look like in the near future. One was Democracity, built inside the gigantic Perisphere, beneath the towering Trylon. The other was the General Motors Futurama.

Democracity was conceived in the ideal of interdependence articulated in the articles of H. G. Wells and Arthur Compton. Here in the interior of the perisphere people mounted "the longest moving electric stairway in the world" which "swept upward, soundlessly" delivering them on two revolving balconies "which form huge rings seemingly unsupported in space."

> As the interior is revealed, you see in the hollow beneath the sky, "Democracity"—symbol of a perfectly integrated, futuristic metropolis pulsing with life and rhythm and music. The daylight panorama stretches off to the horizon on all sides. Here is a city of a million people with a working population of 250,000, whose homes are located beyond the city-proper, in five satellite towns. Like great arteries, broad highways traverse expansive areas of vivid green countryside, connecting outlying industrial towns with the city's heart.
>
> After you have gazed at the model for two minutes, dusk slowly shadows the scene. The light fails, and the celestial concave gleams with myriad stars. To the accompaniment of a symphonic poem, a chorus of a thousand voices reaches out of the heavens, and there at ten equi-distant points in the purple dome loom marching men—farmers, stamped by their garb; mechanics, with their tools of trade. As the marchers approach they are seen to represent the various groups in modern society—all the elements which must work together to make possible the better life which would flourish in such a city as lies below.[8]

The workers of Democracity all live in gardenlike apartments outside the city, commuting on the sweeping highways and electric interurban railways. The key to their happiness is the interdependence and collectivity incarnate in the technological wonders they themselves have built.

These ideals are articulated in one of the most extraordinary cultural statements to be found in this era, the opening passage describing the building of the fair.

> The true poets of the twentieth century are the designers, the architects and the engineers who glimpse some inner vision, create some beautiful figment of the imagination and then translate it into valid actuality for the world to enjoy. Such is the poetic process; the poet translates his inspiration into terms that convey vivid sensations to his fellow men. But instead of some compelling pattern of words you have a great articulation that is far more tangible and immediate; exhibits that embody imaginative ideas, buildings, murals, sculptures and landscapes. Tribute to the men who designed the Fair, but tribute, too, to the many men, celebrated and obscure, who actually built it! The designer's dream on paper and charts is only a tentative gesture toward reality, for the engineer and the workers are the indispensable middlemen who translate a dream into a fact.[9]

The pictures illustrating this passage show manual laborers constructing the fair.

Although superficially resembling Democracity, the science fiction model world of GM's Futurama was actually based on radically different assumptions. Twenty-five million people were to have their idea of the future, the America of 1960, shaped by this vision. It is practically all I can remember of the fair, which I visited at the age of five, and it is the salient feature in memory of every person I known who was there. We rode around in easy chairs as a soundtrack told us what we were viewing. What we saw was an animated scale model larger than any that have ever been constructed. And what we experienced was the thrill of interstate superhighways with streamlined brightly colored cars racing smoothly and with precision at spectaclar speeds, slicing right through cities on steel and concrete pylons, with futuristic ramps giving access to these fairy-tale paths. The excitement of cars and roads was overwhelming. Here is how GM described the Futurama.

> Covering an area of 35,738 square feet, the "futurama" is the largest and most realistic scale-model ever constructed. As visitors in the moving chairs tour this "futurama" they experience the sensation of traveling hundreds of miles and viewing the scenes from a low-flying airplane. As they travel on several levels of the building in their magic chairs, they view a continuous animated panorama of towns and cities, rivers and lakes, country and farm areas, industrial plants in operation, country clubs, forests, valleys and snow-capped mountains. The "futurama" contains approximately 500,000 individually designed houses; more than a million trees of eighteen species; and 50,000 scale-model automobiles, of which 10,000 are in actual operation over super-highways, speed lanes and multi-decked bridges.
>
> Projecting a basic theme of highway progress and possible trends in motor transportation facilities of the future, the Exhibit shows how, by multiplying the usefulness of the motor car, the industry's contributions toward prosperity and a better standard of living for all are tremedously enhanced.[10]

General Motors had constructed a model of America's future. It is the corporation that plans and builds, while the people are purely passive, comfortably watching the creation in motion as mere spectators. This contradicts the vision of Democracity and is antithetical to the ideal of the fair expressed in the section "Theme and Purpose" of the *Guidebook*, which presents an extremely active and thoroughly democratic conception of the relation between the present and the future. This remarkable passage also presents the main element missing from that 1939 *Astounding*, with its multiplied views of lone geniuses and lone capitalists creating our future. For in this conception it is the people who will build the future.

We are convinced that the potential assets, material and spiritual, of our country are such that if rightly used they will make for a general public good such as has never before been known. In order to make its contribution toward this process the Fair will show the most promising developments of production, service and social factors of the present day in relation to their bearing on the life of the great mass of people. The plain American citizen will be able to see here what he could attain for his community and himself by intelligent coordinated effort and will be made to realize the interdependence of every contributing form of life and work.

From this inspiring determination arose the slogan: "Building the World of Tomorrow." The eyes of the Fair are on the future—not in the sense of peering into the unknown and predicting the shape of things a century hence—but in the sense of presenting a new and clearer view of today in preparation for tomorrow. To its millions of visitors the Fair says: "Here are the materials, ideas, and forces at work in our world. Here are the best tools that are available to you; they are the tools with which you and your fellow men can build the World of Tomorrow. You are the builders; we have done our best to persuade you that these tools will result in a better world of Tomorrow; yours is the choice."[11]

"Yours is the choice," we were told. But was it?

In that March fifth article, William Ogburn had warned of the veiled totalitarian state that might come from a marriage between big business and big government, especially a marriage arranged under the shotgun of war. But actually the process was already far advanced. GM's Futurama allows us to peer deeply into the process and its relations with science fiction.

Way back at the Columbian Exposition of 1893, there was also a vision of the transportation system of the near future. "One of the wonders of the fair was the electric Intramural Railway. . . . Fair visitors were sure they were witnessing the transportation of the future."[12] And these visitors were right. Within three or four decades American cities were being served by a highly efficient, pollution-free network of interurban and intraurban electric railways.

But in the depths of the Depression, the giant automobile companies, led by General Motors, began consciously, systematically, and ruthlessly destroying the electric urban railways, along with all other forms of competing mass transportation. The story is spelled out in detail in *American Ground Transport*, a book-length report published in 1974 by the United States Senate Subcommittee on Antitrust and Monopoly. As this report documents, between 1935 and 1956, General Motors alone bought up "more than 100 electric surface rail systems in 45 cities,"[13] disposed of them as scrap, set up subsidiary bus companies with fleets of GM buses, and used its enormous political leverage to have the cities designed for automobiles and buses. Nowhere was the vision of the Futurama carried out so completely as in Los Angeles, as eloquently described in that 1974 United States Senate report, which begins the tale with a picture of Los Angeles in 1939.

> Thirty-five years ago Los Angeles was a beautiful city of lush palm trees, fragrant orange groves and ocean-clean air. It was served then by the world's largest electric railway network. In the late 1930s General Motors and allied highway interests acquired the local transit companies, scrapped their pollution-free electric trains, tore down their power transmission lines, ripped up their tracks, and placed GM buses on already congested Los Angeles streets. The noisy, foul-smelling buses turned earlier patrons of the high-speed rail system away from public transit and, in effect, sold millions of private automobiles. Largely as a result, this city is today an ecological wasteland: the palm trees are dying of petrochemical smog; the orange groves have been paved over by 300 miles of freeways; the air is a septic tank into which 4 million cars, half of them built by General Motors, pump 13,000 tons of pollutants daily.[14]

The GM Futurama was a superbly designed and most effective form of science fiction, helping to turn America away from the democratic future articulated as an ideal of the fair and toward a society built around the automobile and petroleum, a society dominated by the gigantic corporations and banks controlling these industries. That Senate report concludes, "We are witnessing today the collapse of a society based on the automobile."[15] The automobile age, quite different from the worlds imagined in most 1939 science fiction, may perhaps turn out to be just a byway or blind alley. But the ability of the corporate powers, aided by their own forms of science fiction, to shape the future in their own image, has certainly persisted well into the age of the aerospace industry, with its very real capability to generate the apocalypse.

SANDRA M. GILBERT

# Rider Haggard's Heart of Darkness

*Man's timid heart is bursting with the things he must not say,*
*For the Woman that God gave him isn't his to give away;*
*But when hunter meets with husband, each confirms the other's tale—*
*The female of the species is more deadly than the male.*
　　　　　—Rudyard Kipling, *"The Female of the Species"*

More than fifty years ago, Mario Praz famously wrote about the
nineteenth century that "In no other literary period . . . has sex been
so obviously the mainspring of works of imagination"[1] In his ground-
breaking study of *The Romantic Agony*, however, Praz amassed evidence to demonstrate, almost overwhelmingly, that as the century
wore on it was not just "sex" but specifically the female sex, and even
more specifically the power of the female sex that increasingly obsessed male writers in France and England. It should not be surprising,
then, that one of the major best sellers of the period was a novel whose
terse title was an unadorned female pronoun, suggesting that the book
might be an abstract treatise on the female gender or a fictive exploration of the nature of womanhood. Published in 1887, Rider Haggard's
*She* sold a nearly record-breaking 30,000 copies within a few months,
and most of its charisma seems to have come from the regal radiance of
its heroine.

　　The formal title of this woman (whose real name was Ayesha)—
She-Who-Must-Be-Obeyed—was hardly less shocking than the title of
the novel in which She starred, yet it was as crucial to the book's power
as it was in representing her power. For Haggard's heroine was in
many ways a definitive *fin de siècle* embodiment of fantasies that
preoccupied countless male writers who had come of age during a
literary period in which, to go back to Praz's remark, the (female) sex

124

had been "obviously the mainspring of works of imagination." Unlike the women earlier Victorian writers had idealized or excoriated, She was neither an angel nor a monster. Rather, She was an odd but significant blend of the two types—an angelically chaste woman with monstrous powers, a monstrously passionate woman with angelic charms. Just as significantly, however, She was in certain important ways an entirely New Woman: the all-knowing, all-powerful ruler of a matriarchal society.

I will argue that it is especially because of this last point that Haggard's portrait of her was so popular (and so popular with male readers in particular). In addition, I will try to show that her story was both a summary and a paradigm of the story told by a number of similar contemporary tales, all of which were to varying degrees just the kinds of fictive explorations of female power that Haggard's title promised and his novel delivered, and many of which solved what their authors implicitly defined as the problem of female power through denouements analogous to—perhaps even drawn from—the one that Haggard devised for *She*. Finally, I will suggest that both the fascination of Haggard's semidivine New Woman and the compulsiveness with which he and his contemporaries made her "the mainspring of works of imagination" were symptoms of a complex of late Victorian sociocultural and sexual anxieties that have until recently been overlooked or even ignored by critics and historians alike.

At first, of course, as Haggard's hero Leo Vincey, his aggressively misogynistic guardian Horace Holly and their servant Job begin their journey toward her land, they may not seem to be adventuring into a realm whose strangeness inheres primarily in its femaleness. The African coast on which they are shipwrecked, for instance, seems a standard adventure story setting, complete with wild beasts, fever-inducing mists, and mysterious ruins. As they travel inland, however, through vaporous marshes and stagnant canals, the landscape across which they journey seems increasingly like a Freudianly female *paysage moralisé*. When they are finally captured by a band of fierce natives whose leader is a biblical-looking Arab called Father, our suspicions are confirmed. Lifted into litters, the explorers yield to a "pleasant swaying motion" and, in a symbolic return to the womb, they are carried up ancient swampy birth-canals into "a vast cup of earth" that is ruled by She-Who-Must-Be-Obeyed and inhabited by a people called the Amahaggar. About these people, moreover, they soon learn that

in direct opposition to the habits of almost every other savage race in the

world, women among the Amahaggar live upon conditions of perfect
equality with the men, and are not held to them by any binding ties.
Descent is traced only through the line of the mother, and . . . they never
pay attention to, or even acknowledge, any man as their father, even
when their male parentage is perfectly well known.[2]

Given the brief appearance of Leo's ancestor, Kallikrates, in
Herodotus's history of the Persian Wars, it is notable that there is an
eerie correspondence between the strange land of the Amahaggar and
the perverse Egypt Herodotus describes, a country whose people "in
most of their manners and customs, exactly reverse the common
practice of mankind. The women attend the markets and trade, while
the men sit at home at the loom; . . . women stand up to urinate, men
sit down."[3] In each case the country is described as uniquely alien, and
alien in particular because relations between its men and women
inhabitants are exactly antithetical to those that prevail in normal
civilized societies. Thus both Egypt and Kôr, as Haggard's explorers
learn the Amahaggar land is called, are realms where what patriarchal
culture defines as misrule has become rule.

She herself, however, manifests the severity of her misrule only
after some delay. At first, it is her subjects who enact and express the
murderous female sexuality that She herself tends to deny. Thus we
learn before meeting her what it means for her to be the queen of a
people who, bizarrely, "place pots upon the heads of strangers," for
shortly after the explorers arrive in Kôr they are invited to a feast at
which a group of the Amahaggar try to kill the Englishmen's Arab
guide, Mahomed, by putting a red-hot earthen pot on his head. This
astonishing mode of execution, a cross between cooking and decapita-
tion which seems to have had no real anthropological precedent, is
such a vivid enactment of both castration fears and birth anxieties that
it is hardly necessary to rehearse all its psychosymbolic overtones.

But if the hot-potting episode is grotesquely sexual in its elaboration of the ways in which female misrule can cause a vessel associated
with female domesticity to become as deadly as female anatomy, the
inner landscape of Kôr itself is both more melodramatically sexual and
more unnervingly historical. She-Who-Must-Be-Obeyed inhabits a
great cave in the wall of an extinct volcano. As Holly describes it,
moreover, entering her domain is at least as symbolic as being hot-
potted, though (in several senses) graver. Blindfolded, the explorers
are carried (again) on litters "into the bowels of the great mountain
. . . an eerie sensation." Their destination is just as eerie, for the

cavern palace where She dwells is both luxurious and sepulchral, half a set of elegant apartments "under the hill," like the Venusberg of Wagner's *Tannhäuser* or Swinburne's "Laus Veneris," and half a set of "vast catacombs," a sort of Hades where "the mortal remains of the great extinct race whose monuments surrounded us had been first preserved" (p. 142).

Not surprisingly, therefore, She herself turns out to be an interesting cross between Venus and Persephone. As Venus, for instance, She commands the absolute erotic devotion of any man who looks upon her unveiled, while as Persephone She is married to death and queen in a country of shadows. Shrouded in a "white and gauzy material" that makes her look like "a corpse in its grave-clothes," She judges and condemns the hapless Amahagger with the lucid indifference of eternity, and for recreation She takes her visitors on a tour of her domain, a "whole mountain peopled with the dead, and nearly all of them perfect" (p. 179). Besides commanding a realm of tombs and ruins, moreover, She has spent, it soon appears, more than twenty necrophiliac centuries watching, praying, cursing, and sleeping by the side of her dead Egyptian lover Kallikrates, who has been miraculously preserved in a secret catacomb. Finally Kôr, the name of the dead city She rules, links her even more definitively to the bride of Dis, for Persephone is also, after all, called *Kore* or *Kora*. But of course the ambiguity of the word *Kôr* emphasizes the crucial ambiguity of the city's queen. Ruling this domain which is at the *core* or heart of the earth, She-Who-Must-Be-Obeyed is part a *Kore* collecting *corpses* in the "dead heart of the rock" and part a Venus collecting *coeurs* or hearts, and seducing or enchanting the flesh that is the living *corpus* of the earth.

Finally, then, in her striking duality She transcends the traditional archetypes of Venus and Persephone to become a more mysterious and resonant figure than either of these goddesses alone. In fact, She is absolutely identical with the Byronic femme fatale who haunted nineteenth-century writers from Keats and Swinburne to Pater, Wilde, and Macdonald, so much so that her character in a sense summarizes and intensifies all the key female traits these artists brooded on. Having lived under the hill of ordinary reality since classical antiquity, for instance, She chats familiarly about Greek and Arab philosophers with the bemused Holly; clearly, like Pater's Gioconda, she has "learned the secrets of the grave." Wherever She studied, moreover, She has strange herbal wisdom, esoteric healing powers, and arcane alchemical knowledge. In addition, because She is a connoisseur of a language strange as that spoken by Keats's Belle Dame, only She can decipher the writing on the walls of the tombs among which She lives. Nevertheless, despite her supernatural powers, She is tormented by desire and regret, burdened by what seems almost the prototype of an alien consciousness. Finally, indeed, one suspects that just as the name *Kôr* applies at least as much to her as to the lost city She rules, the name *Kallikrates* has as much to do with her as with the dead priest who was her victim. For, like Kali, the Indian goddess of destruction, She is murderous: She condemns men casually to death by torture and is capable of "blasting" those she dislikes with a Medusan glance. In Kallikrates' first incarnation, She murdered him, and now, in his second, She murders the Amahaggar woman who seems to be a reincarnation of her hated rival.

Like the Indian god Brahma, however, or like the Great Mother as Neumann and others have defined her, She is not merely a destroyer; because She is a combined Persephone and Venus she is a destroyer *and* a preserver. In fact, She has evidently learned many of her techniques of preservation from the dead priests of Kôr, and perhaps the most peculiar feature of Haggard's discussion of her kingdom is his ruminative, obsessive, even at times necrophiliac interest in the mummies that surround her as well as the embalming techniques through which they have been preserved. The Englishmen are shown a "pit about the size of the space beneath the dome of St. Paul's" (p. 190) filled with bones, they regularly dine in a cave decorated by bas reliefs that show it was used for embalming as well as eating, and they are invited to a ceremonial feast at which the torches are flaming human mummies as well as the severed limbs of those mummies.

The literal as well as metaphorical piling up of all this dead flesh reminds us, of course, that the womb of the Great Mother is also a tomb. But such mysterious preservation of the flesh also implies other and perhaps more uncanny points. In fact, the way in which the very idea of embalming is dramatized throughout *She* suggests that for its author this practice paradoxically evokes anxieties about both the ordinary world the Englishmen represent and the extraordinary realm She rules. With their perpetual repetition of the same character and the same message, for instance, the mummies evoke the dullness and dread associated with the imagined persistence of the self through history and thus the patriarchal horror of belatedness. At the same time, however, the alien practices that have preserved the mummies evoke an alien culture—Herodotus's peculiar Egypt as well as the strange Egypt that was being diligently studied in the nineteenth century. More metaphysically, the opacity, inertness, and silence of the lifelike but embalmed bodies quite literally incarnate the horror of otherness and specifically the horror of the body that is other than one's own and therefore opaque to one's thought. She herself, for instance, is both powerful Mother Goddess and shrouded mummy. In fact, She herself seems to be the most theatrical example of unnatural preservation that we encounter in the book that tells her story. More than two thousand years old, She has not only been embalmed, She has been embalmed alive. Both destroyer and preserver, She has been, if not destroyed, at least spectacularly preserved. Significantly, however, She lacks the crucial third ability of creation, and just as significantly, She lacks the ultimate power of *self*-preservation. Implicit in such lacks, moreover, is the spectacular moment of her destruction, a sexual climax that can be defined as a sort of apocalyptic primal scene.

She is destroyed, of course, by the very flame of life that has heretofore preserved her (and which at one time presumably created her). Ironically, too, She is destroyed because, wishing to share her magic longevity with her lover, Leo Vincey, whom She regards as a reincarnation of the dead Kallikrates, She has brought the Englishmen on a quasi-sexual journey even more perilous than the approach to her kingdom or to her palace at Kôr. After crossing a terrible abyss and crawling down narrow labyrinthine passages, the explorers have at last reached the secret "place of Life," a rosily glowing cavern that is "the very womb of the Earth, wherein she doth conceive the Life that ye see brought forth in man and beast" (p. 299). Here, She promises the Englishmen, "ye shall be born anew!" And here, quite unexpectedly, in a consummation that seems to be the opposite of what anyone would wish, She is annihilated by the "rolling pillar of Life" that has heretofore preserved her.

Wishes for Ayesha's destruction, however, have been carefully cultivated in the chapters that precede the catastrophe in the "place of Life," for her actions and ambitions are shown to become increasingly satanic as the novel progresses and her willful desire for complete possession of her lover gathers energy. Soon, we are told, She is planning, like some monstrous anti-Victoria, to "assume absolute rule over the British dominions and probably over the whole earth" (p. 267). "It might be possible to control her for a while," speculates Holly, "but her proud ambitious spirit would be certain to break loose and avenge itself for the long centuries of solitude" (pp. 267–68). The terrible punishment in store for such a transgression begins to emerge when, still en route to the "place of Life," She and her companions reach an abyss that they must cross on a narrow plank. Plunged into darkness for most of every day, this gulf can only be bridged when, passing through a cleft in the rock, "like a great sword of flame, a beam from the setting sun [pierces] the Stygian gloom" (p. 285). The moment of illumination that follows, says Holly, is exhilarating, for "Right through the heart of the darkness that flaming sword was stabbed." Prefiguring phallic weapons of light and hearts of darkness in Haggard's literary descendents from Conrad to Lawrence, Holly's imagery also both illuminates and foreshadows Ayesha's doom. For She is, metaphorically speaking, destroyed during a moment of unholy intercourse with the phallic "pillar of Life" whose sexual comings and goings, as the Englishmen now learn, eternally shake the secret "womb of Earth." Thus She herself represents a "heart of darkness" into which the flaming sword of patriarchal justice is ritually stabbed.

The "rolling pillar of Life" that brings Haggard's romance to its apocalyptic climax is an almost theatrically rich sexual symbol. At regular intervals, it appears with a "grinding and crashing noise . . . rolling down like all the thunderwheels of heaven behind the horses of the lightning" (pp. 300–301) and, as it enters the cave, it flames out "an awful cloud or pillar of fire, like a rainbow many colored," whose very presence causes Haggard's narrator to rejoice "in [the] splendid vigor of a new-found self." Such celestial radiance and regenerative power suggest that this perpetually erect symbol of masculinity is not just a Freudian penis but a Lacanian Phallus, a fiery signifier whose eternal thundering return speaks the inexorability of the patriarchal Law She has violated in her satanically overreaching ambition.

Like the stars whose imperturbable order defeats Lucifer in George Meredith's "Lucifer in Starlight," this Phallus comes and goes on an "ancient track," indifferent, omnipotent. Like the "pillar of fire by night" that helps Moses lead the children of Israel out of an Egypt even more perverse than Herodotus's, it expresses the will of the divine Father, and in doing so it will lead Holly and Leo out of her degrading land back into the kingdom of their own proper masculinity. Moreover, flaming out "like a rainbow many colored," it recalls the covenantal rainbow of Genesis, and thus it becomes, in a sense, the pillar of society, an incarnate sign of the manly covenant among men (and between men and a symbolic Father) that is the founding gesture of patriarchal culture. In addition, as a powerful male sexual symbol, it comments dramatically upon the less powerful female symbols deployed by the misruled Amahaggar in the earlier hot-potting episode, for it is radiant, insubstantial, transcendent, where the hot-pots were inert, earthen, grotesque. In fact, the novelist Henry Miller grasps the purpose of this pillar of fire quite accurately when he notes that Ayesha's fate "is not death, . . . but reduction,"[4] for as Harold Bloom observes of Pater's Gioconda, Ayesha "incarnates too much, both for her own good and [from a masculinist point of view] for ours."[5] Finally, therefore, naked and ecstatic, in all the pride of her femaleness, She must be fucked to death by the "unalterable law" of the Father.

As Henry Miller also notes, however, Ayesha's death is not just a death or even a "reduction" but, quite literally, a "devolution" in which her very flesh is punished for her presumption. As She passes through the stages of her unlived life, aging two thousand years in a few minutes, the "language strange" of her beauty shreds and flakes away, her power wrinkles, her magic dries up, and the meaning of her "terrible priority" is revealed as degeneration rather than generativity. The Mosaic reality behind the false commandments of She-Who-Must-Be-Obeyed, Holly and Leo learn, is and always was a bald, blind, naked, shapeless, infinitely wrinkled female animal "no larger than a big ape" who raises herself "upon her bony hands . . . swaying her head slowly from side to side as does a tortoise" (p. 308). More terrible than the transformations of Dr. Jekyll or Dorian Gray, this "reduction" or "devolution" of goddess to beast is the final judgment upon her pride and ambition. "Thus She opposed herself to the eternal law," concludes Holly, "and, strong though she was, by it was swept back into nothingness—swept back with shame and hideous mockery" (p. 309).

*She* is not only a turn-of-the-century best seller but also, in a number of dramatic ways, one of the century's literary turning points, a pivot on which the ideas and anxieties of the Victorians begin to swivel into what has come to be called "the modern." If She is a classic Belle Dame Sans Merci, for instance, the stony wasteland that She rules is modern in its air of sexual and historical extremity, and certainly in England the ceremonial sexual act that brought about her "reduction" or "devolution" was followed by a number of similar scenes in turn-of-the-century and modernist tales, ranging from Wilde's *Salome* (1894), Macdonald's *Lilith* (1895), and Stoker's *Dracula* (1897), to T. S. Eliot's "The Love Song of St. Sebastian," D. H. Lawrence's "The Woman Who Rode Away," and Faulkner's "A Rose for Emily." In all these works, a man or a group of men must achieve or at least bear witness to a ceremonial assertion of phallic authority that will free all men from the unmanning enslavement of her land.

To notice that common anxieties impel these tales toward an uncommonly ferocious denouement is not, however, to understand the real psychological, social, and historical anxieties that underlie them. What, after all, worried Rider Haggard so much that he was driven to create his extraordinarily complex fantasy about Her and her realm in just six volcanically energetic weeks? Why did thousands and thousands of Englishmen respond to his dreamlike story of Her with as much fervor as if he had been narrating their own dreams for them and to them? I want to suggest that the charisma of this novel arose from the fact that the work itself explored and exploited three intimately interrelated contemporary phenomena: the nineteenth-century interest in Egypt, the nineteenth-century fascination with spiritualism, and the nineteenth-century obsession with the so-called New Woman.

As Edward Said has noted, Egypt in the nineteenth century became more than ever a focal point for imperialist anxieties and passions. In the alien, barely decipherable hieroglyphs of its history and in the many mysteries of its ancient and modern religious practices, it must always have seemed to many Europeans to symbolize, as it had for Herodotus and as—together with Kôr—it did for Haggard, the power of what we might call geopolitical otherness. But now such otherness was being dramatically redefined through philological analyses, translations of sacred texts, and theological studies which clarified the coherence of what had traditionally been defined as a paradigmatically alien society. Such studies, moreover, were part of a larger surge of scholarship that was drastically revising Western notions of prehistory, of comparative religion, and of "primitive" social structures. Increasingly revealing the complexity of cultures that had been thought simple and the cultivation of societies that had been thought crude, these researches increasingly dramatized the enigma of human otherness that is not, as Europeans had believed, inferior, but merely different. It is significant, therefore, that *She* broods on one manifestation of this newly haunting enigma not only in Haggard's use of the preclassical goddess Isis but in his naming of her and her land: *Ayesha* or *Aïsha* was the second and favorite wife of the Islamic prophet Mohammed, to Christian readers the incarnation of alien theology, and her strange land of *Kôr*, besides recalling hearts of darkness, corpses, and the pagan goddess *Kore*, evokes the *Kor-an*, the Islamic holy book which is in its essence other than the "good" (Western) book of the bible.

It is significant too, however, that the wisdom of other cultures, and specifically the wisdom of ancient Egypt, was gradually emerging in the nineteenth century through the work of spiritualist adepts like Madame Blavatsky, for spiritualism, with its different but equally serious emphasis on a realm of otherness was the second contemporary phenomenon that Haggard's novel exploited. The novelist himself had actually been a spiritualist in his youth, attending séances, presided over by women, which dramatized yet again the fragility of the control the rational Western mind had achieved over a world of things and people that might at any moment assert a dangerously alien autonomy. Where both materialist science and traditional Christian theology declared that there was nothing (for the dead were, if anywhere, elsewhere), spiritualism seemed to prove that there was something. When theosophy, fostered by spiritualist ideas, summarized a set of radical hermeticist propositions about reality, reminding readers that, as Madame Blavatsky argued, such mysticism had always flowed below Western thought like an underground river, patriarchal rationalism was even more seriously shaken. Finally, the appearance of Madame Blavatsky's notorious *Isis Unveiled* (1877) must have not only cemented the connections between the adepts of Egypt and such challenges to a commonly agreed-upon reality, but also emphasized the link between, on the one hand, the alternative intellectual possibilities propounded by theosophy and, on the other hand, the possibilities of female rule, or misrule.

The third contemporary phenomenon that concerned both Haggard and his readers, then, would in a sense have integrated the first two, for the figure of the New Woman, with its evocation of such unruly females as the Egyptian Cleopatra and the pseudo-Egyptologist Madame Blavatsky, vividly suggested an ultimate triumph of otherness. Feminist thinkers had long understood this point, quite consciously identifying their work for women's rights with such related challenges to patriarchal authority as spiritualism, abolitionism, and the Home Rule movement in Ireland. But even without overt articulations of the links between feminism and other antipatriarchal movements, the very idea of the New Woman was so threatening that her aspirations would tend to evoke all the other subversive aspirations that were suddenly, or so it seemed, being voiced throughout the British Empire, with some even being conveyed from the invisible world of the dead. For of course the rise of feminism, with all its attendant "ills"—the suffrage campaign, education for women, female literary production—was very likely the most remarkable and most remarked-upon social phenomenon of the late nineteenth century. As Theodore Roszak astutely observes, twentieth-century historians have until quite recently tended to ignore the massive effects of this cultural event, but in fact "one would be hard pressed to find many major [thinkers] of the period . . . who did not address themselves passionately to the rights of women."[6] Given such a preoccupation moveover, even the increasingly bulky and extraordinarily durable figure of Victoria herself might have come to seem a threatening emblem of matriarchal dominance.

Whether by the queen or, as is more likely, by some of her less decorously domesticated sister subjects, Haggard clearly was threatened, for in addressing himself to a fantasy of Ayesha and her land, he was confronting the frightening yet fascinating possibility of both political and literary female power, as well as the mythic and psychological meanings of such power. The son of one of the many nineteenth-century "scribbling women" who not only read romances to their children but actually wrote such works themselves, he had special personal reasons to be absorbed by "the woman question": when he was a teenager, his literary mother had scornfully called him "heavy as lead in body and mind," and when he was even younger an unscrupulous nurse had bullied him with a fierce-looking rag doll which he named She-Who-Must-Be-Obeyed. But it is notable, too, that Haggard's adult reading as well as his childhood listening was at least at one point importantly focused on the work of a female imagination: the first best-selling novel ever written about Africa was, after all, a book by a woman, and a feminist one at that—Olive Schreiner's *The Story of an African Farm* (1883). Like Englishmen from Gladstone to Rhodes, Haggard read the book with fascination and excitement. At his first opportunity, he sought out its author to express his admiration, and his charismatically fierce Ayesha may even have been half-consciously modeled on Schreiner's fierce but equally charismatic Lyndall. At the same time, moreover, *She* may also have been half-consciously patterned on yet another work about the problem of feminist assertiveness: Tennyson's 1847 *The Princess*, in which, as in *She*, three bewildered men penetrate a female stronghold and explore the perils of role-reversal.

Certainly at least a few sophisticated women readers seem to have understood, as Schreiner and Tennyson also might have, the extent to which Haggard's novel enacted and exploited masculine worries about female dominance/male submission. Visiting London in the 1920s, the American writer Mary Austin asked him "Whether he hadn't figured 'She' as the matriarch [and] he admitted that he had."[7] A few years earlier, moreover, another American woman—the feminist theorist Charlotte Perkins Gilman—imagined in *Herland* (1915) a female utopia which, like Haggard's Kôr and Tennyson's women's college, is explored by three bemused misogynists. Revising and reversing the values implicit in both *The Princess* and *She*, her novel nevertheless clarified the anxieties about the "rights of women" (and the wrongs of men) that Haggard's work, in particular, had so vividly dramatized.

It is no coincidence, therefore, that within a decade of *She*'s publication two of Haggard's most sophisticated contemporaries recorded dreams and recounted adventures which drew upon just this elaborate configuration of anxieties that *She* enacted. First, Sigmund Freud had a dream that, as his self-analysis revealed, depended heavily on details borrowed from *She*. In this dream, Freud wrote, he had been given a strange task which

> related to a dissection of the lower part of my own body, my pelvis and legs, which I saw before me as though in the dissecting-room. . . . Finally I was making a journey through a changing landscape with an Alpine guide who carried me [part of the way]. The ground was boggy; we went round the edge; . . . Before this I had been making my own way forward over the slippery ground with a constant feeling of surprise that I was able to do so well after the dissection. At last we reached a small wooden house at the end of which was an open window. There the guide set me down and laid two wooden boards, . . . so as to bridge the chasm which had to be crossed over from the window. At that point I really became frightened about my legs, [and] awoke in a mental fright.[8]

As Freud himself rather dryly remarks, "a full analysis of this dream" would take up quite a number of pages, but he does undertake a partial explanation which, significantly, emphasizes the influence of imagery drawn from *She*, a work he calls "A strange book . . . full of hidden meaning . . . The eternal feminine, the immortality of our emotions," and which, as one critic has recently argued, may have helped him conceptualize the psychic geography that was to be so crucial to his theory of "layered personality."[9] What are we to make, though, of the fact that Freud's Haggardesque adventure begins with a pelvic dissection that implies a desexing and that his journey ends in feelings of impotence and terror? Like Leo and Holly, who have to be

carried on litters into the womb/tomb that is Her land, Freud seems to
have been castrated and infantilized early in this dream, so that when
he is borne inward over slippery, boggy ground it is hard, given his own
hermeneutics, to avoid seeing his journey not as a classic trip into the
self but as a voyage into the other, and specifically into an other who is
horrifyingly female. His final despairing vision of "the chasm which
had to be crossed" would inevitably, then, lead to a sense of failure and
"mental fright," not because (as he suggests) he wonders how much
longer his legs will carry him toward the end of his self-analysis, but
because he fears that he *will* reach an end that must inevitably include
an impotent confrontation of—even an engulfment in—the otherness
of the female, whose power is shrouded in a darkness that lies at the
heart of his own culture.

It is significant, however, that Freud's dream broods so insistently
on "the chasm that had to be crossed" by means of narrow planks, for
this frightening image derives, we should remember, from what is
essentially the turning point of Haggard's tale. Holly, Leo, and
Ayesha can only bridge the gulf they must cross in order to reach the
"place of Life" when, "like a great sword of flame, a beam from the
setting sun [pierces] the . . . heart of the darkness" (p. 285) and they
are given a symbolic preview of the fate in store for Ayesha. It is
possible, therefore, that in his dream-allusion to this moment, Freud
was not only enacting crucial male anxieties but offering himself a
paradigmatically patriarchal hope, the hope of renewal through a
reiteration of the Law of the Father.

Interestingly, the most important *fin de siècle* work that we can
associate with *She* also pays tribute to this crucial moment, for in his
*Heart of Darkness* (1899), written not long after Freud dreamed this
dream, Conrad designs for Marlow a pilgrimage whose guides and
goals are as eerily female as those Holly and Leo must confront and
conquer. Just as Leo and Holly must ritually pass through the matriarchal territory of the Amahaggar in order to reach Her deadly land of
Kôr, for instance, Marlowe must pass through an antechamber ruled
by two "uncanny and fateful" women who are "guarding the door of
Darkness"[10] When he reaches a key way station on his African journey, moreover, he is "arrested" by "a small sketch in oils" done by the
mysterious Kurtz, a totemic-seeming image of "a woman, draped and
blindfolded, carrying a lighted torch" (p. 25). Vaguely evoking an
image of Justice, the picture disturbingly suggests the contradictions
between power (the torch) and powerlessness (the blindfold) and thus

it introduces the idea of the other who has been excluded and dispossessed but who, despite such subordination, exercises a kind of indomitable torchlike power.

Finally, Marlowe's discovery of the dying Kurtz in the center of the "dark continent" and at the end of the serpentine river definitively establishes the meaning of such a female totem. For when Marlowe and his "pilgrim" companions try to rescue the sick man from the spell of his black Venus and her people, they fail abjectly. Muttering of his "immense plans" (p. 67), Kurtz crawls back into the jungle, back toward the African queen of night into whose power he has fallen. Destroyed by his greed for the ivory bones of her country as well as by his enthrallment to the alien passions she represents, he has become, himself, "an animated image of death carved out of old ivory" (p. 60) like the dead bodies that litter Ayesha's terrible realm or the "pale Kings and Princes" who haunted Keats's knight-at-arms. Even his name, *Kurtz*, with its incorporation of *Kôr*, suggests that he is ultimately meant to signify the nightmare corpse at the core of the anxious patriarchal/imperialist mind, the dead father who has been "blasted" into impotence by "the horror, the horror" of otherness. There is nothing now for Marlowe and the "pilgrims" to do but prepare to sail away, bearing the alive-in-death body of this ruler like a sacred relic back to the illusory (and female) world of the "Intended," whose secret (female) intentions have now been clarified.

As the Europeans prepare to sail away, however, She-Who-Must-Be-Obeyed actually makes a brief but dramatic appearance at the edge of the night wood she inhabits, as if she were a silent hieroglyph in the language strange that articulates both her mysterious history and her threatening hystery. Shadowing the marble-pale "Intended" the way Ayesha shadows the matriarchal Victoria, she walks "with measured steps . . . treading the earth proudly, with a . . . flash of barbarous ornaments. She [carries] her head high; her hair [is] done in the shape of a helmet. . . . She [is] savage and superb, wild-eyed and magnificent; there [is] something ominous and stately in her deliberate progress" (p. 62). Like Haggard's queen, she is "wild and gorgeous," "tragic and fierce"; like Haggard's queen, she is guarded by subjugated males. And like Haggard's queen she generates quite reasonable terror and quite inevitable plans for revenge in the hearts of most European men. "If she had offered to come aboard I really think I would have tried to shoot her," remarks the Russian "man of patches" (p. 62), a fellow-traveler who has been as certainly (if not as dramatically) destroyed by her land as Kurtz was. Whether or not it is justified, his sense of the imminent danger She represents was shared not only by anxious romancers like Keats and Swinburne, Macdonald and Wilde, but by such disparate figures as Joseph Conrad, Rider Haggard, and Sigmund Freud. There *is*, after all, "something ominous and stately in her deliberate progress" through the nineteenth century.

SUSAN GUBAR

# *She* in *Herland*: Feminism as Fantasy

*I saw no Way—The Heavens were stitched—*
*I felt the Columns close—*
*The Earth reversed her Hemispheres—*
*I touched the Universe—*

*And back it slid—and I alone—*
*A speck upon a Ball—*
*Went out upon Circumference—*
*Beyond the Dip of Bell*
             —Emily Dickinson *(J. 378)*[1]

And when I ask how did we come to envision a world without rape, I am asking about the shape of revolution because when one dreams of a new world, this world immediately becomes possible.
             —Susan Griffin *(Rape)*[2]

What is the relationship between women and the fantastic? The epigraphs for my essay point to the crucial role played by amazing voyages in women's thinking about women: Emily Dickinson, knowing even the heavens to be stitched closed, imagines herself advancing through the sliding doors of the universe until she is poised, alone upon circumference; Susan Griffin reminds us that women abused by the probable refuse it by imagining the possible in a revolutionary rejection of patriarchal culture. What the subtitle of this essay—"Feminism as Fantasy"—means to point toward is the realization that women's fantasies have frequently been feminist in nature and that, concomitantly, feminism imagines an alternative reality that is truly fantastic.

We are, of course, much more accustomed to think about *male* fantasies, as any literary history of speculative fiction will prove, male fantasies not infrequently centered on women. Especially in the heyday of fantastic literature, the late Victorian period, the curious girl-child and the raging queen reign supreme. What exactly is the relationship between men's and women's fantasies in this period? Is it possible that one man's utopia may be one woman's dystopia? Or, do misogynist dystopias fuel feminist utopias of another Eden, a once and future queen, a somewhat different Paradise? If woman is dispossessed, a nobody, in the somewhere of patriarchy, is it possible that she might be somebody only in the nowhere of utopia? What Julia Kristeva calls intertextuality, the transposition of one system of signs into another,[3] can help us trace the dialectic between the father's curse and the mother's blessing in the relationship between H. Rider Haggard's *She* and Charlotte Perkins Gilman's *Herland*, because *She*'s power and popularity transformed the colonized continents into the heart of female darkness that Charlotte Perkins Gilman would rename and reclaim in a utopian feminist revision of Haggard's romance.

If we take *She* (1886) as a touchstone for literature, painting, and philosophy of the *fin de siècle* femme fatale, as Sandra Gilbert has done, it becomes clear that Leo Vincey's trip into the savage origin of life and death, like Marlowe's trip in Conrad's *Heart of Darkness* to the more pretentiously evoked "inscrutable" and "ineffable" wilderness, is a voyage back not only to the infancy of the race but also to his own infancy with its feelings of rage at dependency on the will and whim of the inscrutable, omnipotent female. Certainly the image of Freud dissecting his own pelvis before the journey over the "cleft" into the "womb of the world" illuminates the male anxieties that initiate the colonial trip to an undiscovered country, be it the blank places on the map of Africa or the blank spaces Freud explicitly associates with the female genitals. Actually his dream implies that men experience themselves as haggard riders into the volcano of female transformation that still echoes the roaring inside her. If even Freud's dream of *She* implies that castration anxiety is a male response to female power, then we may find that feminists like Susan Lurie are right in interpreting psychoanalytic theories of female penis envy as a reaction formation to male womb envy.[4] Actually, this is exactly what the American feminist Charlotte Perkins Gilman implies.

By coming to terms with Haggard's *She*, Charlotte Perkins Gilman confronted the misogyny implicit in the imperialist romance. Gilman specified her critique by situating *Herland* on a "spur" of land "up where the maps had to be made,"[5] even in an extinct volcano: in fact, it is a volcanic blast that destroys all the men who are fighting a war and seals the women in a community of their own. As in *She* where the Amahaggar trace descent through the line of the mother, the society in Herland is matrilineal. As in Haggard's novel, moreover, this isolated community ruled by women worships a woman who has solved the riddle of life and death, for while Haggard's She is personally immortal, the inhabitants of Herland are an immortal species, each woman capable of parthenogenically reproducing herself: they gained this parthenogenic power, Gilman explains, 2,000 years ago, 2,000 being the approximate age of She. Just as three self-proclaimed misogynists penetrate into the caves of Kôr, *Herland* is told by one member of a three-man team of explorers whose misogyny is acutely analyzed by Gilman.

Gilman presents Terry Nicholson, Jeff Margrave, and the narrator, Vandyck Jennings, as three stereotypical and faintly ludicrous specimens of masculinity, each with his own all too predictable fantasy of what to expect in a country of no men. But, when they actually enter the no man's land of Herland, all three find their stereotypes of women disabused. Lo and behold, women do not bicker; they are well organized; they do not admire aggression in men; they can invent. As each of the sexist stereotypes of the men is discarded, we see the "flip-flop" or the "diametric reconfiguration" that Eric Rabkin considers so central to fantastic literature.[6]

> We had expected a dull submissive monotomy, and found a daring social inventiveness. . . .
> We had expected pettiness, and found a social consciousness. . . .
> We had expected jealousy, and found a broad sisterly affection. (p. 81)

The satiric critique generated from the utopian reconfiguration here means that the better Herland looks as a matriarchal culture, the worse patriarchal America seems in contrast.

Especially in the introductory chapters of Gilman's utopia, the men experience culture shock when they are treated like the minority they, in fact, are. Secondary creatures, they are herded in like cattle, bedded down like babies, and put on display as anatomical curiosities marketable only for matrimony. Considered inferior for their secondary sexual characteristics, they become petulant, irritable, jealous, vain of their physical appearance, in need of reassurance, rivalrous for approval, as Gilman humorously diagnoses the faults ascribed to her own sex as symptoms of a disease called "marginalization." While the three misogynists in *She* valiantly hold on to their masculine grace under pressure, the quarrelling men who are cooped up in a fortress of *Herland* try, like fairy tale princesses, to escape at night by tying together bedsheets and lowering themselves to a ledge so as to reach their airplane, only to find what they call their "machine" in the garden "swaddled," literally sewed up in a bag (p. 42).

Part of what they must discover is that there is no central, secret interior place to penetrate, for there are no mines or caves in *Herland*. Bold and brave, the three men of Haggard's romance penetrate not only the womb/tomb but also to the single source, She, who is everywoman, the essentially feminine. They will either possess her or be possessed by her, the plot implies. But the men in Gilman's utopia are "tamed and trained" (pp. 72, 73) into the realization that there is no She, but instead there are many Hers, some of whom are cautiously willing to welcome them as an experimental opportunity to restore "bisexuality." What Gilman seeks to call into queston is the idea that there is or can be or should be a single definition of what constitutes the female. There is no Kôr in *Herland*. Historically such a core definition has fixated on the sex-function, and therefore Gilman gives us women with no sexual desire at all. Decentering definitions of the real woman, the total woman, the eternal feminine *is*, after all, the project of feminism.

What makes this project utopian is the imaginative leap it requires beyond empirical data to postulating the possibility of the primacy of the female. The contemporary anthropologist Sherry Ortner reminds us that "we find women subordinate to men in *every known society*" (emphasis mine).[7] Gilman would not have disagreed. Fifty-five years old when she wrote *Herland*, she had explained just this fact in such influential texts as *Women and Economics* (1898), *The Home* (1903), and *Human Work* (1904). For Gilman, the economic dependency of women means that female sexual arts become crucial for attracting and keeping a man: woman therefore identifies herself with the sexual function completely, while man is considered the human prototype. This is the reason why sexuality becomes highly exaggerated in women. As if writing about *She*, moreover, Gilman claims that economic dependency works "to make a race with one sex a million years behind the other":[8] "in her position of arrested development, she has maintained the virtues and the vices of the period of human evolution at which she was imprisoned" (*WE*, p. 350). Haggard's denizen of the darkness with her massive lengths of hair, her gauzy veils, her turbulent desires, contrasts strikingly with the short-haired citizens of Herland who wear tunics quilted with functional pockets for greater free-

dom of movement in their work at creating and maintaining ethical
and physical culture. Not merely a reflection of the dress reform
movement, the desexualizing of women in *Herland* also shifts the
emphasis onto the multiple "livings" open to women in a society that
no longer opposes reproduction and production. Although Gilman
could point to no matriarchal, or even egalitarian, culture in recorded
history, her feminism consists in imagining a society in which the word
"woman" conjures up the whole world of exploring and toiling that
have made a two-thousand-year-old civilization, while the word
"man" means only male, the sex (p. 137). To imagine alternatives to
patriarchy, to speculate on the consequences of female primacy, even
if it may be damaging to men, is to engage in a strategy of role reversal
that is central to the feminist rhetorical tradition from Anna Denton
Cridge's *Man's Rights; or, How Would You Like It?* (1870) to the
recent essay by Bette-Jane Raphael entitled "The Myth of the Male
Orgasm."

Not content to reverse gender hierarchies, however, Gilman
would replace the parasite-siren with the fruitful mother, for she
believes that "Maternal energy is the force through which have come
into the world both love and industry" (*WE*, p. 126). The middle
chapters of *Herland* portray motherhood completely transformed,
divorced from heterosexuality, the private family, and economic dependency. Maternal feeling in Herland flows "out in a strong, wide
current, unbroken through the generations, deepening and widening
through the years, including every child in all the land" (p. 95).
Motherhood therefore serves as a paradigm of service so that labor
and nursing become the model for work. Similarly all the evils of the
private home—isolation of women, amateur unhealthy cooking, the
waste of labor and products, improper upbringing of children, lack of
individual privacy—are avoided not by destroying the idea of home
but by extending it so the race is viewed as a family and the world as its
home. Redefinitions of work, of the home, of motherhood itself
confuse the male visitors who had initially insisted that in any "civilized" country there "must be men" (p. 11). Eventually they are forced
to renounce not only this assumption but the definition of "civilization" that makes it possible.

"Civilized and still arboreal—peculiar people" (p. 17). This is
how Van first comments on the unique culture of Herland. His first
perspective of its inhabitants is a glimpse of three girls leaping, like
wood nymphs, in the branches of a huge tree. With its forests that are
cultivated like farms and gardens that look like parks, Gilman's

Earthly Paradise banishes wilderness, replacing it with cultivation. From Frances Hodgson Burnett's to Nancy Friday's secret gardens, the landscapes of women's fantasies have mediated between the extremes of savagery and civility that have defined women to their own bewilderment.[9] In fact, the crucial difference between Herland and our land is the feeling Gilman strives to give us that culture there is no longer opposed to nature. This binary dualism, resulting in the domination of nature by culture, is presented in Gilman's utopia as resolved more harmoniously, through the intercession of the female. Women, considered closer to nature because of their role in perpetuating the species, break down the dichotomy between mind and matter. The architecture Gilman uses to signal art and nature thus allied includes airy gazebos, ceilingless temples, open-air theaters. Because the all-female Herlanders define the human as female, mother earth is no longer an antagonist. The implications of the mother as landscape are quite different for the two sexes, as the strong link between feminist and ecological movements suggests.[10]

Parthenogenesis functions symbolically, then, to represent the creativity and autonomy of women, mother-daughter reciprocity, and the interplay of nature and human nature. At the same time it releases women from the female Oedipus complex, as defined by Freud: the daughter's rejection of the mother, her resulting sense of self-hatred, the extension of her desire for a phallus to desire for the man who possesses the penis. Haggard valorizes the phallic pillar of fire that strikes She dumb. Antithetically, by envisioning a race of woman born, Gilman valorizes the creativity of the womb which is, and always has been, after all, the tangible workplace of production.[11] As the male visitors admit the greater power of the overmothers, two of them are converted to what they call "loving up," a phrase that evokes "the stirring" within them "of some ancient dim prehistoric consciousness . . . like—coming home to mother" (p. 152). Analyzing the imperialist project in light of this regression, Gilman implies that the white man's burden is bound up with his not being a woman. The female, far from seeming castrated or mutilated or wounded or envious of the penis, derives her energy and her assurance from the fact that, having no penis, she cannot be castrated.[12] Gilman's radical rejection of Freud's identification of the penis with power is probably made clearest in her emphasis on the erotics of motherhood in *Herland*; "before a child comes," we are told, "there is a period of utter exaltation—the whole being is uplifted and filled with a concentrated desire" (p. 70). Yet another consequence of Gilman's refusal of the phallic law of the fathers is her dream of a common language: linguistic activity in *Herland* is characterized by extreme lucidity, the simplicity that stimulates collectivity.

Gilman is understandably vague about how a mother tongue would constitute a different kind of linguistic activity from the father's law. Yet the very word "Herland" implies that this language, mirroring the two-in-one of mother-and-child, would allow for simultaneous expression of the self as self and the self as object. Certainly Gilman criticizes the closed revelation of the Word of God, contrasting it to the "Indwelling Spirit" of service that Herlanders' worship as the accumulated mother-love of the race. Haggard's She, you remember, is obsessed with obtaining eternal life for herself and for her lover Vincey. But while Haggard criticizes the barbaric vanity of this desire of every woman for personal physical immortality, Gilman claims that the Christian doctrine of personal spiritual immortality is no less egocentric on the part of every man, "a singularly foolish idea . . . And if true, most disagreeable" (p. 116). Instead of desiring to go on growing on earth forever, her heroine wants her child, and her child's child, to go on forever. Identification with the species replaces personal identity, as Gilman insists on the importance of accepting death as an aspect of life. Therefore, while She reigns over a kingdom of perfectly preserved embalmed bodies, Gilman is careful to point out that Herlanders practice cremation. Replacing transcendent God the father with "Maternal Pantheism" (p. 59), the Herlanders expose the narcissism of Christianity, as Gilman criticizes Western civilization for the faults ascribed by Haggard to the barbarism of savages.

Gilman's garden of parthenogenesis replaces the Judeo-Christian garden of Genesis, by claiming that the authority of the father—biological or spiritual—is a myth fast degenerating to the status of a fiction. Writing at the turn of the century, Gilman implies that the disappearance of God reflects and perpetuates a weakening in patriarchal domination. But parthenogenesis, besides symbolizing the autonomous creativity of women, mother-daughter bonding, the secondariness of the male, and the disappearance of God, also effectively solves the problems of the pains and pressures produced from motherhood's status as a political institution in patriarchy: these include male dispensation of birth control and abortion, the economic dominance of the father and the usurpation of the birth process by a male medical establishment.[13] In her own time, women were becoming more vocal about the risks of venereal disease, unwanted conception, dangerous parturition, and abortion.[14] In her own life, Gilman had been profoundly afflicted by not a few of these factors. The painful experiences Gilman describes in her autobiography—of being deserted by her father at an early age, of being brought up by an economically and psychologically impoverished mother who denied her physical affection, of severe postpartum depression, shading into madness, following marriage and the birth of her daughter—are at least partially the result of the problem sexuality constitutes for nineteenth-century women.[15] In *Herland*, she gives us this experience transmuted into an enabling fantasy celebrating mother-daughter bond and hinting at her desertion of the father who, in fact, deserted her.

Gilman's inability to nurture her daughter, as well as her difficulty sustaining concentration in her work, are brilliantly dramatized in "The Yellow Wallpaper," (1892) where a nameless woman, denied pen and paper by her physician-husband during a severe postpartum depression, can neither nurture her baby nor herself as she becomes obsessed with the yellowing wallpaper in the upstairs bedroom to which she is confined. Even in the midst of her despair at her confinement in the bedroom with the baroque wallpaper in which she reads the terrible script of women's lives in patriarchy, the narrator glimpses through her window a horde of women ranging freely outdoors where everything is green instead of yellow. Moving toward these "mysteriously deep-shaded arbors, the riotus old-fashioned flowers and gnarled trees,"[16] where can these women be fleeing if not toward the groves of *Herland* where Gilman, who begins her autobiography with a reference to her identification with Queen Victoria, radically revises Ruskin's Queen's Gardens.

Yet the contrast between the fantasy women crawling in the greenly growing country, and the narrator horrified by the patterns in the yellow book of her wallpaper also reminds us that Gilman's utopia has its Gothic shadows too. Certainly part of what drives the narrator of "The Yellow Wallpaper" mad is the bedroom she is made to share with her husband. In *Herland*, men are banished from the bedroom in a fantasy that goes so far as to eliminate both desire and difference. While tenderness and friendship characterize the relationships between women in *Herland*, as they did in Gilman's life, sexuality is fairly closely identified with heterosexuality, as it is in "The Yellow Wallpaper." Even as the climax of Gilman's utopia moves toward "bisexuality"—a word that implies optimistically that heterosexuality is as singular a choice as any other form of sexuality—in fact the plot works to reduce the three male visitors to women's tools or to banish them altogether. In the final chapters of *Herland*, Terry, Jeff, and Van must accept marriage in radically new terms: without a home, without a wife, without sex. For unregenerate Terry who attempts what constitutes marital rape, there can be nothing but anaesthesia, confinement, and expulsion. Weir Mitchell's rest-cure treatment, which had caused Gilman the anguish documented in "The Yellow Wallpaper," is turned against the oppressor. The Herlanders' treatment of Terry is, moreover, similar to their response to all aberrant behavior; they use "preventive measures" instead of punishment: sometimes they "send the patient to bed" as part of the "treatment" (p. 112). The sinister ring to their rest-cures reminds us that Gilman's strategy of reversal threatens to invalidate her feminism by defining it in precisely the terms set up by the misogynists it would repudiate.

Gilman's draining away of the erotic no doubt contributes to the boredom experienced by some readers, even as it perhaps unconsciously perpetuates the Victorian ideal of the chaste angel in the house. At first glance, "negative eugenics" (p. 69)—women controlling the population by denying themselves motherhood—turns parthenogenesis into voluntary motherhood, an ideal form of birth control. On the other hand, Gilman describes how "the lowest types" of girls (those with sexual drives) are "bred out" (p. 82). While eugenics empowers woman, it entraps her in the maternal role: she is important not for herself but as the Mother of a Race that is judged in terms of the racial purity of an Aryan stock. Presumably maternal in their respect for life, moreover, the women of *Herland* are presented as innately pacifist, yet their society originated out of war. Similarly this industrialized land, capable of producing motorized cars, seems magically unpolluted by the language, by-products, labor alienation, or technology of industrialization.

While such contradictions are not uncommon in utopia fiction, their content here specifically points to tensions in feminist ideology at the turn of the century. Nineteenth-century social thinkers repeatedly associated men with war and women with peace, but the women's rights movement was born in the crucible of the Civil War. As Nina Auerbach argues, "Union among women . . . is one of the unacknowledged fruits of war."[17] Similarly, nineteenth-century feminists schooled in the abolition movement found themselves competing (often with racist arguments) against the claims of black men and generally insensitive to the double bind of black women. Finally, nostalgia for the supposed power of women in preindustrial times and hostility toward the role of science in destructively controlling women's bodies combine in feminist thinking at the turn of the century to evade the hard issue of feminism arising in and having to address itself to a postindustrial world. The daughters of *Herland* are fittingly

called "New Women" (p. 56), then, not only because they embody
Gilman's vision of a society of women born again, brand new, at the *fin
de siècle*, the beginning of a female coming of age; not only because
they represent Gilman's version of herself, now adequately nurtured
and nurturing; but also because both the strengths and the contradictions of feminism at the turn of the century are reflected so clearly in
the world she imagines.

Yet the very radicalism of Gilman's biological solution in *Herland*
pays tribute to the obdurate difficulty of altering patriarchy in a way
that her other, supposedly more utilitarian plans did not. Utopian
strategies have a special place in feminist intellectual history because
they solve two problems: rather than attacking what women have
been, they celebrate what women can yet become; instead of admitting that the political and economic strategies for creating a different
world are unclear, they imagine them already having taken place in a
different dimension, a world elsewhere. In America, we catch the
tones of fantastic speculation in Elizabeth Cady Stanton's speech to
the International Council of Women in 1888: comparing women to
"the children of Israel . . . wandering in the wilderness of prejudice,"
Stanton explains that "Thus far women have been the mere echoes of
men. . . . The true woman is as yet a dream of the future."[18] In
England, at the turn of the century, we hear those same speculative
notes sounded forcefully in Mary Elizabeth's Coleridge's poem "The
White Women."

> *Where dwell the lovely, wild white women folk,*
> *Mortal to man?*
> *They never bowed their necks beneath the yoke,*
> *They dwelt alone when the first morning broke*
> *And Time began.*[19]

Finally, in South Africa, the fantastic dreams and allegories of Olive
Schreiner, as well as her *Woman and Labour*, explore the barren
ground of female impoverishment with an eye toward a new "dream of
a Garden" which "lies in a distant future" where men and women
"shall together raise about them an Eden nobler than any the Chal-
dean dreamed of, an Eden created by their own labour and made
beautiful by their fellowship."[20]

Not only does *Herland* uncover the utopian strain of feminist
rhetoric; it also reveals the dispossession that valorized colonization as
a metaphor of female socialization,[21] leading suffragists to proclaim
punningly "No votes for women—no Home Rule." In *The Story of an*

*African Farm* Olive Schreiner most clearly explicates the anti-imperialist tradition in women's literary history. The colonies, which had been a dumping ground for redundant women in search of husbands, also served as a punishment for fictional female rebels like Moll Flanders and Hetty Sorrel. There had actually been plans by men as sober as Gladstone to solve the prostitution problem in England by shipping prostitutes to outposts of the Empire.[22] Along with numerous nuns and nurses, such women might have turned transportation into transport. As if explaining why Mary Taylor, Gertrude Bell, Mary Kingsley, Winifred Holtby, Annie Besant, and the Pankhursts did travel to the colonies as a release from the constraints Victorian culture placed on women, the African explorer Elspeth Huxley wrote a book about Florence Nightingale's life-saving exertions in the Crimea. No wonder the idea of African farming quickens the imagination of women from Schreiner and Gilman to Isak Dinesen, Doris Lessing, Margaret Laurence, and Nadine Gordimer. Even more brutally colonized than these contemporaries, Alice Walker goes "In Search of Our Mothers' Gardens": reminding us of all the silenced black women of the past and present, Walker celebrates her mother's cultivation of the wildest and rockiest landscapes in her gardens resplendant with colorful blooms. Perhaps 200 years ago, she concludes, there was such a mother in Africa.[23]

The shift from *She* to *Herland*, from the caves of Kôr to the South American or African Farm, epitomizes the dialectic between turn of the century misogyny and feminism. For, even though no simple division of labor, no neat point counterpoint, no tidy conception contraception shapes the literary contributions of the two sexes in the twentieth century, an inheritance of double colonization did reveal to women writers the utopian dreams in which they revel, of transforming psychological, social, political, religious, and even biological secondariness and disease into speculations of primacy and health. From their white dresses and hunger fasts to their shattering of mirrors, paintings, and windows, the suffragists exploited fantastic images that empowered the rhetoric of their movement. It is hardly surprising that this dream of female supremacy, being enacted as well as written, in turn aggravated male anxiety, resulting in figures like Jack the Ripper, who haunted the poorer districts of London as if they were exotic climes, hunting down prostitutes whose contamination was punished and perpetuated by the law. He became famous, in 1888, the year after *She* was published, for cutting out their wombs.

GEORGE E. SLUSSER

# Death and the Mirror: Existential Fantasy

To man today fantasy may not ultimately, as Eric Rabkin claims, be so "wholly dependent on reality for its existence" as it is on death.[1] Or, to turn the formula around, our own existence, our sense of existing in a world where life can be a dream and the dream life, has itself perhaps come to depend on a new relationship between fantasy and death. The fantasy-reality axis can operate, it seems, as long as there is belief in the self and the world as distinct and knowable entities. This is the axis of Plato's Cave, where the soul defines itself in the act of being "educated," literally led up out of illusion to reality, and where true and false seeing is not only a function of visual position, but where it is the object that determines the mode of seeing, as with *idein*—to see the "ideal" or real. This relation becomes problematical however when considered in the context of the epistemological crisis associated with empiricism. For here emphasis shifts from delineating states of illusion and reality to examining modes by which we perceive we cannot know such states. Indeed Hume, in his analysis of the perceptual process, cannot assert the existence either of a "world" or of a "self." Both then become fictions, fantasies that skepticism—the admission that we are unable to know their existence—can only rename a higher "reality." By further saying however that we cannot live in this condition of skepticism, Hume repositions the problem of the relation of self to other on a new, existential axis whose poles are fantasy—now clearly named as this reflexive encounter with an experiential world no longer composed of things but of perceptions of things—and death, the antifantasy that is absence of all perception.[2]

This empiricist relation of self and world then may be seen as a mirror relation. To Hume for example, "ideas" have become mental images, external projections of the inner imagination.[3] If there is no way beyond these images to a perception of "real" forms—that is, an external or objective realm that is not in some way a reflection of the perceiving self—then speculation becomes speculum. Introspection, too, it seems, leads to similar mirror play. In corresponding manner Hume posited a receptive "surface" within the mind that expands to create what he called a "theater" in the original sense of *theatron* or "seeing place." Here are arrayed a succession of impressions that may be no more than reflections of our external projections—mirror images of mirror images. As such these can in no way define an existential locus for a "soul" or self. In this context then the mirror assumes a special relation to what we are calling here fantasy, becomes less its condition than its vehicle. For it is the mirror that liberates fantasy, allows what was once neatly confined to the "imaginary" realm of the mind to extend its field to the surfaces of external phenomena, to shape its world theater as *speculum mundi*. Those same phantasms or shadows that once served the Platonic system as means of setting boundaries to illusion and reality, to self and other, are now proliferated by mirror surfaces that simultaneously designate their fundamental reflexivity. Thus if all images are now our shadows, then it is the mirror itself, as perceptual medium, that becomes our true double, the shadow of a perceptual dilemma from which we cannot escape.

   This is a shadow however that we do not simply project but learn to direct and adjust as well, and as such the mirror becomes a technology. Indeed, running parallel in a historical sense to this shift in epistemological focus from object to medium of perception is an increasing fascination with optical instruments and mirror effects.[4] The word "mirror" itself, to return to its root ambiguity of *mirare* and *mirari*—to see (self) or to wonder at and admire (self)—presents what is a potential vehicle for our desire to see ourselves reflected in the world. That potentiality is gradually realized through advances in optical technology that expand and extend, from the Renaissance to modern times, the function of the mirror in terms of clarity, size, and most significantly mobility and versatility. Though he bemoans the replacement in the world at large of the "glasse of trustie steele" by one of crystal—the ancient mirror by its modern counterpart—the Renaissance poet George Gascoigne nevertheless describes a mirror operation that is now seen, under the impetus of the new technology, as not merely defective or deceptive but as symbolic or, more precisely, metaphoric in nature. Gascoigne's mirrors are metaphoric because they assert that what we see in them is not simply our bare reflection or its distortion, but a reflection framed and completed by being placed in relation to some microcosmic structure—a "chain of being" that now replaces in the mirror the unmediated textures and things formerly rendered there, just as that mirror in turn is called upon to replace the phenomenal world itself.[5] Increasingly however the new mirrors come to assume a function we may by contrast call metonymic. Here alterations in the size of frame and angle of location permit the observer to displace his perceptions along a chain of reflective associations that leads not only into but through the looking glass, through the eye of the reflected self hopefully into the alien other.

Already operating in a metonymic sense is the mirror on Arnoldfini's wall in the Van Eyk painting, a mirror that promises to reveal the painter in the act of painting only to deny any such neat reflexivity. For in this convex glass, its frame in turn studded with static scenes in miniature from Christ's passion that act as metaphorical counterpoint to its extensive power, we see beyond the couple's backside to two standing men. As neither paint but only witness, they displace along the visual axis of viewer and mirror the privileged position of the single creator demanding to be reflected in his work. And by extension, in displacing the creator they displace us as well—perceivers of the painted scene who as its potential re-creators are now alienated from this perceptual system by the very mirror that promises to include us.[6] Even more radically metonymic are the later mirrors of Cocteau's *Orphée*. Here again a mirror search for self is displaced in the form of a literal passage through the mirror to the "other world" where the hero, if at first a surrogate for the self-seeking poet, increasingly drifts in his adventures beyond the mirror away from all role as explicating simile, becomes in this labyrinth of mirror exchanges recalcitrant to symbolic interpretation.[7] We witness here a desire to detach the projected image from its projector by extending it through the mirror, and in that way hoping to render the self an alien presence, the split mirror personality of Rimbaud's "je est un autre." Stranger yet however is the retention in this metonymic process of the mirror as point of transfer, as if its presence were needed to remind us constantly that reflexivity is still the base of all perceptual acts such as this exploration by association. This may explain why other optical instruments as well—indeed those apparently one-way devices such as scopes and binoculars originally conceived to help us see farther and anew—come to function eventually as mirrors. Already to a writer like E. T. A. Hoffmann, these aids to science were seen as diabolical engines that fatally limit vision in the very process of extending it. For Hoffman we become, in the act of constructing and perfecting such optical instruments, increasingly aware that sight itself is a mediated experience,

hence that these windows we would pierce in the walls of the phenomenal world are mirrors to the extent that, as media of sight rather
than just empty holes, they shape the new to our angle of vision, thus
qualify our desire to see it as an essentially reflexive operation. We
witness here the curious, even grotesque spectacle of man seeking to
liberate vision by means of the very devices—mirrors—that circum-
scribe it.

To Hoffmann and his century, this grotesqueness conceals a
lapsarian impulse. Indeed, the figure inscribed by man and his mirrors
is no longer seen to be a circle but rather a spiral whose direction is
downward. In this perspective, what appear to be neatly solipsistic
fantasies actually generate, through this insatiable desire to extend the
mirror, a continuous fall from self, the never-ending dread that, if we
may never in the act of seeing see anything that is not in some way a
reflection of ourself, we still cannot know that self through this seeing.
What we have here it seems, in the eyes of this century, is a fatal
corruption of the idea of fantasy itself, where what seems to impel this
perceptual fall is the addition of these same mirror extensions to the
original activity of *phantasein*. At its root *phantasein* means to cause to
appear in the mind. Through movable mirrors however man can frame
similarly reflexive visions outside himself, extend these reflective surfaces until, ultimately, they seem to coincide with those of the phenomenal world itself. At this point then he is forced to realize that all
percepts—in fact the very ideas and words by which he seeks to
organize external reality and in doing so fix his own relation to it—are
perhaps themselves no more than projections in a mirror. The Classical mind may have taken comfort in this ability of human art and
artifice to polish the external world so as to make it man's mirror.[8] The
Romantics however, their sense of nature as a vast profusion of
phenomena calling desperately for more and varied glasses to reflect
and contain it, saw this desire turn to anxiety, to a fear of dissipating
the self as perceptual center in a compulsive proliferation of mirror
images. Thus we have, in Baudelaire's *Fleurs du mal*, the poet's search
for self which is simultaneously an expense of self through the multi-
plication of reflexive images and scenarios. We have the passive and
voyeuristic odyssey of Rimbaud's "Bateau ivre," or De Quincey's
Piranesi sequence where the work of art itself has now become its own
internal gallery of mirrors, a new perceptual prison where man lan-
guishes in the endless recurrence of reflexive visions.

Rooted then like some primal curse in the very act of seeing, this
fear of expending and losing self in the mirrors of our fantastic percep-

tion seems to modern man increasingly an existential rather than an epistemological problem. On this level perceptual man appears to be moving toward what John Vernon calls the state of "schizophrenia," in which the act of seeing bars us finally from even knowing ourselves as existing, and we become the transparent eyeball that in seeing all must become nothing.[9] If this rift proclaims itself a sickness, it is one which, in the act of coming aware of itself as such, considers itself incurable, a sickness unto death. As such it is a condition continually reactivated by our perceptual endeavors themselves—by that *hubris* which, in developing mirrors to extend its fantasms, does not enact so much as reenact the Fall, a plunge this time directly proportionate to the rise of mirror technology and figuring the dark shadow of despair that doubles the rise of humanist science.

But the mirror also is an archetypal symbol, and on this existential level the condition of our new fantastic man may be derived from the old story of Narcissus. As Ovid tells the tale, Narcissus desires to "separate himself from his body."[10] Not content simply to gaze on his mirror image he would become that image, live his mirror adventure by transferring his "self" or soul to it, bestowing independent being upon it. Reaching however toward this image in the pool only to see it shatter, he learns that man cannot have his image both other and the same, cannot project the self and retain his own existence as imager as well. In this existential world there is no passage through the mirror but merely a drift toward it, a gradual and ultimately fatal transfer of existential locus from the projector to the projected image. Narcissus' condition then could be resumed in this distortion of Descartes' dictum: "I see, therefore am not." For instead of willing himself into being through an act of consciousness, he abdicates all possibility of being by transferring concept—the framing power of the mind—to the realm of purest percept—the mirror frame. Thus as both world and self are bound by the mirror, both these poles—in their interaction the dynamic of human existence—are contained as antithetical directions in the same closed system symbolized and actualized as mirror reflection. This system however is a self-destructive one, for to achieve pure mirror existence is to die, to have the shadow totally claim the being that has projected it.

Death then, to Narcissus, is the sole and final opponent of reflexivity. And yet as such it offers him *in extremis* a final mirror, a blank one this time which, as counterfantasy to the fantasy of the mirror of life, gives him at least the potential means of reversing both the direction of desire and the fatally reflexive process of perception itself. In the limbo that is his journey across the Styx, Narcissus looks down to catch a last glimpse of his face in the dark waters. Faced however with the inexorable pull of boat and current that marks the end of one fantasy, Narcissus embraces (we imagine) a new fantasy that does not deny the mirror so much as seek to return it to a primal role as device that reflects not the seen image but the unseen self. In his desire to see himself in the Styx, Narcissus encounters the blank mirror, the possibility of a simulacrum of death that acts as a mirror in reverse, inviting him to retrieve the sense of self lost in this fatal rift between seeing and existing by repossessing, in the split second that separates illusion from annihilation, the very images that through their mirror projection first precipitated this fall from self.

In this situation Narcissus joins—his reverse image perhaps in this mirror of death—another archetypal figure: Orpheus. Indeed it is Orpheus, moving in the opposite direction, who seeks to return from the realm of the dead to that of life. Patron of the nonvisual arts, it is he to whom it is given to reclaim his images by *not* looking at them. He then, rather than Narcissus, ultimately presides over the counterfantasy of the blank mirror. For by suspending the curse of sight—and with it the restless desire of human reason to project us farther and farther from our existential core—he strives to return to a sense of existence that is endless and immanent only because it endlessly hovers on the verge of that fatal look that precipitates our fall. In this context, Orpheus' animation of the stones takes on new meaning. For once its images are withdrawn, the mirror in its blankness becomes the place where we hope to recover what to Jung is the true self—the stone which, in becoming aware of its self-contained obduracy, localizes our return to a sense of unmediated existence.[11]

But if these mythical destinies offer a paradigm for the condition of perceptual man, they do so only in a potential sense. Indeed at the point where these two stories intersect—their respective journeys to and from the underworld meeting at the mirror which becomes the interface of life and death—the elements of a system are present. There is the possibility of a general dilemma—an inability simply to see in the intransitive sense, whose corollary is an inability simply to exist, to live free of the fatal ties we forge between the sense of sight and the pretensions of reason to control the seen world by organizing it reflexively in our own measure. There is also, to this mirror dispersion of self, the counterpossibility of reversing the function of the mirror and, at the point where it ceases to register our projected desires, using it to recapture our images and return them to their existential source.

As it exists however, such a system of desire and counterdesire is a historical product, shaped in the matrix of a technology that has allowed Narcissus to extend his mirror far beyond the original pool. Indeed with our Narcissan inventions we have gradually substituted the vehicle of perception for the object, and come to know only the mirror. Out of the reflexive isolation of this mediated condition however arises the need to perceive some primal, unmediated thing that cannot serve as vehicle to reflect us. But to us in our mirror state this is chaos, the Gorgon we cannot bear to gaze upon except in another mirror. Fear then drives us to manipulate the optical apparatus all the more frantically in hopes of preserving the reflexive mode we associate with ordered existence. Reaching the limit of existential tolerance, this tension resolves into two irreducibles—the mirror and death.

In terms of literary history this impasse is reached, it seems, in the nineteenth century. Indeed we see in the increasing frequency of Dionysian manifestations in fiction across this century—where some ineffable thing rends the fabric of our Apollonian visions of order—life flowing toward death, sight toward the heart of darkness, fantasy toward the triumphant anti-fantasy of Conrad's Kurtz facing, and uttering,the nameless Horror. This seems a realistic outcome for a literature characterized as supremely realist. And it is to the most "realistic" writers that we must turn for revelations of this blankness, for its emergence as pivot point at which the fictional act, beneath surface variances in "plot," polarizes into a psychodrama between man's now clearly Narcissistic fantasies and chaos, between reflections and the unreflecting. Such a conflict, for example, lies at the center of a work of purest "naturalism" like Stephen Crane's *The Red Badge of Courage*. Its hero Henry Fleming does not wander a battlefield so much as a field of changing focal lengths, his existence a self-reflexive space comprised of the varying mirror angles critics designate as Romantic or Stoic, dreamer or pragmatist, and which he continuously shifts or adjusts to accommodate the changing stream of impressions. This optical exercise is interrupted however, throughout the text, by a series of encounters with death that are so horrifying because what is encountered is inscrutable, a thing that cannot be accommodated to reflect the self and through that self the human form divine. The blank eyes and faces of these dead soldiers force Henry to withdraw within his now clearly tautological network of images and words; he closes his perceptual field much as the line of troops reforms around these obtrusive corpses in the hope of excluding the imageless from that eminently imaged domain he finally asserts to be that of Man.[12]

What is more, it is in what seems one of Dostoevsky's most unrelentingly realistic tales that we find this same encounter of the mirror and death specifically cast in terms of fantasy and anti-fantasy. It is customary perhaps to think of reality as some restrictive order that fantasy, with its power to change things at will, constantly abrogates. Dostoevsky however, in the Author's Note to the sparse "The Gentle One," a husband's self-indulgent monologue as he sits before the corpse of his wife who has just committed suicide, clearly inverts the meaning (and with it the function) of these two terms. What stands for the real here is an inscrutable set of acts and things that now lie forever beyond the protagonist's ken—the perceptual barrier actualized by the dumb body of the wife lying on the table, by the empty shoes standing beside the bed "as if waiting for her." The fantastic, on the other hand, is now explicitly the power that frames and adjusts the succession of mirrors by which the narrator simultaneously extends and isolates himself in his own perceptions.[13] These latter are the actions of what Dostoevsky calls his "hypothetical stenographer." Yet in the case of this perceiving subject, it is clear that he is less the glass that passively records "reality" than himself a framer of glasses that he hopes, as he frantically manipulates words and perspectives, will organize this bewildering flux of observed and remembered phenomena and ultimately shape it in his own reassuring image. If then like Crane's hero, Dostoevsky's narrator hopes endlessly to skirt the dead body that lies at the center of his perceptions, he nevertheless drifts in his mirrorings—like the analogous "stenographer" in the cited example of Hugo's *Dernier Jour d'un condamné*—inexorably toward a final meeting with blankness: "Everything is dead, the dead lie everywhere. Just solitary people, and all about—silence."[14]

If anything, Dostoevsky's terrible impasse is more acute today. Indeed the field of fantasy and the fantastic, as he defined it, may now extend (beyond even his imagining) to all imageable perceptions whatsoever, so that there are no longer even any empty shoes, and all perceived phenomena are given purpose or being to the exact degree that they reflect our desire to expand or complete ourselves in the mirrors of images or words. Correspondingly, the result of this universalization of fantasy is a radical sense of loss of self, our perception of self as existing diminishing in inverse proportion to the rise of this compulsion for mirror seeing that is now, as with Hugo's aptly named *condamné*, a sickness unto death. It is then at the point of maximum inversion between these extremes—the meeting of the mirror with death—that the counterfantasy we will examine here is generated. In the apocalyptic desires and fears of our age the mirror dream is felt to have run its course, the terrible awakening to be at hand. Modern man's response then to this sense of an ending—the blank mirror— may tap resources of the instinctual mind perhaps uncalled for till now. We are dealing here, it seems, with psychic reflex, reacting at the heart of what is a real schizophrenia—not Vernon's metaphor for a split between self and world but a deeper rift within, the alternating current of attraction and repulsion inside the single mind as it faces irreducible psychic facts: the mirror and death, the endlessly mediated and the unmediatable—to recommit existence to the act of perception so that both our images and the need to form those images are projected beyond the mirror to the darkness that is death.[15] The purpose, it appears, is to effect a swerve, at the moment of contact, that declares this blankness a mirror in reverse. It is a maneuver then that uses the proximity of death much as a drowning man could be said to use his accident—to retrieve the brute fact of self, that deep and imageless sense of existence ignored in life but now recalled in a flash in its entirety again as the drowning man is said to "see"—now perception turned inward beyond seeing—his whole life pass before him at the instant of death. The struggle then that began as we sought to transpose phenomenal to mental space is ultimately resolved within those minds as fantasy seeks to figure the unfigurable—death—in hopes of returning mind and being to their existential limits. On this profound level of man's psychic activity fantasy, facing this mind-forged blankness, turns against itself in a strange Orphic quest for life-in-death, and in doing so reveals a fundamental connection between fantasy and human existence itself.

Born then of existential pressures at the psychic core, this figure of the blank mirror forms in a sense the subtext to what are the most representative modern "texts" or fictional mirrors. We see this figure today rising from within—and transfiguring—what are our most fantastic narrative forms: the collective mirror fictions of wonder and horror. Gradually forming for example at the center of science fiction's "alien encounters"—where all too often the glass that promises to reveal the alien in the end only yields the human form that projected this promise in the first place—are presences like the black slab of Kubrick's *2001: A Space Odyssey*: organized opacity which embodies, if anything, man's growing psychic resistance to the act of mirror

perception itself. As a figure of our fears and desires, the slab materializes each time at a point of maximum tension between the individual's
narcissistic urgings to imprint his face on the universe and the void
toward which he drifts in his "odyssey." And in the final "star gate"
sequence it functions openly as the blank mirror that allows Bowman
literally to reinhabit, at the moment of death, the series of self-
projections that constitute life as reflection. As Bowman follows the
slab beyond the star gate, the images that have thus far dominated the
film—the spaceships and computers that are both our surrogates and
our extensions in space—give way to a run of "negative" visions.
These, familiar landscapes photographically inverted and alientated
so that they may be retrieved on the blank retina of Bowman's eye,
lead to a rendezvous with death in the shadowless white room. And in
this space that itself acts as a blank mirror, each time Bowman perceives another self, it is only to disappear as perceiver, to inhabit and
*become* the perceived image. In this scene the mirror fantasies of
man—beginning with Bowman as disembodied eye at the farthest
point of separation from self—devolve toward a moment of existential
awareness which is simultaneously the moment of death. As he expires
Bowman, like Narcissus staring into the Styx, reaches yearningly
toward the slab that has appeared at the foot of his bed. The slab
however does not reflect so much as literally deflect back on him the
"star child"—the embryo that in its mandala-like casing may represent
the potentiality of a self. But if life here is superimposed on death,
death in turn stares out of the too-knowing and weary eyes of this
child. In the blank mirror then such potentiality is not realized or
transcended so much as simply encapsulated, presented in death as a
stone experience that has already turned its experiencer to stone.[16]

Also, there is evidence that this same figure of the blank mirror is
working to transform the image of the monstrous at the heart of our
fictions of horror. For if before monstrosity—from its root word *mo-
nere*, to warn—was perceived in terms of portent, its ability to make
the alien take our shape or part of our shape so as to point back to us
reflexively in warning, it now shows signs of retreating toward opacity,
of becoming less the figure in the fog than the fog itself. Taking cinema
again as example, horror may be devolving toward what we experience
in those celebrations of blankness—the Bruce Lee films. The hero of
mute muscle and empty face, Lee does not reflect our fantasy projections so much as absorb them. And within the narrative, through his
ever-intensifying dance of death, he not only defeats but subsumes all
the hybrid forms of monstrosity our imagination can project—the

snake-fist fighters and demons with iron hands—causing all such images to vanish in a cinematic vortex as the camera zooms in on the
vacant surface of Lee's eye at the instant of the kill. Indeed, the great
success of these films may come from their ability to isolate each
individual viewer (on a level beyond differences of race or creed) in his
mirror posture facing as adversary death in the role of taker of images.
As the white of Lee's eye fills the screen to efface and finally deny the
image, the usual Narcissistic direction of film fantasy is reversed. We
are not drawn to lose ourselves in the chain of visual associations, to
transfer our sense of self to an image through whose eyes we experience, vicariously, more images. Instead we witness, in the erasure of
such images, the blockage of these avenues of perceptual escape until
we are brought face to face with death as absurdity in the original sense
of imperceptible blankness. We react here as we do to the final frames
of *The Chinese Connection* where Lee, in a flying death leap into
enemy guns, leaps at the same time into the screen and toward us.
Held in a final freeze frame as the guns that kill him continue to be
heard, he abides at a point that blurs all distinction between life and
death, forcing us (as image and non-image become one) to avert our
gaze from the screen not only into movie house darkness but inward
toward sightless depths of the self. Seeking to repress this merger of
mirror and death formed as Lee springs at us, we retreat psychically
toward what we hope is a state of awareness that exists *before* all
images, even those that in this film invite us again and again to expend
that existence in fantasy projections that only end each time Lee
returns the mirror to blankness.

This existential direction of modern fantasy then is equally dis-
quieting and revealing. On the one hand, as the figured mirrors of film
gradually fill with black slabs or the whites of Bruce Lee's eyes,
blankness usurps not only such surface forms as plot and character but,
in a way that has troubling implications for the future of the art itself,
the mirroring power of the image per se. And the same is true for the
verbal image. For beyond mere "non-referentiality" an opacity is now
spreading from the individual words of our growing formula literature
that is beginning to negate their very capacity to form images. As brute
things such words, in their refusal to be extended either metaphorically or metonymically, deny us access to the figured mirror in what is
no longer merely a problematic but now a highly questionable hope of
returning us to a sense of existing if only in the death of literature itself.
The future of such existential fantasy, of course, can only be specu-
lated upon. Its forms however, and the conscious elaboration of these

forms by thinkers and writers well aware of their implications, are both present and real, and can tell us much about the nature and evolution of fantasy in general. What is revealed then on the other hand, as we look back from this existential reflex emerging from our mirror fictions toward traditional works of the fantastic and traditional theories of the fantastic, is perhaps no less than a new direction of study—a new angle of approach to the problem of fantasy and a new anchor for speculation. Deeper study of the workings of these reverse mirrors will help us, in the rest of this essay, both redraw the critical map of fantasy and, finally, rename that fantasy as the basic reflex of life in the face of death.

The breadth of this fantasy response to modern man's mirror condition, and the urgency this response gives to his encounter with death, is suggested by two otherwise disparate texts: Søren Kierkegaard's *The Sickness unto Death*, and Yukio Mishima's *Sun and Steel*. Converging on a common center from wide angles of cultural variance, these texts affirm, as they consider the relation of death to the mirror structures of human perception, the operation of an existential mode of fantasy.

What Kierkegaard calls despair, his "sickness unto death," is a condition where mortal man, striving to suspend himself on the verge of certain annihilation, hopes in his endless dread to experience eternity, and through that experience regain a wholeness of existence in the present moment that is tangible and palpable. "For dying means that it is all over, but dying the death means to live to experience death, and if for a single instant this experience is possible, it is tantamount to experiencing it forever."[17] For Kierkegaard man is led to this extreme by a situation he explicitly calls "fantastic." Indeed the fantastic is "that which so carries a man out into the infinite that it merely carries him away from himself and therewith prevents him from returning to himself." Not only is man in this condition carried away from the self yet never able to reach the other of infinitude, but he is caught in a maze of mirrors in turn echoed, on the level of the text, in an incredibly reflexive prose where "imagination" becomes both the medium and the reflection of this process of infinitizing, and where in consequence "the self is reflection, and imagination is reflection . . . the counterfeit presentment of the self, which is the possibility of the self."[18] Nor can Kierkegaard's man halt this fantastic dispersion of self by embracing the opposing impulsion of finitude, for in this case flight through visions is merely replaced by total adaptation to the vision of other men, to an image of social conformity that is but another projection of our desires. Such an act again only affirms the mirror, this time by declaring us the reflection rather than the reflection us.

For man then in this fantastic condition Kierkegaard sees a dangerous gap arising between seeing and existing—between image of self and knowledge of self—that is both characterized and realized by the mirror. "Even in looking at one's *self* in a mirror it is requisite to know oneself; for, if not, one does not behold one's *self* but merely a man."[19] To Kierkegaard both finitude and infinitude are modes of the possible. And what is more, this possibility functions explicity as a mirror, indeed as no ordinary one. "For of this mirror it is true in the highest sense that it is a false mirror. That the self looks so and so in the possibility of itself is only half truth; for in the possibility of itself the self is still far from itself, or only half itself." In this field of the possible the act of seeing then, because it is mirror seeing, becomes the means by which we lose ourselves. Yet because such seeing is linked existentially to the mirror, so that we can speak of a mirror condition, we must work within this condition to invent a new form of seeing that can reverse the action of the mirror, one that leads back from the man to a sense of self, from the virtual images of the fantastic to what Kierkegaard calls "actuality," the fixing of an existential "spot" in the midst of existential drift.

At this point in his dialectic Kierkegaard introduces, as the other half of self, the element of necessity in the form of death, and asks how this necessity determines that self, otherwise lost to possibility, more precisely. The strategy is, through this counterforce, to effect an "intensifying" of the imagination, a condensation of the mirror medium itself, that will transform possibility into "the possibility of the intensity of the self."[20] But if, as implied here, necessity is also to act as a mirror, it is explicitly as a blank one. Indeed to Kierkegaard, man in the state of necessity is "dumb." Deprived of all possibility by the constant presence of death, his words and images are reduced to a blank sequence of consonants. To articulate these anew is to revive possibility at the imageless center of necessity, to make bodily contact with the absolute certainty of our death and yet not succumb to it. Using the consistently physical and kinetic imagery associated with this mode of fantasy, Kierkegaard calls this recovery "the fight of faith." The medium of this struggle is a new language beyond language, the blankness of obliterated mirror images respoken and reseen by a form of expression that is silent, immanent awareness of self as pure unmediated existence. Out of this unending contact with death then we wrest the promise of an endless and shadowless present—the existential self retrieved from the fragmentation of the mirror world, from those projections of self backward and forward, toward the past or the future, that designate our Fall. This process is condensed in the phrase "dying the death," where it is language itself that now steals the abstract image from its own mirror in hopes of infusing it with the dynamics of an impossible existence.

In Mishima's text as well we find a like yearning to restore to man—again caught in a "logical gap" between existing and seeing that only death can wholly close because its source lies in the human mind and its fatal need to project self out of self, to perceive the self in its fantastic reflections—a "loquacity" which is that of immanent physical existence itself, a "splendid language of the flesh" that denies the mirror condition and yet (insofar as it is a language) is shaped in that mirror darkened as we recuperate one by one the images by which we extend ourselves to people the surfaces of our "world." For Mishima however the fight of faith is a literal one, and the language of new possibility he cultivates that of the martial arts—the rigorous training for an encounter with self that is flesh-awareness operating in an existential space always a hairbreadth from death.

For Mishima the true existential ground for our words and perceptions is not the figured mirror but rather what he calls "the vast white walls in the waiting room where we await the arrival of the physician, the absolute."[21] It is onto this blank continuum, this "void of the progressive," that our words and images project their "false endings," striving to articulate and hence mitigate its terror. Caught in a paradoxical situation, where a more and more urgent cultivation of these fantasies of finitude only leads to the infinite projection of self outside of self, "the unhealthy tendency of the soul to soar off in a boundless quest after truth, leaving the body where it always was," man must find a means of retrieving the images he projects, of returning the mirror he animates to its original blankness. Mishima recounts a boyhood experience in which this return occurs. Watching monks carry a heavy shrine through the streets, he looks into their upturned eyes and imagines himself, looking through their rapture, seeing divine visions in the sky. But later, as he shoulders the same shrine, he experiences only fatigue, and realizes that the true nature of the "intoxicating vision" produced by such "violent physical stress" is emptiness—"In their eyes there was no vision, only the reflection of the blue and absolute skies of early autumn."[22] The revelation is that of a controlled exhaustion that returns us to our fundamental selves as it turns dreams into muscles. To achieve that revelation the empty sky acts as a mirror in reverse. A "strange compound of lucidity and madness," its blankness forces us to recover substantiality for our phantasms not by alienating them but by shaping them in what is the ultimate distorting matrix of death. In this experience images become the "opponent," the "thing" that stares back where ideas do not, "the great black bull of the toreador" bearing down on us "without any agency of the imagination." It is this death that unifies apple and core—the seen exterior and the unseen interior—in the act of destroying both.[23]

Like Kierkegaard, Mishima presents this effort to retrieve one's sense of existence from the mirrors of perception as both a fall and a leap—a leap that simultaneously designates our perceptions as our shadows and detaches us from these shadows, moves us into a shadowless realm where, in the split second before death, we reexperience existence at the heart of blankness. Mishima finds such detachment and awareness in a jump from a parachute tower. "Beneath the summer sunlight, I had seen, thirty-five feet below me, people's shadows sharply etched and firmly attached to their feet. I had jumped into space from the summit of the silver tower, aware as I went of how the shadow that I myself would cast among them the next instant would lie isolated like a black puddle on the earth, untied to my body. At that moment I was, beyond all doubt, freed from my shadow."[24] In the same manner as Mishima's living-statue impersonations of the martyrdom of St. Sebastian, or his movie enactments of a hara-kiri he was later to commit, the parachute jump is a fantasy that operates existentially in this same shadowless space where the moment of death and that of revelation conflate—that repeatable yet impossible moment when the seer makes tactile "acquaintance with the world of those who are 'seen.'"

Mishima's living statues and film parables however only emphasize the paradox that ultimately circumscribes all such acts of existential fantasy in those arts dominated by the visual imagination—the necessity of using images to render the negation of image that marks these creative encounters with death. Mishima feels this problem even more acutely in the case of words. He is painfully aware that, in such locutions as the "waiting room" of the void or the "physician" of the absolute, language in its very yearning to express the imageless seems doomed to fall back on the image. Moreover, he constantly blames words for being the most mirrorlike of media, in whose use we most completely lose the sense of ourselves as existing. As writer of words then, he is driven to find strategies that allow him to replace reflexivity—the domain of the image—with intransivity—the domain of pure, progressive existence in and for itself. Hoping in his death-drenched parables to restore to words themselves the opacity of that death, he proposes to convert the text itself into a blank mirror that will effect (in the writer and the reader) a transfer from possibility to necessity, from a state of seeing (that fantastic dissipation of the stuff of self in the mirror images of what, to Mishima, is all other prose today) to one of simply existing. "The steps it was necessary to take to acquire another existence involved flinging myself bodily on the side of the phantom evoked and radiated by words; it meant changing from a being that created words to one that was created by words; it meant . . . using subtle and elaborate procedures in order to secure the momentary shadow of existence."[25] The writer then must learn to write (and by analogy the reader to read) existentially, to reframe his words as blank substance by projecting himself bodily into these "radiated" phantasms, giving them opacity (and hence existential locus) through his own linguistic death leap. Mishima's desire to write intransitively however—not to write something or about something in order to write oneself, but simply to write free of all mirror constraints—confounds the reflexivities of language only by confounding those two ultimate intransitives: to exist and to die. For in his existential grammar we do not perceive ourselves as writing until we become the thing that is written, do not then perceive ourselves as existing until we cease to do so. As we hurl our flesh at it, the word (and beyond it the image in general) is simultaneously inhabited and assassinated.[26]

Mishima attributes his obsession with the mirror "sickness" of words to a boyhood fixation on Western Romanticism—on "Novalis's night and Yeatsian Irish twilights." To heal this sickness then, he must blank these self-indulgent glasses, seek to retrieve from them the momentary shadow of his own existence by making language itself, the Romantic medium par excellence, an alien aggressor, by pressing from words a hostile dumbness that increasingly devolves toward the point where self-expression coincides with suicide. Words then he finally subjects to the elaborate—and instinctively wordless—procedures of the martial arts. Through these he longs to recover a sense of existence no longer "endorsed" by words but by muscles alone; he would force these muscles—what he calls the "essence of non-communication"—through contact with mute discipline and blank steel to communicate the self to the self in an immanent fashion. In such a manner Mishima yearns "to revive the dead language . . . to change the silence of death into the eloquence of life." His strivings then, not "simply to see, without words" but to create actual "words of flesh," both call for a new language arising from the blank mirror of death and point to the difficulty of realizing such a language in the verbal context of fiction. In this sense his desires gloss what has been called in E. T. A. Hoffmann's work "verbal music"—music that in the text ultimately seeks to devolve beyond either word or sound to the pregnant silence of gesture. At the same time they designate Hoffmann's first story of music and musical creation, "Ritter Gluck," the *locus classicus* for such a fictional encounter of death and the mirror. Indeed in "Ritter Gluck," what is called "music" operates as a counterlanguage that gradually reclaims the divisive images projected by words, seeking to resolve the fatal distortions that arise between man and his mirrors—between the musical idea and its performance, the artistic dream and boorish reality, the ideal past and philistine present—in a kinetic realm of gesturally immediate expression, the endlessly renewable moment of pantomimic creation. What we have in the "music" of this "Gluck"— two entities significantly for whom the word alone cannot fix an image—is a dance that whirls away the bright figures and false endings from those mirrors of human fantasy that have become the all-embracing "reality," a dance of death in which we cannot tell the dancer from the dance, and as such a counterfantasy of life-in-death where is reborn, beyond word and image, the endless hope of reexperiencing self in some silent and shadowless prelapsarian wholeness as seer seeing, as creator creating.

The existence of the strange musician "Gluck" in Hoffmann's tale has generally been explained as a figment of the narrator's imagination, his mirror double. This narrator may initiate the fantasy, but in the story he is reclaimed by it, the shadower absorbed by his shadow. Indeed the problem here is not whether "Gluck" exists but how he exists, and how in coming to exist he restores the narrator to a sense of his own existence. "Ritter Gluck" then is about the process whereby we, as the double of the narrator, change from a being that creates words and images to one that is created by them. It is about learning to fling ourselves bodily on the side of the phantoms we project in order to experience ourselves as existing. But it is also, ultimately, a story about blanking the mirror, about man at the heart of his perceptual dilemma converting the image into an alien "thing." In "Ritter Gluck" the narrator releases the aggressor that would create him rather than he it. In doing so he is made to operate in a frame of life-in-death where the impossibility of this musician's existence and the very tangible fact of that existence have become one.

The narrator of Hoffmann's tale is his "traveling enthusiast." As such he is the archetypal observer, the man of vision and visions, perceptual man incarnate. What is more, in this particular context of the *Fantasiestücke*, he is the artist who desires to work "in Callot's manner." Indeed, as the story opens he sits in a café on a busy Berlin thoroughfare in late autumn of 1809 observing the comings and goings of the crowd. Soon it is obvious however that what at first seems accurate and "realistic" description of external phenomena is instead the elaboration of a projected mind frame, the cultivation of mirror "reflexes" that do little more than fix the phantasms of a narrational existence that is being dissipated in the very act of seeing.[27] It is clear, in the short sketch that frames the *Fantasiestücke* and "Ritter Gluck," that Callot himself, as addressed by this narrator, is both his double and one in the process of breaking away from his creator. The same dynamic is inherent in Callot's art, which is presented at one and the same time as a mirror activity and the obfuscation of such activity. Considering the "grotesqueness" of Callot's images—especially the resurgence of animal traits in human forms—the narrator describes a process of regressive, atavistic distortion that gradually clouds the images in the mirrors the artist creates. Indeed, it is this hybridizing of forms that is the visual grotesque that provides the paradigm, in "Ritter Gluck," for the increasing split between projector and shadow, respectable critic and "mad" musician, that occurs as sound and gesture distort and finally usurp the functions of visual and verbal images altogether. In "Ritter Gluck" the agent of this grotesque is explicitly music. And it is under the sign of music that the narrator's descriptions, once uttered, are refracted toward caricature, then displaced by the cacophony of a street band, only to be dispelled entirely by the appearance of an image that cannot be an image, the impossible "Gluck" who as incarnation of music is Callot's mix of scurrility and mystery come to independent life. The narrator's progress in this opening paragraph then is less a withdrawal from the real to the fantastic than a displacement from words to music, from a visual to a nonvisual mode of fantasy.

In general, Hoffmann is fascinated with the possibilities and consequences of losing one's mirror image. Significantly, in the story "The New Year's Adventure," he doubles Peter Schlemiehl's loss of his shadow with his hero Spikher's loss of a "Spiegelbild." In doing so he shifts the emphasis from what in Chamisso was social stigma—others' perceptions of our loss of shadow or image—to a process that is fundamentally intransitive and existential in nature.[28] For Spikher in reality does not lose his image so much as it simply ceases to obey, falls out of synchronization with its projector in the grotesque distortions of the mirror until it begins to move independently of him. In the case of "Gluck" then, it is this alienated shadow of the narrator who must now struggle not to throw its own shadow, to retrieve all possible projections that might tie it to a past or a future so as to abide at the high noon of a shadowless present, existence aware of itself as simply existing. This is what "Gluck" means when he calls himself "gestaltlos"—the shadowless condition he maintains in those performances where, through a language of sound and flesh that reverses the process of reflection and turns creation into a thing-in-itself, he now captures the narrator this time as his double, drawing the man of visions and words—and with him the Berlin society that has debased Gluck's music by severing the image (here the contemporary productions that have dissipated its existential soul) from the creative source in the instant of composition—back to an unmediated sense of self.

Such a performance, and mutual *prise d'existence*, is the so-called "conducting" scene. Here "Gluck," in response to the small street band's playing of the overture to *Iphigenia in Aulis*, begins to mime as if conducting an orchestra. This scene would be comic were it not for the immediate and unreflecting acceptance of the narrator. The rationalist vision, dependent upon observation and the reflective distance between entities, could only apprehend such a spectacle as the faintest image of an image, the travesty of a work of art. Just the opposite is true however. What we have is a case of the image, through a process that is the reverse of reflection, reclaiming its own independent existence. For if "Gluck" begins his pantomime tied to this street band as its debased image, through his movements he gradually transfers this paltry music—the shadow of an opera written by Gluck and itself debased by the critics and musicians of Berlin until it has become a vulgar street tune—back to his own vital existence, incarnates it in the facial expressions and almost involuntary "Muskelspiel" of his physical being. In this way, explicitly, a "bare skeleton" is "fleshed out," and the musical composition returned to the existential moment of its conception.[29] And simultaneously, as the shadow breaks free to existence, so "Gluck" himself, the narrator's shadow, through his incredible mimic activity, draws his own projector to participate body and soul in the re-creation of his refurbished "music"—to "hear" it sensually with the inner ear of physical empathy, to re-create it at the center of a being itself re-created in the process. The narrator then hurls himself bodily on the side of a phantom just as that phantom had hurled himself, in his gestural music, on the side of an image "radiated," dispelled by the words of his age—the sterile critical disputes or "Schwatzen von Kunst" in which the existential act of composing is lost.[30]

Explicitly, however, this danger of words proves much greater in that inner "realm of dreams" that the musician revisits and describes in the next episode. For here the expense of the creative self through the proliferation of images is not so easily countered, as in the outer world of Berlin society, by a mute language of nerve and muscle that "expresses," in the literal sense of pushing forth, the hidden and resistent core of existential man. Through the ivory gate, though, the direction is inward, to that inverted world of reflections where the mind's surface has become the mirror. This then is a world of pure image that cannot be reached by sound or flesh. As such it is a hollowing out of the existential core, a vortex where in dreaming we dream away the dream, melt to insubstantiality (*zerfliessen*) in the flow of images, of uttered or "radiated" words that have totally displaced the radiating power of music. Here to cast no shadow is to be the imager absorbed by his images, the speaker swallowed by his words. But to attach and secure these images, to reestablish the bond of shadow between them and their creator, the speaker seeks to transform words into something like "verbal music." This does not mean making them more "melodious" in the sense of free-flowing, but rather the opposite, more solid and obdurate. It is no accident that to "Gluck" opera is the highest form of musical expression, for it anchors melody in the existential substance of drama. Thus as the musician thrusts himself into the realm of free-floating forms, pushing confrontation with this inner mirror of dream to the existential extreme of *Liebestod* where the leap into the nothingness of the image becomes a tangible fall into a vortex through this action reconstructed as a giant sunflower, the images are automatically restructured as opera, and the verbal description of this adventure solidified into what is clearly musical drama.

What is fleshed out here gradually, as the speaker begins to repossess his words, is no less than the theoretical skeleton of the Gluckian opera itself, and the images that literally awaken and stride through this landscape of dream are the tonic and dominant chords that define its particular structure.[31] Through the musician's actions light itself—as pure visual medium the ethereal "soul" of the mirror relationship—is made a protagonist in this struggle of life and death, its beams devolving first to notes, then to palpable entities that finally fuse with the images they would project in a union of agent and act. In

like manner the eye, as organ of perception forfeiting all claim to
existence in its closed relationship with the mirror, is liberated from
this circuit. As the musician-hero encounters this same eye in precise
physical loci—first in an organ, then in the giant sunflower—it reverts
from means of dissipating self to one of recovering self, projecting
images backward so that they gather thickness and sensual bulk,
passing from the audible through the edible finally to the tactile. This
"grosses helles Auge," in this new function, is the blank mirror of
death. Reflected in it, this moment of greatest synesthetic totality, the
living union of five scattered senses, coincides with the moment of
greatest fall—the hero sucked into the eye of the sunflower where light
has become consuming fire. As death then, in the manner of Mishima,
finally transfers "Gluck" from the state of seeing to that of being seen,
the moment of his disappearance becomes that in which we are most
aware of his fantastic presence as shaper of existential opera, as teller
in words of flesh.

Both in these pantomimes and in this verbal music the creative
self is reconstituted in a dark mirror which is that of death—the limits
that decree that Gluck cannot exist in 1809. For the musician in this
story to create is to exist, and it is through such "performances" that he
strives to abolish those "endings" that to Mishima banish existence in a
creative present to some particular and perishable locus in time and
space—in this case the past of a music written by a historical figure long
dead, and the future of Gluck's compositions misperformed. Contrary
to what has come to be the accepted fantasy of permanence through
art, in Hoffmann's tale projections of self into the mirror of art do not
free the creative being from time so much as bind him all the more
firmly to a given time and place. In "Gluck's" final rendition of the
overture to *Armida* however all such projections—the dated work and
its subsequent dated performances—are taken back from this mirror.
Taking the narrator to his room, the strange musician announces that
he will now substitute for all distortions past or future a true version of
*Armida* in the emphatic present—"Sie sollen *jetzt* Armida hören." As
he begins to perform, his old-fashioned furnishings and decor—images
that seem to anchor him in a historical past, hence make him, as
madman or imposter, but another corrupter of Gluck's work—fall
away like masks. Once again he captures a single image, this time not a
street band but the overture to a representative work, the beginning
point for this elaborate process of retrieval. Now combining both
gesture and music he transfers external forms to the ultimately silent
eloquence of the flesh, and in doing so liberates the "essential ideas" of

Gluck's music altogether from their accretions of time and space, returns them to life in "verjüngter Gestalt." This musician then, who as the narrator's double was in the beginning all form and no substance, has now himself, as he becomes less the spirit of music (another image) than the existential process of musical creation, become timeless, "gestaltlos" in the sense of ties to any specific period or school.

"Gluck" then works to close that gap between composition and performance that Hoffmann and his contemporaries saw as the curse of the musician—the necessary dispersion of the creative self in the images of that self which are the works, as Plato calls them in the *Phaedrus* "parentless" shades to be distorted at will as they are reprojected, reuttered.[32] First the score, then the audience—the music's past and its future, the source and goal of musical performance—are rendered empty, blank surfaces, mirrors that no longer reflect. The audience for this Ur-performance, the lone and nameless narrator, dwindles in turn, as the primal moment of creation is reborn in this gestural and kinetic present, to a vanishing point. Taking up the gold-bound volumes of what he believes to be Gluck's complete works, the narrator opens the one marked *Armida* only to find empty lined note paper. Accepting in the heat of performance to turn these empty pages "zur rechten Zeit," he further relinquishes all role as music critic to become another such blank form, one literally read in reverse by the musician. Through this experience the narrator is displaced in time and space ("Was ist das? Wer sind Sie?"), dispossessed of those images of self that serve to anchor him in Berlin in 1809. As the visible notes, then the sounds themselves are taken from him, he comes to perceive with his innermost physical being, and as he does so loses himself to the other, becomes "gestaltlos" as well. The double here has absorbed his projector, and as "Gluck" steps forth in the final scene with his candelabra, the image or creature of light has become the vital source of that light. Again however, the gap between seeing and existing closes only at a moment of interface with death. For here the final union of musican and narrator, of word and flesh, in a mutual *prise d'existence*, is shattered by the musician's statement of identity and last words in the story, "Ich bin der Ritter Gluck." For if through the musician's actions Gluck lives, through his words he dies, for in this very declaration of his existence he names himself as titled, outmoded—a dead man.

What happens in "Ritter Gluck" then, the transfer of the fantasy process from the plane of seeing to that of existing, is important for understanding the nature of this mode. For more than simply a way of seeing, fantasy has become a means (precipitated by this need to see anew) of recovering the self from the mirrors of a very real perceptual crisis. Curiously, both reigning views of the fantastic mode are oriented toward the visual faculty, toward the idea of fantasy as a means of seeing anew. To Eric Rabkin the fantastic, as a basic mode of human knowing, ultimately extends our field of vision in order to effect revolutionary change.[33] And Tzvetan Todorov, in asserting that the role of the fantastic has been taken over in modern times by psychonanalysis, claims for the genre the status of protoscience, and considers it the means of imagining or visualizing causal relationships between apparently unrelated facts that have since been corroborated by science.[34] Both these views are basically rationalist, and as such tend to ignore the fears that haunted Hoffmann and Mishima—the dread of a fall that is prolonged by fantasy, by the dispersion of being that is a necessary consequence, in our fallen world, of the very act of seeing itself. To both these writers it is such faculties as art and reason—and their extension which is visual fantasy—that perpetuate this fall by allowing man to polish the opaque things of nature so that they reflect him, and in doing so permit him to locate the center of his being outside himself at the point of admirative attention defined by this act of seeing. The counterdesire however—the need to blank these mirrors we erect in our seeing, must also be called a fantasy. Indeed, to call it so is to reposition what Todorov designates "hesitation" on a deeper level of tension—that between reflection and reflex, between the rational impulsions of eye and ego and a prerational drive to return to the original obdurate wholeness of selfhood. It is significant in this regard that Hoffmann's "Gluck" refuses this dispersion of self along the visual axis in both directions—outer and inner, that of Rabkin's fantastic of social progress and that of Todorov's fantastic of expanding consciousness. On the contrary, "Gluck's" gestural fantasy works counter both to the historical realm of opera houses and music critics, and to the "eternal" realm of dreams. His "performances" suspend time on both levels as changes in critical taste and as cyclical mutations of myth—at a point of hesitation that returns man to a state of existence. Hoffmann's musician then, transposing fantasy from an epistemological realm to an existential one, has placed it on the side not of light but of life.

In addition, by relocating the hesitation that has been said to define this mode on an existential level, we may have a means of clarifying the terminological problems that till now have beset it, of distinguishing between the rival claims of "fantasy" and the "fantastic" for predominance in the definitional system. This relocation permits us to rename the places on Todorov's map of the fantastic, for example. Todorov considers the "uncanny" and the "marvelous," modes tangential to his central figure of hesitation, as structures other than and opposed to the fantastic. But by calling these two forms themselves (in agreement with both Hoffmann and Freud) fantastic, we can bring them into a systematic relationship with the existential reflex of the blank mirror, and in contrast name that reflex fantasy. Indeed, in the workings of the uncanny and the marvelous, as Todorov defines them, we can retrace the now familiar patterns of that perceptual dilemma associated with the rise of the mirror consciousness. On his grid Todorov relates, on the level of how we read the text, the allegorical to the uncanny insofar as that uncanny presents a supernatural that is explained and explainable, and the poetical to the marvelous where the supernatural resists all such explanation. In the former then the text could be said to function as a vertical mirror in which, as its images "place" us as viewer in its larger illustrative context of order, we lose our literal to its figurative being.[35] In the latter, on the other hand, the text serves as a horizontal mirror in which the viewer does not exchange a literal for a figurative existence so much as project that same literalness along the axis of the poetic image, and in doing so transfer it to those images so as to render them alluring passage points into another world. To embrace the marvelous then is to extend the glass outward until the viewer loses all sense of the self as point of resistance to this drift through the mirror. To embrace the uncanny, on the other hand, is to return the mirror to the mind. Though initiated by reason, this retraction of the field of perception can lead to consummate irrationality wherein the mind, as final figurable space, declares itself the only knowable realm—a substitution of figurative for literal mirror that ultimately denies even the possibility of seeing and knowing an external world. The difference then between these two fantastic impulsions is subtle but real—for the marvelous life is a dream, for the uncanny the dream is life. Behind the latter impulsion lies that centripetal motion designated as "classical," where reason draws in the radius of its mirror vision until it ends in the perceptual isolation of skepticism. Behind the former is the centrifugal reaction we call "romantic," where the existential center of being is not lost through contraction but rather through dispersion—the uncontrollable profusion of images toward an ever-receding perceptual horizon.

At their core these are less quandaries of literature than of life.

And it is on this plane of living, we contend, that the mind is drawn to deal with this mirror condition in a way that resists both of these fantastic impulsions. To Todorov, the marvelous represents a drift toward the not-yet-seen, the future, while the uncanny, in its retreat toward the *déjà vu*, embraces limits that constitute a past. Both forms then function in constant denial of a present—indeed to such a degree that for Todorov the present in this system exists only as "pure boundary" between these two impulsions. "Hesitation" then defines a genre that, in terms of narrative and its tendency to develop and resolve a story in terms of narrated and narrational time and space, must as this boundary point necessarily remain "evanescent." Even Todorov however suggests that beneath these language forms lie those of life, indeed that these forms of life and the mind may even generate the literary superstructure of the fantastic.[36] To be sure, it is at the point where this evanescent literary present intersects with the fatal dread of an existence endlessly lost in the act of seeing that the fantastic becomes the central means of understanding our modern mirror dilemma. At this same point however arises the counterstrategy by which the mind strives to resolve this dilemma. Indeed, if the anti-verbal and anti-imagistic acts of Mishima and Hoffmann's "Gluck" are fantasy, they redefine fantasy perhaps in its most primal sense as man's existential reaction to the fantastic. This fantasy then is a desire to obscure and solidify the hesitational instant which would endlessly tip us back one way or another into the mirrors of the fantastic, to make it the obtuse place to which we recall our images, the place of intersecting life and art, death and the mirror, that in its opacity is pregnant with the possibility of self-awareness—the awareness of self existing in this present suspended hesitationally beyond the fatal fall into sight. In this darkness sensed and sensible then, our existence seeks to reconstitute itself as anti-narrative, as a thing untellible, hence unlocatable in imaged, articulated time and space. And finally, it would reconstitute itself in a way that reverses the normal path of existentialism. For in this mode of fantasy he who hesitates is not lost but on the contrary regains his sense of existing. We have then, in the opposite direction from Pascal's "vous êtes engagé," existence through resistance to all commitment to the flow of time and image.

Finally, the operations of this existential fantasy may be located in the involuntary mental processes Freud calls "dreamwork," that dream within the dream of our mirror projections that displaces and condenses all images toward and around that center of resisting obduracy which is the self.[37] If Freud does not openly trace the new fantasy direction of this dreamwork, he nevertheless responds in his formulations to the specific psychic pressures of his age. This new direction however is clearly seen by one of Freud's most recent commentators, J.-F. Lyotard. For if Lacanian psychology still reinforces the separation between seeing and existing by binding us to the "orthopedic" function of our projected images, Lyotard sees the dreamwork drawing these same images toward reintegration with more primal forms of the mind and self, the opaque "phantasms" of that dream activity he designates (with the word Freud borrowed from Hoffmann) as *phantasieren*.[38] Going farther than Freud, Lyotard claims the dream not only does not think but does not speak either. Again by contrast, in the Lacanian mirror, language is the prime means of reaffirming the ego (here the entity that predicates objects and in doing so creates a "dialectic of identification" in which linguistic patterns themselves become a mirror of words) in its function as subject. Lyotard however sees the action of dream as obscuring this verbal mirror, closing the distance between image and perceiver, and thus between ego and self, by closing the linguistic space Lacan says creates and perpetuates it. The work of displacement and condensation then is less a "travesty"—our images "dressed" in the forms of some ultimately unknowable external world—than a retraction of the words and images of this dream of life toward the original opacity that generated them.[38] As this dreamwork compresses and rearranges the linear projections of word and image around some primal and unyielding matrix of the mind, surprising us with a redistribution of elements that is "tout à fait improbable," we discover what Lyotard calls the "figure," the fundamental (and fundamentally existential) form created at this point where image meets imager. Language then does not "express" a figure so much as it is "habité, hanté" by it. Language becomes, in this "figurative" state, the blank mirror in which we can no longer tell the figurer from the figure. Yet the sense of unity regained in these phantasms—as they figure the pure activity of dreaming rather than any imagistic content of the dream—is ultimately that of the unreflecting and prereflexive Id, the inscrutable desire within that corresponds to Mishima's "vast white walls" of the material world without. Once again, the matrix in which we recover the immanence of self is death, the negation of selfhood.

It is Hoffmann of course, not Freud, who first located these reverse mirrors in the mind, who first saw in them a subconscious survival response to what is a precise historical act of consciousness—the development of the mirror through a technology that, as agent of the fantastic, endlessly reactivates the fall of man. Hoffmann however does not stop here. For if he finally considers fantasy, in its ultimate form, as an existential reflex, it is in order to show man all the more terribly in the grips of a perverse destiny. In his great tale of scientific curiosity, "Der Sandmann," we discover of course the temptation of the image as a profusion of eyeglasses is spread before the bewildered hero Nathanael, so many potential angles of vision on the world. And all prove reflexive, for we look with Nathanael through the fatal glass in which he discovers that each man, mirrorlike, perceives his own reality and is isolated in it. But if Nathanael in response seeks to cultivate, in his poems and his actions, the blank mirror of death in hopes of retrieving some sense of self from the fatal vortex of images that lures him, his acts ultimately reveal that such fantasies of dying the death do not abolish death but summon it instead. Indeed, with Nathanael, Hoffmann exhausts fantasy in order to show that even blank mirrors remain mirrors, that through them man has sought to engineer his response to reality down to the very level of instinct. This ultimate hope of escaping fate then becomes its most gruesome twist, and the blank mirror the final illusion of that "devil" that (to Hoffmann) man in his *hubris* has loosed and continues to loose upon himself. Nathanael begins his dance of retrieval only to spin "like a wooden doll." In that spinning dance he does not withdraw into the pregnant silence of "words of flesh" but utters slurred nonsense, glass and eye are "condensed" only to be twisted atavistically into the pidgin-German "Sköne Oke." And in his final encounter with the mirror, he does not (like "Gluck" or even Mishima) suspend the fall but merely reenacts it in a particularly gruesome way. On a high tower, spinning in a destructive rage that devolves through animal bruteness to the inanimate "life" of the wood doll, Nathanael looks down at the crowd below and perceives his fatal mirror creation—the "sandman" Coppelius—looming up at him. Leaping from this tower, he seeks to rejoin the shadow by the familiar plunge into the mirror. This time however there is neither freeze frame nor parachute, no blank mirror in which existence is recovered in the split second before death. All such mirrors of the mind yield here to hard pavement, the stone of self to real stone. Nathanael reclaims his shadow in a final breakthrough to reality—to the real blankness of real death.

**Notes**
**Biographical Notes**
**Index**

# Notes

## The Descent of Fantasy

1. The term "semiobiology" was suggested by Wladyslaw Godzich at a "Conference on Theories of Narrative" held in Bloomington, Indiana, 24–26 October 1980, under the auspices of the Department of English of Indiana University and the Society for Critical Exchange. It was at that conference that I first began to organize diverse ideas I had had into a form that led to this essay. I wish to thank many people for their stimulation and comment at that conference, especially David Bleich, Ralph Cohen, Jonathan Culler, Paul Hernadi, Mary Louise Pratt, Gerald Prince, Leroy Searle, and James Sosnoski. In addition, much of my thinking about evolution in particular and science in general has been stimulated by conversations with colleagues at the University of Michigan and in particular with Richard Alexander, Gordon Kane, Matthew Kluger, and Roy Rappaport. I thank them all.

## How New is New?

1. See Judith Merrill, "What Do You Mean: Science? Fiction?" in *SF: The Other Side of Realism*, ed. Thomas D. Clareson (Bowling Green, Ohio: Bowling Green University Popular Press, 1971), p. 60 and, in the same volume, James Blish, "On Science Fiction Criticism," p. 167.
2. See Merrill, "What Do You Mean," p. 54; Samuel Delany, "Interview," *Argol* (1976), 17–18; and Kingsley Amis, who quotes Heinlein in his *New Maps of Hell: A Survey of Science Fiction* (New York: Harcourt, Brace, 1960), p. 61.
3. See Stéphane Spriel and Boris Vian, "Un Nouveau Genre littéraire: la 'science fiction,'" *Les Temps Modernes*, no. 72 (Oct. 1951), 626; David Ketterer, "The Apocalyptic Imagination, Science Fiction, and American Literature," in *Science Fiction: A Collection of Critical Essays*, ed. Mark Rose (Englewood Cliffs, N.J.: Prentice-Hall, 1976), p. 149; and Peter

Nicholls, "Science Fiction: The Monsters and the Critics," in *Science Fiction at Large*, ed. Peter Nicholls (London: Victor Gollancz, 1976), p. 178. I am quoting and paraphrasing, respectively, Nicholls's account of De Bono's and Toffler's contribution to the same volume.

4. Ray Bradbury, *The Martian Chronicles* (Garden City, N.Y.: Doubleday, 1946), pp. 49–53.

5. Ibid., pp. 31–32.

6. Michel Butor, "Science Fiction: The Crisis of its Growth" in *SF: The Other Side of Realism*, p. 157.

7. See Mark Rose's introduction to *Science Fiction: A Collection of Critical Essays*, p. 1; Robert Scholes and Eric S. Rabkin, *Science Fiction: History, Science, Vision* (New York: Oxford University Press, 1977), p. 131; John Huntington, "Science Fiction and the Future," in *Science Fiction: A Collection of Critical Essays*, pp. 156–66; and Stanislaw Lem, "Robots in Science Fiction," in *SF: The Other Side of Realism*, pp. 307–25.

8. C. S. Lewis, "On Science Fiction," in *Science Fiction: A Collection of Critical Essays*, p. 109.

9. Eric S. Rabkin, *The Fantastic in Literature* (Princeton, N.J.: Princeton University Press, 1976), p. 119.

## Jules Verne: Journey to the Center of Science Fiction

1. The present essay in somewhat different form is reprinted by permission of the publishers from *Alien Encounters: Anatomy of Science Fiction*, by Mark Rose, Cambridge: Mass.: Harvard University Press, Copyright © 1981 by the President and Fellows of Harvard College.

2. "The *Nautilus* and the Drunken Boat," *Mythologies*, tr. Annette Lavers (New York: Hill and Wang, 1972), pp. 65–67.

3. *Journey to the Center of the Earth*, tr. Robert Baldick (Harmondsworth: Penguin Books, 1965), p. 47. Further citations are given in parentheses in the text. English translations of Verne being notoriously unreliable, I have checked the relevant passages in Baldick against the original in *Le Grand Jules Verne* published by Librairie Hachette.

4. In supposing the pole to be marked by a volcano opening into the earth's interior, Verne was employing the notions of the early nineteenth-century American proponent of the hollow-earth theory, John Cleves Symmes. Poe's *Narrative of Arthur Gordon Pym*, in which the seas become warm as the explorers approach the South Pole, was probably also influenced by Symmes and was of course a major influence on Verne; see *The Narrative of Arthur Gordon Pym*, ed. Sidney Kaplan (New York: Hill and Wang, 1960), pp. xii–xiv.

5. *Last and First Men and Star Maker* (New York: Dover, 1968), p. 183.

6. *Science and the Modern* (New York: Macmillan, Free Press, 1967).

7. See, for example, Eric S. Rabkin, "Determinism, Free Will, and Point of

View in Le Guin's *The Left Hand of Darkness*," *Extrapolation*, 20 (1979), 5–19. John Huntington, "Science Fiction and the Future," *College English*, 37 (1975), 345–52, proposes that science fiction "answers a craving, not for a new and plausible technology, but for a science which will mediate between a conviction of the necessity of events—that is, a strict determinism—and a belief in creative freedom."

8. *Science and the Modern World*, p. 76.

### Manifest Destiny: Science Fiction and Classical Form

1. *The Known and the Unknown* (Kent, Ohio: Kent State University Press, 1979), p. 105–6. Much of what Wolfe says about "the icon of the city" (chapter four) can be applied to empires as well; see especially the subsection on "The Imperial City" (pp. 105–9).

2. I draw my sense of the classic from T. S. Eliot, "What Is a Classic?" *On Poetry and Poets* (London: Faber and Faber, 1957), 53–71, and Frank Kermode, *The Classic* (New York: Viking, 1975).

3. Kermode, *The Classic*, p. 40, specifies two kinds of classics, those which imitate previous models and those which renounce them. Each of his four chapters examines a different culture that offers examples of both kinds of classics.

4. Joseph E. Patrouch, Jr., *The Science Fiction of Isaac Asimov* (Garden City, N.Y.: Doubleday, 1974), pp. 61–62.

5. Eliot, "What Is a Classic," p. 68.

6. Isaac Asimov, *Second Foundation* (1953; rpt. New York: Avon, 1972). My abbreviation cites the title and the book and chapter numbers. Subsequent citation refers to this reprint.

7. Donald Hassler, "Asimov's Golden Age: The Ordering of an Art," in *Isaac Asimov* (Writers of the 21st Century Series), ed. Joseph Olander and Martin Harry Greenberg (New York: Taplinger, 1977), pp. 116–17. Hassler notes that this sense of burden from tradition increases as science fiction writers become more sophisticated and more aware of their antecedents, and that the ambivalence is expressed through an ironic treatment of inherited material.

8. Eliot, "What Is a Classic," p. 58.

9. Kermode, *The Classic*, p. 55. Kermode goes on to draw a contrast between Milton and Marvell similar to the distinction I make between Asimov and Herbert (pp. 55–67).

10. Paul, of course, can also figure Mohammed, another prophet/messiah to a chosen people. Just as Gibbon provides a subtext for the *Foundation* series, so T. E. Lawrence's *Seven Pillars of Wisdom* underscores *Dune*.

11. Frank Herbert, *Dune* (New York: Ace, 1965).

12. Kermode, *The Classic*, p. 114.

*"All you have to do is know what you want": Individual Expectations in* Triton

1. Georges Simmel, "The Metropolis and Mental Life," tr. H. H. Gerth, 1950; rpt. in *Classic Essays on the Culture of Cities*, ed. Richard Sennett (Englewood Cliffs, N.J.: Prentice-Hall, 1969), p. 53.
2. Richard Sennett, *The Uses of Disorder: Personal Identity and City Life* (New York: Knopf, Vintage, 1970), p. 171.
3. Ibid., pp. 149, 181.
4. Samuel R. Delany, *Triton*, (New York: Bantam, 1976), p. 234. All further references are to this edition.
5. Simmel, "The Metropolis and Mental Life," p. 57.
6. Robert Park, "The City: Suggestions for the Investigation of Human Behavior in the Urban Environment," 1916; rpt. in *Classic Essays*, p. 128.
7. Ibid., p. 126.
8. Peter S. Alterman, "The Surreal Translations of Samuel R. Delany," *Science Fiction Studies*, 4 (Mar. 1977), 25–34.
9. Delany, *Out of the Dead City*, in *The Fall of the Towers* (New York: Ace, 1966), p. 99.
10. Delany, "To Read *The Dispossessed*," in *The Jewel-Hinged Jaw: Notes on the Language of Science Fiction* (New York: Berkley, Windhover, 1977), p. 278.
11. Delany, *The Einstein Intersection* (New York: Ace, 1967), p. 155.
12. Delany, *The Jewels of Aptor* (New York: Ace, 1962), p. 156.
13. George Edgar Slusser, *The Delany Intersection: Samuel R. Delany Considered as a Writer of Semi-Precious Words*, The Milford Series, no. 10 (San Bernardino, Calif.: Borgo Press, 1977), p. 33.
14. Simmel, "The Metropolis and Mental Life," pp. 57–58.
15. *City of a Thousand Suns*, in *The Fall of the Towers*, p. 405.
16. For an excellent discussion of the significance of binary, triune, and tetradic relationships in Delany, see Slusser's *The Delany Intersection*.
17. Ibid., p. 40.
18. *City of a Thousand Suns*, p. 392.
19. Sennett, *The Uses of Disorder*, p. 6.
20. Frank E. Manuel, ed., *Utopias and Utopian Thought* (Boston: Houghton Mifflin, 1966), p. vii.

*Autoplastic and Alloplastic Adaptations in Science Fiction: "Waldo" and "Desertion"*

1. Quoted in Paul A. Carter, *The Creation of Tomorrow: Fifty Years of Magazine Science Fiction* (New York: Columbia University Press, 1977), p. 173.
2. This idea appeared early in Róheim's work, in his 1925 study *Australian Totemism*. It also appears in the better-known 1934 work *The Riddle of the Sphinx, or Human Origins*, trans. R. Money-Kyrle (New York: Harper

and Row, Torchbooks, 1974). A summary and critique of the idea can be found in Mary Douglas, *Purity and Danger: An Analysis of Concepts of Pollution and Taboo* (1966; rpt. London: Routledge & Kegan Paul, 1978), pp. 114–18.

3. Bruno Bettelheim, *Symbolic Wounds: Puberty Rites and the Envious Male*, rev. ed. (New York: Crowell-Collier, Collier Books, 1962); Norman O. Brown, *Life Against Death: The Psychoanalytical Meaning of History* (New York: Knopf, Vintage, [1959]).

4. J. J. Pierce, Introduction, in *The Best of Cordwainer Smith*, ed. J. J. Pierce (New York: Ballantine, 1975), pp. xiv–xv.

5. (New York: Duell, Sloan, and Pearce, 1947), p. 241.

6. Human-machine symbiosis is apparent not only in "Scanners Live in Vain," but also among Smith's "pinlighters," who are neurally connected to spaceship defenses ("The Game of Rat and Dragon") and among the "Go-Captains," whose brains are locked into the guidance systems of spacecraft ("The Burning of the Brain"). The animal-human theme is central to several stories concerning a slave class of remade animals called underpeople (such as "The Ballad of Lost C'Mell") but also appears in the *Island of Dr. Moreau*-like "A Planet Named Shayol." All of these stories may be found in *The Best of Cordwainer Smith*.

7. *Robert A. Heinlein: America as Science Fiction* (New York: Oxford University Press, 1980), p. 54.

8. "Waldo" in *Waldo and Magic, Inc.* (New York: New American Library, 1970), p. 33. Future references are to this edition.

9. The notion of doubt or worry short-circuiting complex technology would seem rather bizarre, but it has occurred in science fiction more than once. An interesting comparable treatment is Theodore Sturgeon's 1957 *Galaxy* story "The Pod and the Barrier" (collected in *A Touch of Strange* [Garden City, N.Y.: Doubleday, 1958]). Philip K. Dick touches on this theme in a number of his novels: see, for example, *Ubik* (Garden City, N.Y.: Doubleday, 1969; rpt. Boston: Gregg Press, 1979).

10. One might call this the Miltonic paradox of science fiction, since it's a little like describing the face of God. It presents a problem to Arthur C. Clarke in his *Childhood's End* (New York: Ballantine, 1956). A more directly parallel example to Heinlein, however, is Jack Williamson's *The Humanoids* (*Astounding*, 1947–48; New York: Simon and Schuster, 1949), in which Williamson goes to heroic lengths to accommodate both mechanical determinism and mysticism.

11. See Bruno Bettelheim, *The Uses of Enchantment: The Meaning and Importance of Fairy Tales* (New York: Knopf, Vintage, 1977), especially pp. 16–17.

12. "Clifford D. Simak: The Inhabited Universe," in *Voices for the Future: Essays on Major Science Fiction Writers*, 1 (Bowling Green, Ohio: Bowling Green University Popular Press, 1976), p. 72.

13. Robert Scholes and Eric S. Rabkin, *Science Fiction: History, Science, Vision* (New York: Oxford University Press, 1977), p. 137.

14. *City* (New York: Ace, [1952]), p. 119. Future references will be to this edition.
15. Clareson, *Voices for the Future*, p. 73.
16. Quoted in Muriel R. Becker, Introduction, in *Clifford D. Simak: A Primary and Secondary Bibliography* (Boston: G. K. Hall, 1980), p. xxii.

## *Science Fiction for the Age of Inflation: Reading* Atlas Shrugged *in the 1980s*

1. Donald R. Katz, "Ruthless Mothers: Money, Values and the Gimme Decade," *Playboy* (Sept. 1981), p. 95.
2. An excellent examination of the contradictions implicit in Rand's epistemology and ethics is William F. O'Neill, *With Charity toward None: An Analysis of Ayn Rand's Philosophy* (Totowa, N.J.: Littlefield, Adams, 1972).
3. *Contemporary Authors*, ed. Clare D. Kinsman, First Revision (Detroit: Gale, 1975), vols. 13–16, p. 655.
4. "The Goal of My Writing" (1963); reprinted in *The Romantic Manifesto: A Philosophy of Literature* (New York: World, 1969), p. 161.
5. *Contemporary Authors*, p. 656; cf. Aristotle, *Poetics*, ch. XXV.
6. Interview (with Alvin Toffler), *Playboy*, March 1964; reprinted in *Playboy Interviews* (Chicago: Playboy Press, 1967), pp. 107–8.
7. Rand discussed the "prophetic" aspects of *Atlas Shrugged*, inconclusively, in the 1964 lecture "Is Atlas Shrugging?" reprinted in *Capitalism: The Unknown Ideal* (New York: New American Library, 1966), pp. 149–66.
8. Rand went to some pains to document the bureaucratic attitudes portrayed in *Atlas Shrugged* from a "horror file" of newspaper clippings ("Is Atlas Shrugging?" passim).
9. Rand clearly had in mind, not the actual transcontinental railroad, but James Jerome Hill's much shorter Great Northern Railroad; Nathaniel Taggart also resembles Commodore Vanderbilt, founder of the New York Central, in his acquiescence to bribery when unavoidable. See Rand, "Notes on the History of American Free Enterprise" (1959); reprinted in *Capitalism: The Unknown Ideal*, pp. 96–103.
10. "Non-Contradiction," "Either-Or," and "A Is A"; cf. Aristotle, *Metaphysics*, book IV, passim.
11. *Astounding Science Fiction* (Feb. 1939), pp. 9–32; reprinted in *Five Science Fiction Novels*, ed. Martin Greenberg (New York: Gnome Press, 1952). For a far-ranging discussion of the capitalist/adventurer subgenre of sf, see H. Bruce Franklin's essay "America as Science Fiction: 1939," in this volume.
12. *Atlas Shrugged* (New York: New American Library, 1959), p. 20. All subsequent references are to this edition.
13. See, for example, the nearly identical descriptions in *Atlas Shrugged*, pp. 107, 119, 242, 680, 1011.

14. Ibid., p. 44.
15. Ibid., p. 39.
16. Ibid., p. 793.
17. Ibid., p. 14.
18. Ibid., p. 34.
19. Ibid., p. 275.
20. See, for example, Robert Heinlein's "Waldo" (*Astounding*, Aug. 1942); and George O. Smith's *Venus Equilateral* stories (1942–45) and his related "Lost Art" (Dec. 1943), among many others.
21. *Atlas Shrugged*, p. 760.
22. Ibid., p. 766.
23. Ibid., p. 1050.
24. In a postscript to "Is Atlas Shrugging?" Rand and her correspondents gloat (the word is not too strong) over the New York power blackout of November 9, 1965 (*Capitalism: The Unknown Ideal*, pp. 165–66.
25. *Atlas Shrugged*, pp. 1075–76.
26. Ibid., p. 1084.
27. "Self-esteem" is a key term in Objectivist psychology. Rand's disciple and hagiographer Nathaniel Branden, who broke with her personally but not ideologically in 1965, has gone on to establish a school of psychotherapy in such works as *The Psychology of Self-Esteem* (1969) and *The Disowned Self* (1971).
28. After her De Mille period (1926–28), Rand worked in the wardrobe department of RKO Pictures, New York (1929–32), and then as a script reader and screenwriter for various producers (1932–49).
29. As a philosophical tobacconist says: "I like cigarettes, Miss Taggart. I like to think of fire held in a man's hand. Fire, a dangerous force, tamed at his fingertips. . . . When a man thinks, there is a spot of fire alive in his mind—and it is proper that he should have the burning point of a cigarette as his one expression" (*Atlas Shrugged*, p. 65).
30. Ibid., pp. 266–77.
31. Ibid., pp. 569–70.
32. A cycle, properly speaking, has neither beginning nor end; a loop (for example, the "if-then-else" and "do while" loops available in high-level computer languages) contains within itself a statement or command that loops the completed function back to its first step. Both images are central to modern science fiction, and to the personal obsessions of writers as different from Rand as Blish, Dick, Bester, Anderson, and Heinlein (cf. George Slusser's "Heinlein's Perpetual-Motion Fur Farm," in *Science Fiction Studies* 9, no. 1 (1982), 51–67. The relation of cyclical imagery to the styles and philosophies of speculative fiction awaits a major study.
33. Especially notable is composer Richard Halley's opera *Phaëthon*, in which (unlike the Greek myth) the son of Helios succeeds in driving the chariot of the sun. The opera is booed off the stage by the decadent audience (*Atlas Shrugged*, p. 70).

34. Cf., for example, the first description of John Galt (Ibid., p. 537).
35. Interview, *Mademoiselle* (May 1962), p. 194; *Atlas Shrugged*, p. 669. Also on p. 669 Galt describes the young woman as "the kind of writer who wouldn't be published outside. She believes that when one deals with words, one deals with the mind."
36. *Atlas Shrugged*, p. 149.
37. "An Answer to Readers about a Woman President," *The Objectivist* (Dec. 1968), p. 1; quoted in O'Neill, *With Charity toward None*, p. 24.
38. Cf. the almost identical language as Dagny expresses her feelings toward D'Anconia (*Atlas Shrugged*, p. 108), Rearden (Ibid., pp. 240–41), and Galt (Ibid., p. 888).
39. Ibid., p. 902.
40. Ibid., p. 976.
41. *Le Camp des saints*, (1973); English translation by Norman Shapiro (1975).
42. Cf. the Professor's definition of "rational anarchist": "I can get along with a Randite. A rational anarchist believes that concepts such as 'state' and 'society' and 'government' have no existence save as physically exemplified in the acts of self-responsible individuals. He believes that it is impossible to shift blame, share blame, distribute blame . . . as blame, guilt, responsibility are matters taking place inside human beings singly and *nowhere else*" (Robert A. Heinlein, *The Moon Is a Harsh Mistress* [New York: Putnam's, 1966], p. 84).
43. Cf., for example: "The depression sets in as you realize that *Atlas Shrugged* is everyday life. The world is strangling at the hands of a man-created monster—government—which grows more out of control each day. . . . Ayn Rand's warnings about the future are no longer applicable to the future; they are applicable to the present. The future has arrived! Men do not tell their government what to do. Government tells men what to do—and backs it up with force" (Robert J. Ringer, *Restoring the American Dream* [New York: QED, 1979], pp. 2–3). Ringer and his school promote Rand as a major philospher unjustly scorned by pseudointellectual professors (Ibid., pp. 247–48).
44. "I consider *National Review* the worst and most dangerous magazine in America. The kind of defense that it offers to capitalism results in nothing except the discrediting and destruction of capitalism. Do you want me to tell you why? . . . Because it ties capitalism to religion. . . . which means that there are no rational grounds on which one could defend capitalism" (*Playboy Interviews*, p. 119). Rand was drummed out of the conservative fold by Whittaker Chambers's attack on *Atlas Shrugged* in the fledgling *National Review*; see William F. Buckley, ed., *American Conservative Thought in the Twentieth Century* (Indianpolis: Bobbs-Merrill, 1970), pp. xxi–xxii.
45. Greenspan was a regular contributor to *The Objectivist* during the 1960s;

several of his essays are reprinted in *Capitalism: The Unknown Ideal*. For Rand's reaction to Greenspan's appointment to the Council of Economic Advisors, see the *New York Times* (July 24, 1974), p. 57; (July 28, 1974), part III, p. 1; (Nov. 17, 1974), part IV, p. 4.

46. A typical Watt reply to his critics: "My responsibility is to follow the Scriptures, which call upon us to occupy the land until Jesus returns" (quoted by Jeffrey Klein, "Man Apart: James Watt and the Marketing of God's Green Acres," *Mother Jones* [Aug. 1981], p. 22).

47. The universal grammar or *calculus ratiocinator*, which could deal equally well with logical, mathematical, psychological, or historical theorems, derives from the dreams of Leibnitz and the early cyberneticists; see Pamela McCorduck, *Machines Who Think* (San Francisco: Freeman, 1979), pp. 39–42. This concept was assimilated into John W. Campbell's recurrent search for the absolute, and can be traced through the 1940s in such *Astounding* contributors as Heinlein (the semantic calculus in "Blowups Happen"), van Vogt (Korzybski's "non-Aristotelean" epistemology in *The World of Null-A*), and Hubbard ("Dianetics"), and later in such Campbell clones as Mark Clifton and Frank Riley (*They'd Rather Be Right*).

## America as Science Fiction: 1939

1. Suzanne Hilton, *Here Today and Gone Tomorrow: The Story of World's Fairs And Exposition* (Philadelphia: Westminster Press, 1978), p. 152.
2. *Book of Nations: New York World's Fair*, Compiled and edited by William Bernbach and Herman Jaffe (New York: Winkler & Kelmans, 1939), pp. 98–100.
3. Ibid., p. 146.
4. *Going to the Fair* (New York: Sun Dial Press, 1939), p. 54.
5. *The Official Guide Book to the New York World's Fair of 1939* (New York: Expositions Publications, 1939), p. 91.
6. *Guide Book*, pp. 199–200.
7. Ibid., p. 66.
8. Ibid., pp. 44–45.
9. Ibid., pp. 29.
10. Ibid., pp. 208–9.
11. Ibid., p. 41.
12. Hilton, *Here Today and Gone Tomorrow*, p. 60.
13. Bradford C. Snell, *American Ground Transport, Hearings before the Subcommittee on Antitrust and Monopoly of the Committee on the Judiciary, United States Senate, 93rd Congress, Second Session on S. 1167* (Washington: U.S. Government Printing Office, 1974), p. A-2.
14. Ibid., pp. A-2, A-3.
15. Ibid., p. A-1.

### Rider Haggard's Heart of Darkness

1. Mario Praz, *The Romantic Agony* (1st English trans., 1933; New York: Oxford, 1970), p. xv.
2. Rider Haggard, *She* (New York: Hart, 1976), p. 85. All pages references, hereafter included in the text, will be to this edition.
3. Herodotus, *The Persian Wars*, trans. George Rawlinson (New York: Modern Library, 1942), pp. 133–34.
4. Henry Miller, *The Books in My Life* (New York: New Directions, 1969), pp. 91–92.
5. Harold Bloom, *Figures of Capable Imagination* (New York: Seabury, 1976), pp. 32–33.
6. Theodore Roszak, "The Hard and the Soft: The Force of Feminism in Modern Times," in Betty Roszak and Theodore Roszak, eds., *Masculine/Feminine: Readings in Sexual Mythology and the Liberation of Women* (New York: Harper & Row, 1969), p. 88.
7. Mary Austin, *Earth Horizon* (Boston: Houghton Mifflin, 1932), p. 344.
8. Sigmund Freud, *The Interpretation of Dreams* (New York: Avon, 1965), pp. 489–90.
9. Norman Etherington, "Rider Haggard, Imperialism, and the Layered Personality," *Victorian Studies* 22, no. 1 (Autumn 1978): pp. 71–87. For a somewhat different analysis of this dream, see Alexander Grinstein, *Sigmund Freud's Dreams* (New York: International Universities Press, 1980), pp. 392–422.
10. Joseph Conrad, *Heart of Darkness* (New York: W. W. Norton, Critical Edition, 1971), p. 11. All references, hereafter included in the text, will be to this edition.

### She *in* Herland: *Feminism as Fantasy*

1. Emily Dickinson, J. 378 in *The Poems of Emily Dickinson*, ed. Thomas Johnson, 3 vols. (Cambridge: Harvard University Press, Belknap Press, 1955).
2. Susan Griffin, *Rape: The Power of Consciousness* (New York: Harper & Row, 1979), p. 25.
3. Julia Kristeva, *Desire in Language: A Semiotic Approach to Literature and Art*, ed. Leon S. Roudiez, trans. Thomas Gora, Alice Jardine, and Leon S. Roudiez (New York: Columbia University Press, 1980), pp. 36–37.
4. Susan Lurie, "Pornography and the Dread of Women: The Male Sexual Dilemma," in *Take Back the Night*, ed. Laura Lederer (New York: William Morrow, 1980), pp. 159–73. Also see Susan Lurie, "The Construction of the 'Castrated Woman' in Psychoanalysis and Cinema," *Discourse* 4 (Winter 1981–82), 52–74.
5. Charlotte Perkins Gilman, *Herland* (New York: Pantheon Books, 1979), pp. 2, 4. All subsequent quotations are from this edition. I am indebted to the excellent introduction by Ann J. Lane.

6. Eric Rabkin, *The Fantastic in Literature* (Princeton, N.J.: Princeton University Press, 1976), p. 8.

7. Sherry B. Ortner, "Is Female to Male as Nature Is to Culture?" in *Woman, Culture and Society*, ed. Michelle Zimbalist Rosaldo and Louise Lamphere (Stanford: Stanford University Press, 1974), p. 70.

8. Charlotte Perkins Gilman, *Women and Economics*, ed. Carl Degler (New York: Harper & Row, Torchbooks, 1966), p. 70. Subsequent quotations are from this edition.

9. Annette Kolodny has studied the relationship between women and the land in *The Lay of the Land: Metaphor as Experience and History in American Life and Letters* (Chapel Hill: University of North Carolina Press, 1975) and, more recently, in "Honing a Habitable Languagescape: Women's Images for the New World Frontiers," in *Women and Language in Literature and Society*, ed. Sally McConnell-Ginet, Ruth Broker, and Nelly Furman (New York: Praeger, 1980), pp. 188–204.

10. Susan Griffin, *Woman and Nature: The Roaring Inside Her* (New York: Harper & Row, Colophon Books, 1980).

11. See Gayatri C. Spivak's discussion of the womb in "Unmaking and Making in *To the Lighthouse*," in *Women and Language in Literature and Society*, p. 326.

12. This is Susan Lurie's point about the male castration fear underlying the Freudian theory of female penis envy.

13. Adrienne Rich, "Motherhood in Bondage," in *On Lies, Secrets, and Silence: Selected Prose 1966–1978* (New York: W. W. Norton, 1979), p. 196.

14. Linda Gordon, *Woman's Body, Woman's Right: A Social History of Birth Control in America* (New York: Penguin Books, 1976).

15. *The Living of Charlotte Perkins Gilman* (New York: Harper & Row, 1975), p. 104.

16. Charlotte Perkins Gilman, *The Yellow Wallpaper* (Old Westbury, N.Y.: The Feminist Press, 1973), p. 15.

17. Nina Auerbach, *Communities of Women: An Idea in Fiction* (Cambridge: Harvard University Press, 1978), p. 161.

18. Elizabeth Cady Stanton's speech is reprinted in *Feminism: The Essential Historical Writings*, ed. Miriam Schneir (New York: Random House, 1972), p. vi.

19. Mary Elizabeth Coleridge, "The White Women," in *Poems by Mary E. Coleridge* (London: Elkin Mathews, 1908), p. 92.

20. Olive Schreiner, *Woman and Labour* (London: Virago Press, 1978), p. 282.

21. For a discussion of the relationship between woman and the colonized, see Barbara Charlesworth Gelpi, "A Common Language: The American Woman Poet," in *Shakespeare's Sisters: Feminist Essays on Women Poets* (Bloomington: Indiana University Press, 1979), pp. 269–79.

22. A. James Hammerton, "Feminism and Female Emigration, 1861–1886,"

and Judith Walkowitz, "The Making of an Outcast Group: Prostitutes and Working Women in Nineteenth-Century Plymouth and Southampton," in *A Widening Sphere: Changing Roles of Victorian Women*, ed. Martha Vicinus (Bloomington: Indiana University Press, 1980), pp. 52–71, 72–93.

23. Alice Walker, "In Search of Our Mothers' Gardens," in *Woman as Writer*, ed. Jeannette L. Webber and Joan Grumman (Boston: Houghton Mifflin, 1978), pp. 193–201.

## *Death and the Mirror: Existential Fantasy*

1. Eric S. Rabkin, *The Fantastic in Literature* (Princeton: Princeton University Press, 1976), p. 28. Rabkin uses the word "fantastic" in this instance, but in his study "fantasy" is defined as the quality of those narratives that use the fantastic. "But in varying measure every narrative that uses the fantastic is marked by Fantasy, and offers us a fantastic world."

2. Hume says the following: "To whatever length one may push his speculative principles of skepticism, he must act and live and converse like other men. . . . It is impossible for him [the skeptic] to persevere in total skepticism, or make it appear in his conduct for a few hours." Quoted in Samuel Enoch Stumpf, *Socrates to Sartre: A History of Philosophy* (New York: McGraw-Hill, 1966), p. 296.

3. David Hume, *Selections* (New York: Scribner's 1955), p. 21: "Let us chace our imagination to the heavens, or to the utmost limits of the universe; we never really advance a step beyond ourselves, nor can conceive any kind of existence, but those perceptions which have appear'd in that narrow compass."

4. See Julien Eymard, *Le Thème du miroir dans la poésie française, 1540–1815* (Lille: Université de Lille, 1975). In his first chapter especially, Eymard discusses the interrelations between the use and development of this literary "theme" and improvements in mirror technology during what is the preclassical and classical age in France.

5. "The Steel Glass: A Satire" (1576), in *Sixteenth-Century English Poetry*, ed. Norman E. McClure (New York: Harper & Brothers, 1954), pp. 141–47. Even this "steel glass" is metaphorical in the sense defined, for in it too "I desire to see myself indeed—/Not what I would, but what I am, or should" (ll. 70–71). Here we are not creating private wish-structures but seeking to mirror self in some higher moral and natural order ("should"). In general, Gascoigne links this mirror fascination with the fall. "I see and sigh (bycause it makes me sad)/That peevish pride doth all the world possess;/And every wight will have a looking-glass/to see himself, yet so he seeth him not" (ll. 14–17).

6. Over the mirror in the painting is a signature, "Johannes de Eyck fuit hic," and a date. But is it really he who is reflected in that mirror? And who is the second figure and why is a second figure represented? The metonymic mirror here could be said to bifurcate into the fantastic.

7. Arthur B. Evans, in his *Jean Cocteau and His Films of Orphic Identity*
(Philadelphia: The Art Alliance Press, 1977), makes the following argument: "But to what extent *is* the Orpheus of Cocteau's film *Orphée* a
cinematic incarnation of Cocteau himself? . . . if *Orphée* parallels the
nature of *Le Sang d'un poète* regarding their respective raisons d'être,
then one should be able to discern a very large amount of Cocteauean
autobiography in this film" (p. 105). My argument is that the fluid nature
of mirrors in this film—Cocteau even used liquid mercury, a surface that in
yielding conceals yet still reflects, in the scene where Orphée thrusts his
hand through the mirror—alters this metaphorical intention, creates a
metonymic drift in which the mirror image (here poet reflected in his
work) becomes increasingly obdurate to such metaphorical interpretation.

8. See Eymard, *le Thème du miroir*, pp. 1–10. To the classical mind in France
truth ("la vraie réalité") comes not from seeing the object in itself but
from a "polishing" activity that renders that object a reflection of the
human form. Eymard cites a statement by a seventeeth-century commen-
tator, the Cardinal du Perron, that neatly points to this reflective or
reflexive nature of knowledge: "Les arbres ont beau estre plantez au bord
d'un ruisseau, avoir la terre grasse, le ciel serein, l'air temperé, le ciel à
propos, et toutes les faveurs de la nature et tout le bien qui est requis à leur
estre, si ne dirons-nous pas qu'ils aient aucun plaisir: pour ce que jouys-
sants de tout ce bien-là, ils ne le cognoissent point." These trees then, no
matter how fortunate in their situation or beautiful in themselves, cannot
*know* themselves as existing because they cannot see themselves reflected
in that stream on whose banks they stand.

9. *The Garden and the Map: Schizophrenia in Twentieth-Century Literature
and Culture* (Urbana: University of Illinois Press, 1973). Vernon biases
the term "schizophrenia" in a different direction. In his view, this state of
modern culture derives from a fall from Edenic oneness with the world, a
fall brought about by that mode of perception that separates perceptions
into what become mutually exclusive opposites: "subject" and "object,"
"I" and "other." Upon this base, I am positing a more recent and radical
fall: a total fascination with reflexive seeing (a desire to resolve this
primary rift from the point of view of the "subject" by turning its objects
into mirrors that reflect that subject) that not only abolishes all sense of an
objective world without but all possibility of returning to a state of pure
existence before—the immanent self-awareness that might precede this
fall into seeing.

10. *The Metamorphoses of Ovid*, tr. Mary M. Innes (Baltimore: Penguin
Books, 1962), p. 93: "My very plenty makes me poor. How I wish I could
separate myself from my body! A new prayer this, for a lover, to wish the
thing he loves away!" Narcissus here is suspended in the paradox of the
mirror existence before actually committing that body to the mirror,
hurling himself at the mirror to shatter it.

11. See M. L. von Franz' essay in *Man and His Symbols* (New York: Dell,

1968), p. 224. Jung's stone experience symbolizes "mere existence at the farthest remove from the . . . feelings, fantasies, and discursive thinking of ego-consciousness."

12. Stephen Crane, *The Red Badge of Courage*, ed. Sculley Bradley, Richmond Croom Beatty, and E. Hudson Long (New York: W. W. Norton, 1962), p. 109: "He had been to touch the great death, and found that, after all, it was but the great death. He was a Man."

13. Fyodor Dostoevsky, *Stories* (Moscow: Progress Publishers, 1971). See Author's Note to "The Gentle One," pp. 271–72. Dostoevsky is aware that he is reversing the sense of his terms here: "Now this hypothetical stenographer (whose notes I have given shape to) is what I call 'fantastic' in my story." I am indebted to Gary Kern for introducing me to this story and to this crucial passage on the "stenographer."

14. Ibid., p. 312.

15. We detect this alternating current already in Pascal. We sense in his work almost irreconcilable tension between two modes of perception: one the desire mode that seeks through increasingly sophisticated mirrors to extend man's image to the ends of the universe; the other a fear mode that methodically seeks to sever all sympathetic or reflexive ties between man and phenomenal nature. Through this latter, what Pascal calls "esprit de géometrie," man is confronted with the unreflecting abyss of space and time. This impulsion in turn however summons a countermovement—the instinctive strategies of the "esprit de finesse" that, on the edge of this abyss, would use these oscillations of desire and fear to return man to a sense of his existential self. In his "thinking reed" passage, Pascal, repositioning thinking man against the fearful "devouring" vastness of the natural universe, not only reveals the *cogito* to be a dangerous mirror tautology, but in doing so seeks to reverse the direction of this mirror. For in this new context, one does not will himself into existence in the mirror of reason but rather in that of certain annihilation. In this extreme *renversement* man can know he exists only by knowing that he certainly will die. We see this same instinctual strategy at work in the much later *Doctor Faustus* of Thomas Mann, where the defeated narrator shapes the same sort of reverse mirror, but this time out of composer Leverkühn's nihilistic dirge—a recessional darker than any cosmic void, where mankind's hope to retrieve from war and holocaust some residual sense of self yields only a ghostly last note, a reverse image echoing impossibly in the silence of death.

16. Giving a Jungian interpretation to the Iranian fairy tale of Prince Hatim in the castle of nonexistence, M. L. von Franz (in his chapter "The Process of Individuation," in *Man and His Symbols*) provides an interesting analogue to *2001*. In this tale the prince is first lured into a closed cupola by a barber with a mirror, who then vanishes in darkness. As waters rise and threaten to drown him, he prays, and escapes only to find himself in another enclosed space—a garden at whose center there is a ring of stone

states. In the center of that ring, in turn, is a parrot in a cage. Given three shots with a golden bow to kill the parrot and break the spell of the place, he misses the first two. With each miss he is partially turned to stone himself, the first time to the waist, the second time to the chest. For the third shot he closes his eyes, again prays, and is granted a hit, bringing himself and all the other statues to life again. The barber with his mirror and the parrot may represent then the lure of the projected image, the reflexive insincerity of a world of objects made to imitate us, thus to confine us in our mirror existence. And we may also admit with Mark Rose (*Alien Encounters: Anatomy of Science Fiction* [Cambridge: Harvard University Press, 1981], p. 150) that the room in which Kubrick's Bowman finally lands also "suggests man's imprisonment in his own mind" and culture as projection of that mind. The retrieval of self, in both cases, involves breaking out of these mirror confines. And in both, in breaking out, the hero encounters death. In the fairy tale the hero's acts (praying in the dark, shooting blind) not only blank the mirror, but in doing so retrieve life from death. In *2001* however, Bowman, increasingly slowing to stonelike awkwardness only to become through his final and leaden death-reach a reborn "star child," may not break through, either to transcendence or to self-awareness. Indeed the final return of the film to the music and dark landscape of the opening "Dawn of Man" scene may imply, instead of some new dispensation, a circular and imprisoning return to the old biological cycle—to the same drama of the mirror and death we have just witnessed in the film.

17. Søren Kierkegaard, *The Sickness unto Death*, tr. Walter Lowrie (Garden City, N.Y.: Doubleday, 1954), p. 151.
18. Ibid., p. 164.
19. Ibid., p. 170.
20. Kierkegaard expands upon this: "The self becomes an abstract possibility which tries itself out with floundering in the possible, but does not budge from the spot, nor get to any spot, for precisely the necessary is the spot; to become oneself is precisely a movement at the spot. To become is a movement from the spot, but to become oneself is a movement at the spot" (ibid., p. 169).
21. Yukio Mishima, *Sun and Steel*, tr. John Bester (New York: Grove Press, 1970), p. 69.
22. Ibid., p. 13.
23. See Mishima's parable of the apple and the core. "The apple certainly exists, but to the core this existence as yet seems inadequate; if words cannot endorse it, then the only way to endorse it is with the eyes. Indeed, for the core the only sure mode of existence is to exist and to see at the same time. There is only one method of solving this contradiction. It is for the knife to be plunged deep into the apple so that it is split open and the core is exposed to the light—to the same light . . . as the surface skin" (ibid., p. 65).

24. Ibid., p. 60.
25. Ibid., p. 63.
26. For another viewpoint on this matter, see Roland Barthes, "To Write: An Intransitive Verb?" (in *The Structuralists: From Marx to Lévi-Strauss*, ed. Richard T. De George and Fernande M. De George [Garden City, N.Y.: Doubleday, 1972], pp. 155–67). In describing the function of the verb "to write" today, Barthes seems to imply a shift toward the reflexivity Mishima fears. "Today to write is to make oneself the center of the action of speech; it is to effect writing in being affected oneself" (p. 165).
27. See the sketch "Jaques Callot" in E. T. A. Hoffmann, *Werke* (Frankfurt am Main: Insel Verlag, 1967), I, 7: "Oder vielmehr seine Zeichnungen sind nur Reflexe aller der fantastischen wunderlichen Erscheinungen, die der Zauber seiner überregen Fantasie hervorrief."
28. See Adalbert von Chamisso, *Peter Schlemiehls wundersame Geschichte*, in *Chamissos Gesammelte Werke*, I (Stuttgart: J. G. Cotta, 1883).
29. Hoffmann, *Werke*, I, 11: "So belebte er das Skelett, welches jene paar Violinen von der Ouvertüre gaben, mit Fleisch und Farben." Hoffmann may have taken his model for these pantomimic performances from Diderot's *Neveu de Rameau*.
30. Ibid., I, 15: "über dem Schwatzen von Kunst, von Kunstsinn und was weiss ich—können sie nicht zum Schaffen kommen."
31. Ibid., I, 14: "da traten zwei Kolossen in glänzenden Harnischen auf mich zu: Grundton und Quinte! Sie rissen mich empor, aber das Auge lächelte." On "verbal music" see Steven Paul Scher, *Verbal Music in German Literature* (New Haven: Yale University Press, 1968). To Scher, the primary technique of rendering the word musical is through a "linguistic approximation" of musical effects and devices.
32. See Wilhelm Wackenroder, "Die merkwürdige musikalische Leben des Tonkünstlers Joseph Berglinger," in *Werke und Briefe* (Heidelberg: L. Schneider, 1967), p. 126: "Ein dreifaches Unglück für die Musik, dass bei dieser Kunst grade so eine Menge Hände nötig sind, damit das Werk nur existiert! Ich sammle und erhebe meine ganze Seele, um ein grosses Werk zustande zu bringen;—und hundert empfindungslose und leere Köpfe reden mit ein, und verlangen dieses und jenes."
33. Rabkin, *The Fantastic in Literature*, p. 227: "Thomas Kuhn has shown that even in the scientific perception of reality, we establish perspectives (which he calls paradigms), and we make revolutionary scientific progress only by fantastically reversing them. . . . Fantasy represents a basic mode of human knowing."
34. *Introduction à la littérature fantastique* (Paris: Editions du Seuil, 1970), p. 169: "Les thèmes de la littérature fantastique sont devenus, littéralement, ceux-la mêmes des recherches psychologiques des cinquante dernières années."
35. Ibid., p. 67: "L'allegorie est une proposition à double sens, mais dont le sens propre (ou littéral) s'est entièrement effacé."

36. Ibid., p. 97: "Le fantastique se définit comme une *perception* particulière d'événements étranges."
37. *The Interpretation of Dreams*, in *The Basic Writings of Sigmund Freud*, tr. Dr. A. A. Brill (New York: Modern Library, 1938), pp. 319–467. What Freud designates for instance as "concern for representability" is the tendency in dreams to replace abstract and colorless images with ones that are fundamentally more concrete.
38. Jacques Lacan, *Ecrits I* (Paris: Editions du Seuil, 1966), "Le stade du miroir comme formateur de la fonction du Je," pp. 93–94: "Le *stade du miroir* est un drame dont la poussée interne se précipite de l'insuffisance à l'anticipation—et qui pour le sujet, pris au leurre de l'identification spatiale, machine les fantasmes qui se succèdent d'une image morcelée du corps à une forme que nous appellerons orthopèdique de sa totalité."
39. Jean-François Lyotard, *Discours, Figure* (Paris: Editions Klincksieck, 1971), P. 245: "Seulement cette réflexion est irréfléchie, préréflexive, et l'on peut comprendre comment: le désir est d'emblée texte boulversé, le travestissement n'est pas le fait d'une intention de tromper qui serait celle du désir, mais le travail même *est* travestissement parce qu'il est violence sur l'espace linguistique. Pas besoin d'imaginer que le Ça a quelque chose derrière la tête. 'Le travail du rêve ne pense pas.' La mobilité du processus primaire trompe par elle-même, est ce qui trompe, donne le vertige aux 'facultés' usant du langage articulé: le figural contre l'esprit."

# Biographical Notes

LESLIE FIEDLER is Samuel Clemens Professor of English at the State University of New York at Buffalo. He is the author of numerous studies of American literature and culture, and has completed a book on Olaf Stapledon.

H. BRUCE FRANKLIN is Professor of English and American Literature at Rutgers University-Newark. His most recent book is *Robert A. Heinlein: America as Science Fiction.*

SANDRA M. GILBERT is Professor of English at the University of California at Davis. She is co-author (with Susan Gubar) of *Madwoman in the Attic.*

SUSAN GUBAR is Professor of English at Indiana University. She is coauthor (with Sandra M. Gilbert) of *Madwoman in the Attic.*

GEORGE R. GUFFEY is Professor of English at the University of California at Los Angeles. He specializes in the seventeenth and eighteenth centuries.

ROBERT HUNT is Director of Publications for Context Management Systems in Los Angeles. He holds a doctorate from the University of California at Los Angeles and has written widely on science fiction.

JOSEPH LENZ teaches English literature at Drake University.

MICHELLE MASSÉ is a member of the faculty at George Mason University, where she teaches English literature.

GERALD PRINCE is Professor of French at the University of Pennsylvania. His field of study is narratology and the grammar of narrative.

ERIC S. RABKIN is Professor of English at the University of Michigan. He is the author of *The Fantastic in Literature* and numerous articles on literary theory.

MARK ROSE is Professor of English at the University of California at Santa Barbara, where he teaches Renaissance literature and science fiction. His most recent book is *Alien Encounters.*

ROBERT SCHOLES is Head of the Semiotics Program at Brown University. His most recent book is *Semiotics and Interpretation.*

GEORGE E. SLUSSER is Curator of the Eaton Collection at the University of California, Riverside, where he also teaches literature and film.

GARY K. WOLFE is Dean of Continuing Education at Roosevelt University, where he also teaches English. He is the author of *The Known and the Unknown: The Iconography of Science Fiction.*

# Index